Interdisciplinary studies are emerging rapidly to meet the demands of the modern age. To bring together biblical interpretation and Christian ethics is a potentially creative undertaking. Such dialogue is attempted in this work, at a time when much attention is being paid to *reading texts* and the *interpretive tradition*. The author's principal concern is to read the Bible in the context of moral concern. Attention is paid to the liberal quest and to eschatology and ethics, before the post-modern age is studied under the rubric 'participation in meaning'.

BIBLICAL INTERPRETATION AND CHRISTIAN ETHICS

NEW STUDIES IN CHRISTIAN ETHICS

General editor: Robin Gill

Editorial Board: Stephen R. L. Clark, Anthony O. Dyson,
Stanley Hauerwas and Robin W. Lovin

In recent years the study of Christian ethics has become an integral part of mainstream theological studies. The reasons for this are not hard to detect. It has become a more widely held view that Christian ethics is actually central to Christian theology as a whole. Theologians increasingly have had to ask what contemporary relevance their discipline has in a context where religious belief is on the wane, and whether Christian ethics (that is, an ethics based on the Gospel of Jesus Christ) has anything to say in a multi-faceted and complex secular society. There is now no shortage of books on most substantive moral issues, written from a wide variety of theological positions. However, what is lacking are books within Christian ethics which are taken at all seriously by those engaged in the wider secular debate. Too few are methodologically substantial; too few have an informed knowledge of parallel discussions in philosophy or the social sciences. This series attempts to remedy the situation. The aims of New Studies in Christian Ethics will therefore be twofold. First, to engage centrally with the secular moral debate at the highest possible intellectual level; second, to demonstrate that Christian ethics can make a distinctive contribution to this debate – either in moral substance, or in terms of underlying moral justifications. It is hoped that the series as a whole will make a substantial contribution to the discipline.

BOOKS IN THE SERIES

BIBLICAL INTERPRETATION AND CHRISTIAN ETHICS

BY

J. I. H. McDONALD

*Reader in Christian ethics and New Testament studies
in the University of Edinburgh*

CAMBRIDGE
UNIVERSITY PRESS

CAMBRIDGE UNIVERSITY PRESS
Cambridge, New York, Melbourne, Madrid, Cape Town, Singapore, São Paulo

Cambridge University Press
The Edinburgh Building, Cambridge CB2 2RU, UK

Published in the United States of America by Cambridge University Press, New York

www.cambridge.org
Information on this title: www.cambridge.org/9780521430593

First published 1993
This digitally printed first paperback version 2005

A catalogue record for this publication is available from the British Library

Library of Congress Cataloguing in Publication data
McDonald, J. I. H.
Biblical interpretation and Christian ethics / by J. I. H. McDonald.
p.   cm. – (New studies in Christian ethics)
Includes bibliographical references.
ISBN 0-521-43059-3
1. Christian ethics – Biblical teaching. 2. Bible – Criticism,
interpretation, etc. 3. Christian ethics – History – 19th century.
4. Christian ethics – History – 20th century. 5. Bible – Criticism,
interpretation, etc. – History – 19th century. 6. Bible – Criticism,
interpretation, etc. – History – 20th century. I. Title.
II. Series.
BS680.E84M43   1993

241 – dc20   93-16555 CIP

ISBN-13 978-0-521-43059-3 hardback
ISBN-10 0-521-43059-3 hardback

ISBN-13 978-0-521-02028-2 paperback
ISBN-10 0-521-02028-X paperback

Contents

vii

viii   *Contents*

General editor's preface

This is the second monograph in the *New Studies in Christian Ethics* series. Fundamental to this series is the attempt to write about Christian ethics in an interdisciplinary context. Authors are encouraged to bring together recent discussions in philosophy, literary studies and the social sciences with the very best in Christian ethics. This is meant to be an intellectually challenging series and, as such, it inevitably makes heavy demands on contributors. In the first monograph Dr Kieran Cronin used his philosophical and theological skills in *Rights and Christian Ethics*. It is an admirable example of interdisciplinary study.

In this second monograph Dr Ian McDonald also adopts an interdisciplinary approach. He is already a well-established scholar with impressive qualifications and books in both biblical studies (specialising in the New Testament) and Christian ethics. He brought these two skills together most notably in the well received *The Quest for Christian Ethics* that he wrote with the philosopher Ian Fairweather. Now he brings them together again in this new study.

The approach that Dr McDonald adopts in this monograph is to view the last century of biblical interpretation in relation to Christian ethics as consisting of three phases. In the first phase liberal scholars responded to the new methods of biblical criticism and sought to make sense of biblical ethics from perspectives derived from the Enlightenment. In the second phase, a more radical disjunction between biblical culture and present-day culture was seen (for example on eschatology). Various attempts were made to cope with this disjunction, ranging from outright scepticism to existentialism. In the third phase, sometimes termed post-modernism, the relation between text and interpretation is seen as distinctly more problematic. There can be no handling of texts – in relation to ethics or to anything else – which is independent of interpretation.

I have no doubt that such an analysis of biblical interpretation and Christian ethics is overdue, and that this new monograph will be a significant contribution to an exceedingly problematic area of scholarship. Biblical scholars themselves are increasingly influenced by literary and sociological theories, and have opened up new and fascinating areas of scholarship as a result of these influences. The 'Bible' is now often seen as a series of texts with lengthy processes of interpretation inescapably attached to them. Biblically dependent forms of Christian ethics are naturally subject to the same processes. Dr McDonald offers a timely guide in these largely uncharted waters.

ROBIN GILL

Preface

Inter-disciplinary studies are rapidly emerging to meet the insistent demands of the modern age. Nowhere is this more evident than in the two areas that provide the title for this work. Biblical interpretation is itself interdisciplinary, drawing together the biblical disciplines and others to address the problem of interpreting texts. Christian ethics is also multidisciplinary and thus no stranger to this new ethos, although in practice its relationship to biblical interpretation is often problematic.

To bring these two areas together is a potentially creative undertaking. It comes at a time when much attention is being paid to *reading texts*. Texts are always read in a context. Our task in this book is to consider how biblical texts may be read in the context of moral concern.

Yet, while interdisciplinary studies are mostly of recent origin, one is aware of a series of scholars who did not allow themselves to be narrowly confined within one discipline or who, like Schleiermacher for example, were at home in multidisciplinary endeavour. The direction taken in modern scholarship has been anticipated in some measure in each generation since the rise of critical studies. Hence, if one reads biblical texts in the context of moral concern, one is aware of standing in a *tradition* of interpretation: one which has had its crises and its fractures and its wrong turnings, but which nevertheless possesses coherence, logic and objectives from which much can be learned. The approach adopted here is therefore by way of the liberal quest, with its enduring results especially for social ethics, and thereafter through the period when eschatology dominated interpretation, differentiating contextual worlds, but emphasising the address of the Other. And so to today: when it is no longer possible for the scholar to dwell in the peaceful haven of assumed objectivity. Participation is the name of the game. We are all together in the bundle of life, values and commitments.

Limited though this work inevitably is, it has been enriched by the interest and co-operation of many who did not even know of its existence: students and colleagues, particularly in Biblical Interpretation and Christian Ethics courses, and also in New Testament classes, at Edinburgh. Some of its material may have a familiar ring to them. More particularly, I must acknowledge gratefully the constant helpfulness and encouragement I have had from several colleagues at Edinburgh: Professor Duncan B. Forrester (Christian Ethics), Professor John O'Neill (New Testament Studies), Dr Kevin Vanhoozer in Biblical Interpretation and Dr Ruth Page in Modern Theology. My erstwhile colleague, Professor Robin Gill (now at Canterbury) and Alex Wright of Cambridge University Press first suggested that the book should be included in the present series, and have maintained a strong interest in it. I am much in their debt, as I am to Gillian Maude and the staff of the Press who have solicitously and industriously attended to the manifold requirements of the publishing process.

Finally – and this is far more than a conventional acknowledgement – I must express my deep indebtedness to my wife, Jenny, whose understanding and forbearance have meant so much to me during the years of increasing preoccupation with this work, and who has even mastered the dreaded wordprocessor in order to assist me materially with the final preparation of the book.

To cover the range with which this book attempts to deal means that procedures have had to be selective. What agony there is when one has to delete a favourite theme or topic! Doubtless, others would have selected on a different basis. Another consequence was that I have been obliged to draw heavily on the work of others: a left-handed compliment to the vitality of tradition! I have not hesitated to make wide use of translations, for biblical interpretation and Christian ethics are world-wide concerns, articulated not only in languages such as French and German in which I have a modest competence, but also in Spanish, Portuguese and others in which I have none.

When all is said and done, however, the final responsibility must be my own. The book goes forth with the hope that it may help to foster interest in this most vital type of study, and that others may be moved to carry the task further.

Abbreviations

BA	*The Biblical Archaeologist*
BAR	*Biblical Archaeology*
BCE	*Basic Christian Ethics*
BJRL	*Bulletin of the John Rylands Library*
CBQ	*Catholic Biblical Quarterly*
DBI	*Dictionary of Biblical Interpretation*
ET	*Ethics and the Gospel*
ENT	*Ethics in the New Testament*
ER	*Epworth Review*
ESP	*The Ethics of Saint Paul*
Exp.T.	*Expository Times*
GL	*Gospel and Law*
HCE	*History of Christian Ethics*
JBL	*Journal of Biblical Literature*
JJ	*Jesus and Judaism*
KGPC	*The Kingdom of God and Primitive Christianity*
MPT	*The Meaning of Paul for Today*
NTS	*New Testament Studies*
PK	*The Parables of the Kingdom*
PRJ	*Paul and Rabbinic Judaism*
PPJ	*Paul and Palestinian Judaism*
REB	*The Revised English Bible*
RGG	*Religion in Geschichte und Gegenwort*
RMT	*The Relevance of the Moral Teaching of the Early Church*
SM	*The Setting of the Sermon on the Mount*
STCC	*The Social Teaching of the Christian Churches*
TJ	*The Teaching of Jesus*
TNT	*The Theology of the New Testament*
ZAW	*Zeitschrift für die Alttestamentliche Wissenschaft*

Introduction: Relating the Bible to Christian ethics

> As drink is pleasant to them that be dry, and meat to them
> that be hungry; so is the reading, hearing, searching, and
> studying of Holy Scripture, to them that be desirous to
> know God, or themselves, and to do his will.[1]

One of the more rewarding features of the current academic
scene is the growth of interdisciplinary studies. As the above
quotation shows, the Reformation viewed interpretation, theology, self-understanding and ethics as part of an organic whole,
an integrated movement in the divine–human symphony. It is
only in recent times that 'biblical interpretation' has re-
emerged as an attempt to co-ordinate and interrelate a variety
of disciplines accustomed to operate with a jealous regard for
their independence: textual study, exegesis, theology, history,
hermeneutics, ethics... Whereas the legacy of the Enlightenment was fragmentation into separate disciplines, detailed
attention is now being given to the process of reading texts,
which involves many disciplines. Diplomatic relations have
been re-established also with the world of literature. Results are
already impressive. 'In the waning years of the twentieth
century, and at the heights (or depths) of secularisation, the
Bible is being reaffirmed and re-examined as one of Western
literature's greatest texts.'[2]

Ethics has resurfaced in hermeneutical debate. Prominence
has been given, for example, to the ethics of biblical interpretation,[3] and new studies have been made of ethics in the
Hebrew scriptures and the New Testament.[4] In the context of
such developments, this book sets out to examine the whole
range of interaction between biblical interpretation and Chris-

tian ethics. Such a project is facilitated by the fact that Christian ethics itself has emerged as a discipline from a long subservience to philosophy, theology, exegesis and social science to stake its claim to its own integrity, although it is unlikely to lose sight of its compound nature, one element of which is its biblical base. Indeed, an intrinsic relation between biblical interpretation and Christian ethics can be claimed with some confidence. The area of difficulty lies not in the general principle, but in the practicalities of this interaction, which involves not two disciplines, but two interdisciplinary areas. Such complexity can lead to the taking of shortcuts, with damaging consequences – thus giving further legitimation to a study such as this! It is well, therefore, to begin by frankly recognising some of the difficulties.

ACCESSIBILITY

The New Testament does not set out to be a handbook or compendium of ethics or moral instruction. The moral teaching which it contains is embedded in the context of the life and mission of the church. It is true that early studies in the field tended to focus on such themes as 'the ethics of Jesus' or 'the ethics of Paul', and some modern books still follow this time-honoured model. But generally speaking, as New Testament studies became more sophisticated, the moral teaching of Jesus was seen to be accessible only in as far as it was preserved, interpreted and transmitted by the evangelists and the communities they represented.[5]

But the world of the New Testament is qualitatively different from that of the modern interpreter, who has not only inherited the bequest of the scientific and technological revolutions, but is living in a time of astonishing cultural transformation. The inherently strange New Testament world view represents a wholly different civilisation, and one which, as Schweitzer demonstrated memorably, was determined and permeated by eschatological expectation. The notion that the End was rushing in to overwhelm the present age, and that the breakdown of the present cosmic order was already evident, deeply affected the way ethics was conceived, whether in epistles, gospels or apocalypse.

Thus interpreters came to accept – in many cases only slowly and with notable reluctance – that one did not have the kind of access to the moral teaching of Jesus or his followers which would readily allow one to read off from the pages of the New Testament definitive solutions to moral problems. At best, one could hope to join in the process of Christian moral decision-making which clearly exercised the minds of apostles and house churches alike and perhaps share, however remotely, in the moral integrity of Jesus. But any investigator who wished to do so had to master the tools of the trade, namely the traditio-historical approach with its emphases on source, form and redaction criticism, and its concern for the socio-historical context of the material in question.[6]

A price has to be paid for such scholarly discipline, and one must ensure that one is not overcharged for it! It may tend to represent the study of ethics in the New Testament as a minor offshoot, almost a by-product, of a relatively arcane academic discipline, to which only the guild of New Testament scholarship has access. E. Schüssler Fiorenza, for example, speaks of the great gulf which separates the communities of faith today and historical biblical scholarship.[7] This is a matter of serious concern; yet, if the extremes of intellectualism and anti-intellectualism can be avoided, the New Testament may impress the reader not only with the strangeness and intensity of its eschatology, but also with the vigour and challenge – the real presence[8] – of its moral concern.

CONTEXTUALITY

Does this combing of the sources enhance or inhibit the contribution of the New Testament to ethics? In a strange way it may do both. The ancient world to which the New Testament belongs is not completely closed to the modern investigator. It is open to historical criticism and to sociological research, and these disciplines not only present the wider moral and cultural milieu of the early Christian communities, but also set their eschatology and moral practice in perspective and thus render them more meaningful to the outside enquirer. As the world of the New Testament thus evinces an ethos of Christian moral concern, an affinity is established between the ancient setting and the modern interpreter who is reading this material in the context of moral concern today.

If, however, one fails to take due note of considerations of context, the attempt to use New Testament material may be invalidated. A non-contextual use of the Bible can perpetrate serious error and prompt overcorrection. Thus Jack T. Sanders:

> The ethical positions of the New Testament are the children of their own times and places, alien and foreign to this day and age. Amidst the ethical dilemmas which confront us, we are now at least relieved of the need or temptation to begin with Jesus, or the early church, or the New Testament, if we wish to develop coherent ethical positions. We are freed from bondage to that tradition, and we are able to propose, with the author of the Epistle of James, that tradition and precedent must not be allowed to stand in the way of what is humane and right.[9]

Several points are being telescoped here. The writer's emphasis on context is entirely appropriate. But one should also point out that tradition is a double-edged sword – Sanders stands in a tradition too! – and that, while tradition can inhibit, it can also guide and inform. The New Testament tradition – and not only the Epistle of James! – contains material which gives pre-eminent recognition to what is humane and right. Contextual considerations in themselves do not justify Sanders' apparent abandonment of a biblical basis for Christian ethics, but his strictures on non-contextual exegesis are certainly in order. B. C. Birch put the matter thus: 'in Christian ethics the Bible is always primary but never self-sufficient'.[10]

Recent developments in the sociology of knowledge have put great emphasis on social context as the ground of all thinking. The logical conclusion is that all documents have to be deconstructed in terms of their socio-historical and material presuppositions. The problem is then to ascertain whether we are dealing simply with a culture-bound phenomenon, a piece of ancient social history, or whether there is an ideological tension in the material pointing to moral and religious issues of perennial or universal significance.

The New Testament – let alone the Bible – is diverse. Not only does it contain many different genres and forms, but there are striking contrasts within the same genre (for example, the Synoptic Gospels and John). Different documents reflect different contexts: such as the Gentile mission, the Hellenistic Jewish milieu and Jewish Christianity. There are also different ways of reading the New Testament: the historical and literary approaches are not always easy to yoke together. Above all, while the New Testament witnesses to the supreme event of Jesus Christ, its understanding of that event is informed by the Hebrew scriptures, which (often in translated form) constituted the scripture of the early church communities. When Old and New Testaments are placed side by side (as they eventually came to be), the diversity is immense and gives urgency to the question of overall structure.[11] The question is complicated by the emergence of the concept of the canon of scripture, which provided the church with a rule of faith and life. In view of the diversity discussed above, we may well ask if there is effectively a canon within a canon. Do we quietly assume the priority of certain books? And if we appeal to ways in which the ancients interpreted the Bible, are the interpretive procedures of a millennium ago defensible today? How then is the Bible to be read?

These questions, though fundamental, are not unanswerable. It is not difficult, for example, to locate the centre or focal point in the structure of scriptural understanding found in the New Testament. It is, in a word, Christ.[12] To put the matter more strikingly:

Christianity was born in hermeneutics. Its primal act of appropriation was the claim that the life and work of Jesus were the preordained fulfilment of earlier prophecies in the Hebrew scriptures. This was the famous 'key' without which there was no access to the Bible.[13]

Hence the importance of the trajectories of understanding which run in both directions from the centre throughout the whole complex of Old and New Testaments. Provided that the centre is clearly located, Christian moral teaching can draw from these trajectories and thus make creative use of selected material from the Hebrew Bible and, indeed, from an even wider cultural context.

APPLICATION

The problems of application in the field of ethics are considerable. Does the New Testament – or the Bible – provide a set of coherent principles or rules for application in all situations? If the exegete has doubts, the ethicist has even stronger misgivings. Even if situation ethics is regarded as extreme,[14] issues may well be specific to the context in which they arise. Many modern issues have no counterpart in the New Testament, and even recurrent issues such as abortion are culturally relative.[15] Further, some ethicists might argue that the autonomy of ethics, which they endorse, is infringed if an external authority such as the Bible is intruded. Against this notion theologians such as Barth and Bultmann protested so vehemently that they denied the validity of human systems of ethics. Human beings must be open to the Word from beyond them, the Word that sets them free. Or, as Iris Murdoch has suggested, they must look outward at Christ. 'The argument for looking outward at Christ and not inward at Reason is that self is such a dazzling object that if one looks *there*, one may see nothing else.'[16]

The use of biblical material in ethics can be controversial and open to challenge, but it is not thus automatically invalidated. On the contrary, by virtue of its transcendent horizon or ultimate concern it may well be in a position to present a radical challenge to conventional ethics. The claim of biblical ethics to serious consideration in moral decision-making today rests on its radical openness to the Other – God, neighbour and (at least in Jesus' teaching) enemy, as well as the poor, the needy and the victims of oppression; and on its insistence that one can attain such openness only through the conquest of those powerful forces, operating both internally and externally, which close mind, spirit and will to transformative possibilities. How such a claim was handled in major phases of modern scholarship and in contemporary debate is the central theme of this book.

BEYOND THE DIFFICULTIES

Merely to outline difficulties, however, would be excessively negative in the introduction to a book such as this. One can be positive about interpretation today. The place of cultural tradition has come to the fore in recent philosophical discussion: all debate takes place within its parameters.[17] Christian interpretation and ethics stand in a tradition that goes back to New Testament and Patristic times, to the Middle Ages and the Reformation, and includes the critical tradition that stemmed from the Age of Enlightenment. But traditional understanding can also be challenged and reworked. In the exciting times in which we live, interpretation and ethics find their context in a time of rapid cultural change where the parameters sketched out by Enlightenment thinkers have been decisively shifted, not least in the era of science post-Einstein. No longer is it acceptable to view the world in simple subject–object terms. Today, there is a recognition of relativity; we *participate* in the reality we study; we are an integral part of the universe whose secrets we would unlock. And, as we do so, we discover *ourselves*. The Enlightenment mode, for all its concern for freedom, rationality and culture, had about it an aspect of domination which had its correlative in alienation,[18] and its critique of religion combined valid appraisal with, at times, neurotic hostility. The relatively open holistic ethos of the emergent modern paradigm may well provide a more promising scene for biblical interpreters and ethicists.

Like all cultural developments, interpretation is part of a developmental chain: to understand where we are at the present time requires awareness of the process by which we got here. In this book, we begin with the liberal modernism which, after predictable apologetic defensiveness, embodied the positive and optimistic response within biblical interpretation and Christian ethics to the new rationalistic spirit. The result was the 'eternal values' (Part One) which the liberals generated through their interpretive approach and which informed their personal and social ethics. But liberalism, with its reliance on historical criticism, nurtured within itself the seeds of its own downfall. Part Two traces the undermining of the liberal consensus, largely through contextual emphases which highlighted eschatology. Eternal values are now replaced by 'interim' or 'charismatic' ethics, by various forms of divine command given in the address of the Word, or by 'faith ethics', while acute difficulties emerge in the realm of social ethics. Part Three is concerned with radically participative paradigms, which mark a new age in interpretation and raise acute ethical issues. These include the ethics of historical reading – and its consequences for ethics; and the ethics of contemporary reading – which holds interpreters accountable for the use they make of the texts. As well as traditional Western paradigms, feminist and global perspectives are also taken into account. Thus, to relate Christian ethics to biblical interpretation is not to impose a strait-jacket upon it, but to empower it, through the horizons which are thus opened up, to contribute meaningfully to global discourse about the priorities and options confronting humankind today.[19]

PART ONE

Liberal principles and practice

The rationalists of the Enlightenment were correct in their view of the mind's ability to know the world. But they claimed too much, too confidently and too soon. They aimed at an omniscience that is not for human knowers to obtain, or even to aspire to.

(Colin Gunton)[1]

PHILOSOPHICAL AND CRITICAL GROUNDWORK

Problematic though it may be, the *Aufklärung* or Age of Enlightenment is the starting-point of our study. How can it be characterised? Sometimes it seems to epitomise a society developing a new confidence, a new awareness of its own potential: a society ready to solve its own problems by initiative and effort, and evincing a belief in its ability both to achieve and to progress materially and culturally. The pre-Copernican, geocentric world was now replaced by an increasingly confident anthropocentric universe. The new confidence could therefore strike a more iconoclastic note. There was a readiness to question, even to overthrow, the structures – whether of authority or power or dogma – which seemed to have retarded freedom and truth. Generally, the *Aufklärung* evinced an enquiring and creative spirit – in this respect, as in some others, the heir of the Renaissance. Human reason and will, human feeling and creative energy: on these foundations humankind would build its house, and neither heaven nor hell would prevail against it!

Sometimes, as in the microcosmic Scottish Enlightenment, the resultant picture is gracious and attractive: like Allan Ramsay's picture of David Hume, a figure of light emerging from the darkness.[2] But the gentler nature of the Scottish Enlightenment must not obscure the extent of the challenge to existing structures: especially when we revert to the macrocosm of Europe, with its many-stranded new initiatives. In Germany,

Wolff and Lessing emphasised the centrality of reason, while the romantics, the *Sturm und Drang* movement to which Schiller and Goethe were related, reacted against rationalism, yet philosophers and romanticists alike challenged the grip of traditional institutions and beliefs. The French Revolution was hailed by the Romantic movement as a great blow struck for the freedom of the human spirit. Wordsworth wrote of it:

> Bliss was it in that dawn to be alive,
> But to be young was very heaven![3]

With its noble principles and horrendous outcome, the revolution was, in fact, an explosive combination of Enlightenment idealism, resentment at social and economic oppression, and political opportunism. Its complex ideological roots included the writings of the philosopher John Locke, on whom Rousseau and Voltaire drew so heavily. His philosophy, which invoked the laws of reason and nature and spoke of 'natural rights', presented a picture of the human being as born free, equal and virtuous, but gradually corrupted by property and luxury, against which it was the role of civil government to give protection. One thing is clear: if existing belief systems were to survive, let alone make a meaningful contribution, they would have to relate to the new age, with its aspirations for freedom and fulfilment, its critical and scientific spirit and its emphasis on human experience.

The position of the apologist was not easy. Among the *philosophes* in France, for example, there was a consensus view that, if the organized churches had legitimate business, their sphere was strictly spiritual and related to the salvation of the soul. The realms of science, government, economics and even morality were autonomous, and had to be freed from the dead hand of ecclesiastical and religious authority. Dogma was rejected as a closed authoritarian system, imprisoning the free spirit, as did autocratic political systems. Thus, as far as possible, religion was marginalised and privatised. The new approach enshrined a reaction, even a neurosis, evidenced in the disowning of the spiritual and cultural heritage of a millennium and a half. It affirmed the dominance of *homo sapiens* over his world, the subject over the object, and declared for human freedom and responsibility. Revelation was rejected in favour of (at best) 'natural religion', although the latter's presuppositions were savaged by Hume. The tendency was certainly in the directipn of the secular, the humanist and the romantic. The effect was to erode Christendom from within.

Ethics was no less embattled. It is true that Kant, who raised in an essay the question of the nature of 'enlightenment', contributed directly to the pin-pointing of a new paradigm of moral understanding. Recognizing the limitations of pure reason, he understood knowledge to be produced through the interaction of thought and sense. In relation to morality, the human moral sense posited categorical imperatives arising from the nature of *homo sapiens* as an autonomous rational being. Such imperatives constituted universal moral laws. Here then was the formal basis of an ethics of obligation (a deontology) in which motive was also important, for Kant emphasised the fundamental importance of goodwill. Moreover, conscience, duty and moral freedom – the hallmarks of the moral life – were held to be guaranteed by the existence of the righteous God who ensured the ultimate outworking of justice.[4]

Other philosophers, however, found different ways of relating the sense of moral obligation to human autonomy and rationality. For example, Fichte focused on the notion of the Absolute Ego as the living moral order. Hegel, the proponent of the all-comprehending, idealist system, operated with the logic of 'becoming', of dialectical process and evolution. Feuerbach took religion and ideals to be projections of human experience, and sought to redirect human effort to the larger natural and social whole to which all belong and which may be called God. Ethics was in danger of becoming the prisoner of ideology.

Another important approach related to the social context of ethics, and came to have increasing importance as Western society underwent radical change with the onset of the industrial revolution, itself the product of scientific and technological advance. New intellectual disciplines were devoted to the study of its implications and effects. George Adam Smith, for example, explored the economics of capitalism and free trade, and Karl

Marx developed the theory of dialectical materialism and the class struggle. The wider framework was provided by, among others, Charles Darwin on natural selection; Sigmund Freud in psychology; E. B. Tyler in anthropology; and Emil Durkheim and Max Weber in sociology. The immense social and political outcomes ranged from communism and revolution to democratic socialism, the welfare state and human rights.

Social and political interests thus came to occupy an important, if not dominant, place in ethical discourse. Attention was turned towards social utility: moral value was assessed in terms of social consequences. The utilitarianism of Bentham and Mill was the logical outcome of this line of thinking. The 'good' was tantamount to that which benefits the greater number. But another significant consequence was that the point of view of working people gradually found articulation in a variety of ways. To be sure, it was frequently manipulated by those in power, and often neutered by paternalism. It was potentially of great moment to ethics – and usually neglected by ethicists. But the long-term consequence is that, when a moral position is outlined or an ethical perspective commended today, it is germane to ask: is this view 'from the top' of the power structure downwards, or is it 'from below' upwards. In other words, what is the hidden political and social agenda?

By contrast, Kant's procedures might be described by some as bourgeois: empirico-rationalist theory developed in the senior common room and discussed over port! A valid ethics, it might be said, must be rooted in the historical and socio-economic processes which effectively determine the scope of moral decisions. But when this is attempted, one is then faced with a wide spectrum of social sciences, each one of which seems to be setting forth rival 'goods' for our attention. Marxists posit the goal of a new order of society, the end justifying the means. Economists indicate the goal of prosperity and the means of attaining it through market forces, with or without controls – together with matching moral attitudes. Psychologists may suggest human fulfilment as the *telos*, and indicate the conditions for its realisation, in whole or part. Biologists may suggest survival as the basic goal, as well as strategies, such as 'adaptation', for achieving it. All these competing, and at least partially conflicting, goals presuppose moral or quasi-moral strategies which may be mutually incompatible. Utilitarianism attempted to find an inclusive social ethics, but could not avoid some of the pitfalls noted above. It, too, assumes the nature of the 'good' end or consequence. Hence the effect of the Enlightenment appears to be the fragmentation of moral values.

It was liberal scholarship that accepted the gauntlet which the Enlightenment cast before it. The contest took place under rules largely dictated by the *Aufklärung*, for what it proposed was in effect a brave-new-world view with its own axioms and taboos. Spurning extraneous claims to authority, the liberal case was that a properly grounded historical engagement with scripture, which would show Jesus as moral teacher and Christian values as liberating and enriching for the human spirit, would lead one beyond life's ephemera into the realms of eternal truth and destiny. It also proposed principles of social ethics. Moreover, historical and biblical criticism were progressively supplying new tools for the job.[5]

Thus, F. D. E. Schleiermacher[6] – theologian and biblical interpreter – proceeded on the basis of a correlation between scriptural hermeneutics and the interpretation of literature in general. A contemporary of Coleridge, who placed 'all-embracing stress on the absolute primacy of subjective experience',[7] Schleiermacher recognised the text's organic unity, adopted a view of symbolism which allowed for a range of interpretations, and spoke in terms of intuitive procedures which comprehended the immediacy of the reader's engagement with the text and the alignment of one's own frame of mind with that of the author. In relation to the Bible, no *tour de force* – effected, for example, by appeal to inspiration or authoritative tradition – could be allowed to displace this interpretive engagement. The New Testament represented the original interpretation of Christian feeling, the complete correspondence of concepts and vocabulary, which translators subsequently struggle to recapture. A presupposition of his hermeneutics is that we can know others because all are fundamentally alike. This notion of psychological affinity has been criticised (perhaps unfairly) as simply a bridge between the feelings of the interpreter and the alleged feelings of the author, and as a 'flattening out' of New Testament hermeneutics.[8] Yet the positive side of his idealism enabled Schleiermacher to understand faith and life in terms of the interaction of the finite and the infinite, and thus to identify a holistic context which strikes a chord with many modern developments. Schleiermacher's hermeneutical work, which was not published in full until a century and a quarter after his death, was somewhat precariously channelled to the wider world by Wilhelm Dilthey,[9] who tended to coalesce Schleiermacher's views with his own.

Another influential theologian whose work had major implications for ethics and interpretation was Albrecht Ritschl, whose Lutheran Reformed hermeneutics had at its centre the proclamation of God's love in Jesus Christ, through whom justification and reconciliation are effected.[10] With God's gift he correlated God's demand; with Christian faith he correlated Christian life. Consequently, 'God's prevenient reconciling action and man's subsequent ethical response are held together in equilibrium'.[11] A key concept is the notion of Christian lifestyle – *Lebensführung* or *Lebensideal* – in which the notion of vocation is prominent. The Christian, 'directs his action towards the end of the Kingdom of God',[12] the kingdom representing the transcendent pole and the other being historical experience. Ritschl followed Kant, Schleiermacher and others in insisting that the Christian faith must not be confined within the narrow limits of church life, but must issue in the furthering of God's moral purpose for the world and in working towards the transforming or Christianising of society.

Ritschl's emphasis on lifestyle has been castigated as rationalistic moralism, his Lutheran emphasis on vocation as bourgeois, and his understanding of history as 'positivistic'. His point was that Christian vocation was not essentially sacerdotal nor was it monastic nor even ecclesiastical. The Christian is called to bear witness to Christ in the world, particularly through a Christian lifestyle. Marriage, family life, work or professional pursuit are thus brought into the front rank of

Christian concern. In these spheres, one is called to perform 'the ordinary duties of love'; in special circumstances, one may be moved to offer 'an extraordinary duty of love'. At all events, moral duties are not conceived in the course of a solitary existence, but through interaction with other people. The dilemma, however, is as follows: to commit oneself to one's worldly vocation may be to embrace, as a given duty, a set of priorities and values, even a relatively closed world view, which are at odds with the Christian *Lebensideal*. As J. Richmond wrote, with emphasis, of Ritschl:

He apparently did not perceive the extent to which the social, economic and vocational structure of the West was determined by secular, impersonal and even ungodly forces and factors, an insight which gathered tremendous momentum throughout his own nineteenth century.[13]

His understanding of society was traditional and insufficiently illumined by the remarkable advances in economics and sociology while characterised the nineteenth century. The result was a superficial and pietistic understanding of social reality.

At this point, note should be taken of developments in historical interpretation. Auguste Comte[14] had attempted to subject history to positive laws of development, and his famous 'law of three stages', which applied to the development of individuals as well as the human race, encompassed on an ascending scale the theological (or fictitious), the metaphysical (or abstract) and the positive (or scientific), each separated by a period of critical negation. He came to apply this model to social science: hence the 'historical positivism' which was influential in his day (J. S. Mill was a notable follower).

Outgrowing such philosophical frames of reference, historical science evinced a classic divergence of view, which might be characterised as the 'interactive' versus the 'objective'. B. G. Niebuhr,[15] who has been called the first great German historian, accepted that the present could only be understood in the light of the past, and that the past could only be understood on the basis of present experience. Thus, on the basis of his political experience and knowledge, he was able to come to a deeper appreciation of the political and constitutional struggles of ancient Rome, and to present them in a vibrant way. Roman history also spoke to him when his own beloved Prussia was in turmoil. But his critical method was central to his achievement. He dissected his literary sources (principally Livy) like an anatomist, carefully pieced together the fragments of the jigsaw, and finally relied on intuition to weigh the worth of the uncorroborated material. His great successor in Roman history, Mommsen, put even greater weight on personal engagement with his subject. However, one of Niebuhr's pupils, Leopold von Ranke,[16] conceived of a more 'objective' goal, namely to write history 'as it actually happened' (*wie es eigentlich gewesen ist*). To this end, he distinguished between primary and secondary sources, the latter being treated with proper caution. But history without presuppositions is a tall order, however committed one is to history 'for its own sake'. Did von Ranke cease to be a Prussian when writing history? His work has been criticised as impersonal and often failing to penetrate the inner core of events. But his judicious sifting of the sources, his identification of bias and perspective, and his awareness of influences and contexts, greatly illuminated the science of evidence. In England, where von Ranke's work was followed up by Gardiner, Lord Acton and others, the moralistic strain, noticeable in party-political writers such as Alison and Macaulay, was exemplified in Carlyle, whose individualistic leanings were evident in his thesis that since most people are foolish it is wise to follow great leaders. Seeley, about whom we shall have more to say shortly, was a distinguished political historian.

In all this we may discern the ethics of historical reading as a critical factor.[17] Historians are active in interpreting their sources and writing history. They may differ in their readings of events; indeed, within limitations, a diversity of view and creative discussion are essential. The limitations are, at least in part, moral. One is the recognition of viewpoint, of bias or prejudice on the part of the historian – and the sources in question. Here, a 'hermeneutics of suspicion' is called for: an estimate of where the historian is coming from, and how far the line he or she takes, is explicable in terms of his or her basic standpoint. Similar questions may be put to the sources. Another is respect for the evidence and the refusal to allow it to be sacrificed to the interests of the interpreter.[18]

Wilhelm Dilthey,[19] whose hermeneutics gave more precise expression to the text's historical strand, posited an imaginative reliving of events as essential to historical interpretation. This required a critical sifting of all available evidence and an assembling of the parts so that coherent meaning and understanding could emerge in the final statement. Dilthey laid weight on the contribution of psychology, and recognised the importance of developmental patterns and common mental structures. He rejected the positivist kind of sociology which set forth a single comprehensive principle adduced from the 'laws' of history – psychology, biology and the like – and produced over-simplification, as in the work of Comte. History is a process, a continuum fed by human purposes, but no all-embracing purpose or absolute principle can be posited. Values arise within it, but no one value transcends it. Idealism is too simplistic. Knowledge comes through the active engagement of the whole mind with its world.

One wonders if the text is still being absorbed into the penumbra of the critic's imagination. Does Dilthey's scepticism lead to total relativism? The answer seems to be 'not entirely'. Dilthey points to the fact that every *Weltanschauung* or world view evinces a unity of outlook, sponsored by religion, art, philosophy or other cultural agent. An overview of these would show what humankind has made of its experiences of life. Philosophers are charged with bringing them together and critically assessing the significance of their combined vision of reality. The study of ethics is therefore, for Dilthey, primarily historical and comparative.

But now it is time to turn to the ethicists themselves and see how they related biblical interpretation to the elucidation of Christian values.

CHAPTER I

Eternal values

> Jesus' teaching is not merely something historical... it also
> contains eternal, unchangeable, divine truths which one
> can fully explain to himself and make comprehensible to
> others, never on the ground of history and grammar alone,
> but rather by one's own spirit...
>
> (C. F. Staudlin)[1]

The concern for historical experience which was a by-product of
the Age of Enlightenment created the demand for an understanding of the Christian faith in which the historical and moral
dimensions enshrined eternal truth. Theologians and biblical
interpreters looked to the historical Jesus to supply the focus
which the times demanded. Was it possible that enlightened
critical studies could now provide the kind of access to the
ministry of Jesus which would highlight its moral and spiritual
dimension, express its moral teaching in universal principles
and set Jesus' message free from its bondage to dogmatic
systems?

England provided several striking examples of a type of socio-
political idealism which illustrated the temper of the times.
Here we shall look briefly at the work of J. R. Seeley.

THE APPROACH OF ETHICO-POLITICAL IDEALISM:
J. R. SEELEY

Seeley's little book, *Ecce Homo*, was published in 1865 to a chorus
of protest, although a few voices were raised in commendation,
including that of W. E. Gladstone.[2] It represented a cultural
phenomenon of some significance, embodying as it did many of

the features of the contemporary cultural process. In his preface, Seeley mirrored the discontent felt by many at the opaqueness of doctrinal presentations of Jesus which veiled his 'motives, objects and feelings'. Truth is to be found not in received tradition nor ecclesiastical authority, but through historical research which will accept only 'those conclusions... which the facts themselves, critically weighed, appear to warrant'. The biographical sketch speedily raises the importance of the kingdom of God which, when set in the context of Old Testament usage, denotes the restoration of theocracy in practice, the recalling of the nation to first principles. Christ's life was therefore devoted to 'proclaiming the new political constitution, to collecting adherents to it, and promulgating its laws'. Hence was established, in Seeley's words, 'the Christian republic'.

That kingdom of God into which he called men he elevates... into the *summum bonum* of human life, and represents it as the secret of happiness and of all enduring good to belong to the divine society, and to understand and keep the rules prescribed for its members.[3]

An utterly this-worldly picture of the kingdom of God is presented: one which can be described by analogy with political societies. Its religio-moral nature is expressed in the positive law which governs it: Christ's rule of universal love, which is to be internalised by believers so that every Christian may be divinely inspired to choose the right course of action: 'which inspiration is the passion of humanity raised to a high energy by contemplation of Christ's character and by the society of those in whom the same enthusiasm exists'.[4] Strengthened by the church's sacramental fellowship, the Christian can undertake the fuller obligations of the divine commonwealth, which are represented as the 'laws' of philanthropy, edification, mercy, resentment (or gratitude) and forgiveness. Admittedly, such a kingdom is an ideal and has never existed on earth. That is why Christ sometimes referred to it in the future tense as well as the present, and why it is always proper to pray for its coming.

Seeley had firm views both on the philosophy of religion and on hermeneutics. In his later work *Natural Religion*, he argued

that, while religion is at the basis of all true morality, society has
outgrown its former adherence to a supernatural law. Morality
must now be seen to rest on a view of religion that has always
been implicit in Christianity, though most often subjected to
supernatural sanctions. It is 'natural' religion, the religion of
the human spirit: intelligent, rational, historical, inspirational.
The Bible enshrines such, and if properly expressed the effect
would be to revolutionise the world.[5] Neither the Christian
tradition nor the Christian documents are obsolete, but one
must engage with them as one would with the classics. Read
them in the wrong way and one will give credence to obsolete
sentiment. One must contextualise ancient literature. In the
case of the Bible, that means making allowance for the lapse of
2 thousand years. In all its variety, it is 'addressed to wholly
different people living in a different period of history'.[6] It must
be read also in continuity with Christian history. By thus
relativising the sanctions of supernaturalism, Seeley is able to
interpret history as the struggle for the emergence of 'the free
morality':

It ought to be related how the free morality, after being successfully
revealed to the world, became the religion of races which were so far
from being ripe for it, that they were but just ready for the legal stage;
and how of necessity a new system of Christian legalism arose which
reigned for centuries; how, after disciplining a barbarian world, this
system, so powerful, though so radically self-contradictory, gave way,
and the language of St Paul about faith and liberty began to be
intelligible again; how the tyranny of a church gave place to the less
intolerable tyranny of a book, while the nations were preparing
themselves to take up once again the freedom of those who live not by
rules but by religion, the religion of ideal humanity.[7]

The reduction of religious teaching to ethical and political
principles is evident.

It is easy to appreciate both the shock *Ecce Homo* occasioned
to the traditionally pious, and its eventual appeal to the age it
addressed. Written with directness and clarity, it reflected the
dominant intellectual ethos with its anthropocentrism and its
emphasis on natural religion, its overriding concern for the
moral and practical, its rejection of supernatural religious

sanctions in favour of rational ideals and its determination to find patterns of historical development.

His approach to interpretation, informed as it was by classical studies, began well enough: in his conversation with history, he viewed history as past politics, and politics as present history.[8] He therefore had a platform from which to launch a contextual study of Jesus and the relation of his moral teaching to the life of the times. But Seeley's interests lay in a different direction. He sought to generalise, to adduce large principles, and to point lessons: history was a school of statesmanship. The moral realm – one of the constraints of politics – combined with religion to project the ideal of humanity. There are overtones of Schleiermacher and romanticism, and some approximation to the *Lebensideal* which Ritschl developed, but there the resemblance ends. Seeley was influenced more directly by historiography and moral philosophy, and he largely reflected the spirit of English empiricism. Important influences were Kant, who not only spoke of duty, but described the kingdom of God as 'a republic under ethical laws', and Comte, with his notions of the 'religion of humanity', the positive laws which govern human behaviour and progress. Thus Seeley sought to interpret Jesus as fulfilling the highest aspirations of humankind, and the church as the divine society on earth. He would certainly have fallen foul of Dilthey's subsequent strictures on simplistic analyses of reality. Seeley's conversation with history was very one-sided.

The historical critical method of biblical exegesis was already becoming more technical and specialised than Seeley allowed, particularly in his later work. His treatment of biblical sources is inadequate. He simply transposed eschatology into idealism, and his hermeneutic lacks the sense of encounter with the transcendent. He was thus led to view Jesus as 'a young man of promise' (in the notorious words of the original preface to *Ecce Homo*) and to refashion him as an ethico-political radical according to accepted philosophical assumptions.

THE 'HISTORY OF ETHICS' APPROACH:
ERNST LUTHARDT[9]

Ernst Luthardt adopted a different approach from the ethico-political perspective of Seeley. In the context of the history of ethics, Luthardt reads the moral teaching of the Bible from a personal standpoint in which idealism and Lutheranism coalesce. He thus poses the problem of subject–object interaction in an acute way.

(i) *The Lutheran standpoint*   The history of ethics perspective lends itself to a broad – almost a global – cultural sweep within which biblical ethics takes its place. Luthardt's sketch of pre-Christian ethics includes the 'ethics of ancient paganism' as well as the ethics of ancient Israel. In the former category, Greek morality from Homer onwards is briefly sketched and consideration given to the ethical systems of the Greek philosophers from Socrates to the Stoics and, finally, to the popular moral philosophy of Hellenistic and Roman times. Note is taken both of the indebtedness of the church to the classical tradition of ethics and the sharp differentiation that must also be made between Christian and non-Christian traditions. The critical difference is that in Christianity 'the chief interest turns upon man's personal relationship to God as the absolute moral Personality'.[10] The ancient world adhered to a natural or philosophical morality which affirmed the moral basis of nature as it is. Hence, for all its insights into 'virtue', it affirmed pride rather than humility, and selfishness rather than love. Luthardt quotes Seeley with approval: 'The selfishness of modern times exists in defiance of morality; in ancient times it was approved, sheltered, and even in part enjoined by morality.'[11] Christianity, therefore, represents 'essential progress', which it is 'against history' to deny. Here is yet another over-simplified view of history: positivistic, optimistic and absurdly self-confident.

(ii) *The ethics of the Old Testament*   In relation to the tradition of Israel, Luthardt resonates to the monotheism of the Old Testament as 'a truth of practical significance', for God as creator transcends the world and maintains it by his power. He is 'self-evidently spirit' and, as such, is 'the object of awful reverence'. Yet, since he transcends nature, it is possible to know him personally as the gracious and holy God whose nature is reflected in the *Torah*, and whose justice is made known in history. With the Psalms as guide, Luthardt explores the notion of divine justice, which is definitive for human justice and which gives unity to the various uses of the term: in particular, faithfulness and constancy, judgment and mercy. In the wisdom literature, he locates the revealed God who works teleologically in the world, and a corresponding human wisdom, a purposive intelligence and will, which finds its ground and goal in Yahweh, God of Israel. This correspondence is the key to the moral realisation of Israel's consciousness of God.

Two emphases stand out: universalism and internalisation. The universalism, he says, 'is still enclosed in the husk of particularism; but the husk encloses a germ with a rich future in it.'[12] The need for internalisation, evident in the Decalogue and emphasised in Psalms and Prophets, was not met in much of Israel's life and passed into the hope of Messianic times (for example, Jer. 31.31–4; Ezek. 36.26f.). Accordingly, Luthardt finds an inviting target in the particularistic nomism and nationalistic fervour of the late canonical and intertestamental period, in the Pharisaic nomism against which he believes Jesus, Paul and, in its latter-day form, Luther inveighed so tellingly, and in the asceticism of the Essenes and others. Finally, in the Hellenistic period he finds Philo's universalism falsely grounded. The fulfilment of Israel's tradition is to be found only 'in the relationship of grace becoming a reality, and, on that basis, of conduct becoming really moral, as being thus founded on a personal reference to God and through it also to the world'.[13]

Luthardt clearly underestimated the complexity of the Old Testament and the need for a more patient and imaginative appreciation of the ethics of ancient Judaism. He essayed a task which required much fuller research into the socio-historical context and a greater willingness to bracket out modern philosophical and theological presuppositions. Yet while his hermeneutical shortcomings are evident, he at least recognised the element of continuity in Old and New Testament ethics and attempted to pin-point the relational core of each system.

(iii) *The ethics of the gospel*   In the ethics of the New Testament, which he subsumes under 'the proclamation of truth in the Gospels' and 'the apostolical proclamation', Luthardt finds 'the actual realization of the previously typified and prepared communion with God in the person and in the work of Jesus Christ by which the objective relationship of the grace of God to men is established'.[14] The relationship of grace, appropriated by faith, effects a new principle of conduct which 'begins with the subjective change of repentance, manifests itself in love to God and to our neighbour, and puts forth its activity in prayer and trust in God'.[15] Here in a nutshell is the difference Luthardt sees between the moral teaching of Jesus and 'the nomistic ethics of Israel and the heathen world'.[16] Jesus' emphasis was upon repentance and turning to God, upon love as the true righteousness and forgiveness as the reflection of the divine forgiveness. The call to perfection arose out of the actualisation of one's relationship to God in Christ, and was therefore neither nomistic nor ascetic. Leading emphases for Luthardt were disposition, the inwardness of the personal life, the independence of the moral from the ritual and legal and, hence, the freedom to act morally and fulfil the will of God in all the varied forms of one's earthly calling. Luthardt's position may here be related to our previous discussion of Ritschl's understanding of vocation.[17]

The kingdom of God, with its roots in the Old Testament, is the new order of things proclaimed by Jesus. Luthardt defined its essence as 'primarily the good which consists of fellowship in the grace and life of God'.[18] The *ecclesia*, the community of believers, was 'the earthly place of the Kingdom of heaven'. It represented the universal fellowship characterised by the forgiving grace of God and of the disposition of love. The nineteenth-century controversies about New Testament ethics which surface in Luthardt's discussion pin-point salient issues such as Jesus' alleged asceticism and indifference to worldly concerns.[19] Jesus, however, activated a living power which impinged dynamically on every side of life, including politics and 'the life of civilisation and culture'.[20]

Luthardt's liberal presuppositions reveal both theological

and sociological limitations. His understanding of the kingdom of God reflects the typical nineteenth-century this-worldly view, although like Ritschl he modified its cruder aspects (but not always convincingly). Eschatology is transformed by sleight of hand into idealism, and the kingdom is embodied in the church. In answering the gauche and unsympathetic criticisms advanced by Strauss and Ziegler, Luthardt presents a picture of Jesus as a reasonable, cultured moral teacher: one who properly underlines religious values, reflects the well-known common places on excessive wealth and worldliness, and knows his civil duty. The cutting edge is removed from any sayings that question the conventional pattern of bourgeois morality. The separation of the spheres of Caesar and God is lauded, but no attention is given to the key question of their interrelationship. What is most obviously missing is that element of self-awareness which leads readers to question their own cherished presuppositions.

(iv) *The ethics of the apostolic message* Luthardt also examined the ethics inherent in the apostolic proclamation, which he viewed in threefold terms: Jewish Christian, Gentile Christian and Johannine.

The first was based on the Epistle of James and expressed Christian morality as the fulfilment of the *Torah*. It emphasised moral activity as the necessary expression of faith. The holy will of God was not expressed as an external ordinance but paradoxically as 'the law of liberty' (James 2.12), 'the perfect law' (1.25): i.e., as the fulfilment of the *Torah*. Christian morality is an expression of the God-given Spirit (4.5), of faith made complete by works (2.22). All righteousness is based on faith and expressed in moral action. Whatever the limitations of the Jewish–Christian community, James clearly defined 'the new principle of the Christian morality'.[21]

The Gentile Christian position leans heavily on Paul – and Luther! Here is, *par excellence*, a theologically grounded and relational understanding of faith and life. The familiar outline of Pauline theology, based mainly on Romans and Galatians, emphasises Christ as the end of the *Torah*, the new relationship with God in Christ through faith and the inner reality and witness of the Spirit, who is the power of the new life freed from bondage to sin and slavery to the law. Faith is the active principle which works through love (Gal. 5.6).[22]

But Paul's ethics also includes paradoxical elements. Christians combine 'the heavenly sense', i.e., the belief that 'home is above with Christ', with the recognition that one must submit to '*the earthly orders* as God has ordained them to this earthly life'.[23] These earthly orders include the magisterial and political, as well as the conjugal and domestic, to which should be added those which pertain in the Christian community. Within this context, Paul relates to questions of marriage, property and acquisition, work, earthly calling and 'the liberty of enjoyment'. Yet paradoxically, liberation in Christ enables the Christian to accept the need for submission to the worldly orders, even to the point of slavery, and to bear with personal injustice in a Christ-like manner (cf. 1 Pet. 2.16–25).

Finally, Luthardt notes Paul's acceptance of a common moral practice, uniting Jewish and Gentile Christians without infringing Christian freedom. This Luthardt takes to be the significance of the so-called apostolic council in Acts 15, which he accepts as 'regulations for practice with a view to the education of the moral feeling'![24] Paul could go along with practical rules and guidelines as a help towards emphasising the importance of moral practice in the Christian communities, provided that these did not infringe 'the principle of evangelical liberty'.

The paradigm is completed by a consideration of Johannine ethics. Luthardt suggests that the Johannine emphasis on the love commandment is to be explained as a response to a 'libertine antinomianism' which arose from the separation of faith and conduct. In Christ, God's will is revealed as love for humankind; therefore, God's will in us is the will to love. The concept of command is therefore explicitly relational: it is not an external or additional imposition but 'contained in the relationship to God Himself'.[25]

(v) *General comment*   The 'history of ethics' approach anticipates in a limited way some aspects of the later 'history of religions' perspective, and in Luthardt's recognition of the variety of bases for ethics in the Bible he helped establish a lasting paradigm for such studies. His Lutheran idealism, however, can lead to interpretive weaknesses. In his discussion of 'paganism', as in his brief appendix on Buddhism, he provides no hint of the imaginative reliving of events in order to allow the position under scrutiny to reveal its positive merits. Luthardt writes out of his commitment to 'the personal relationship to the personal God that carries in it the power of true morality'.[26] The hermeneutics of commitment are by no means uncommon today (liberationist and feminist approaches are obvious examples), and may be more in tune with modern holistic interpretation than approaches which pretend to neutrality or objectivity on the part of the subject. But, while in all scientific investigation there is a sense in which the question conditions the answer, there are grounds for serious concern when the question *determines* the answer. Instead of a fusion of horizons there is a confusion of horizons: that is, there is formal error in the crucial 'distantiation' (Ricoeur) which is the condition for eventual fusion.[27] In other words, Luthardt's employment of the comparative method lacks the element of openness to the subject matter which is essential for encountering truth.

Theologically, Luthardt adumbrated the anthropo-theo-centric position adopted by many liberals in response to the challenge of Enlightenment thinking, and also incorporated a kerygmatic concern as in Ritschl. As in much liberal writing, there is a problem about his use of 'personality' as the key to moral and spiritual awareness; the concept required greater elucidation than he gave it.[28] The weaknesses of his position – including excessive individualism, a shallow view of social ethics and the nature of society, identification with the political status quo and an underestimation of the importance of eschatology for ethics – were typically nineteenth-century shortcomings.

LIBERAL MODERNISM AND THE ETHICS OF JESUS:
ADOLF HARNACK[29]

The kingdom of God in the teaching of Jesus

Harnack's celebrated work, *Das Wesen des Christentums* (1900), focussed on the teaching of Jesus and located ethics at the core of Christianity. While the sources cannot sustain a biography of Jesus, they nevertheless provide 'a plain picture of Jesus' teaching', together with an account of his vocation and the impact he made on his disciples. Taking an overall view of Jesus' teaching, Harnack found that it may be grouped under three heads:

Firstly, the Kingdom of God and its coming.
Secondly, God the Father and the infinite value of the human soul,
Thirdly, the higher righteousness and the commandment of love.[30]

Each of these, as will become apparent, has direct moral implications and immediate consequences for historical existence.

Harnack recognised an inescapable polarity and ambiguity in Jesus' use of 'the kingdom of God'. One pole represented the rule of God as a purely future, external event; the opposite pole related to 'something inward, something which is already present and making its entrance at the moment'.[31] Only mundane, political interpretations were discarded. For all other aspects of it, Jesus had a place: from the cosmic conflict between God and evil, to the proclamation of the kingdom in the midst, 'a still and mighty power in the hearts of men'. But where is one to find the leading edge or – as Harnack would put it – the essence or kernel? Not in the dramatic future hope: great personalities do not simply articulate ideas they share with their contemporaries but have something distinctive to say. Harnack was looking for what we call today a 'criterion of differentiation', which not only saw Jesus in his context, but also valued that which set him apart from it. He found it in the parables which, above all, pointed to the 'realised' pole of the kingdom: to the rule of the holy God in the hearts of individuals. The kingdom, Harnack emphasised, represented God himself in his power. The dramatic, external scenario had been banished. 'It is not a question of angels and devils, thrones and principalities, but of God and the soul, the soul and its God.'[32] Supernatural, religious and experiential, the kingdom is a mighty spiritual force which can be understood only from within, and which renews and brings joy as it unlocks the meaning and the aim of life.

Central to Jesus' teaching was the notion of becoming children of God, for which Harnack cited a fourfold exegetical base. From the Lord's Prayer there is the address, 'Our Father'; there is the notion of being 'safe with God', which is implicit in the assurance that our names are written in heaven; there are the sayings about sparrows and 'the very hairs of your head'; and there is the utterance, 'What shall it profit a man if he shall gain the whole world and lose his own soul?'[33] Here is the transvaluation of all values, presented with the combination of simplicity and profundity which was the hallmark of Jesus' peculiar genius.

Finally, when Harnack took up the theme of the higher righteousness and the commandment of love, he emphasised that to project the gospel as an ethical message was no depreciation of its value.[34] Harnack made four points about the ethics of Jesus: (i) Jesus severed the connection between ethics and the observance of external forms of worship: love and mercy are ends in themselves; (ii) questions of morality were radically evaluated in relation to disposition and intention: only thus can the 'higher righteousness' be understood; (iii) the moral principle was reduced to one root and one motive, viz. love; (iv) there was an intrinsic connection between religion and morality at one point in particular, not easy to define, but perhaps best described as humility: it is well expressed in the parable of the Pharisee and the publican, as well as in the love commandment and in the beatitudes. Thus, said Harnack, 'Jesus defined the sphere of the ethical in a way in which no one before him had ever defined it.'[35]

Having established the fundamental characteristics of Jesus' message, Harnack turned to the relation of the gospel to six problems selected by reason of their intrinsic importance and persistent recurrence in history. Four of them were issues in ethics. They concerned the relation of the gospel to the world (or the question of asceticism); to the poor (or the social question); to the law (or the question of public order); and to work (or the question of civilisation). The two remaining issues centred on Christology and doctrine.[36] Comment is offered here on the four issues in ethics which, as Harnack himself observed, 'hang together'.

Four issues in ethics

Is the gospel a world-denying creed?
The monastic ideal embodied in, for example, St Anthony or St Francis, might argue in favour of this proposition, although it has the disadvantage of suggesting that the gospel has little relevance to ordinary life. The total commitment Jesus required of those who aspired to be his disciples might seem to point in the same direction.[37] To these contentions however, Harnack opposed three weighty considerations. Unlike the Baptist, Jesus was a sociable person – eating, drinking, enjoying company: a 'free and active spirit' not 'bent under the yoke of asceticism'. Moreover, the disciples, however demanding their calling, did not follow an ascetic life-style. The factor which clinched the argument for Harnack was that the keynotes of the life of faith are humility, the forgiveness of sins and mercy: 'there is no room for the introduction of any other maxim, least of all for one of a legal character'.[38] Worldly blessings are not to be regarded as of the devil: 'your heavenly Father knows that you need them all' (Matt. 6.32). Asceticism is not to be confused with the struggle against mammon or materialism, against the anxious care which comes of distrust in God's providence, or against selfishness which is the reverse of the love which serves.

The gospel and the poor
Against a background of claim and counter-claim about Jesus as social reformer, Harnack underlined the fact that, in the socio-religious context in which Jesus taught, 'the poor' represented not simply the economically depressed, but humble people whose hearts were open towards God. It should not be

concluded from this, however, that Jesus either advocated economic poverty as good for the soul or was indifferent to its consequences. The importance he assigned 'to those forces of sympathy and mercy which are expected to counteract this state of things' speaks for itself. Jesus did not promulgate a programme of social reform; but his message was 'profoundly socialistic, just as it is also profoundly individualistic' in that it placed value on 'every human soul' while affirming the need for community and togetherness. It is 'the proclamation of solidarity and brotherliness, in favour of the poor'.[39] Harnack was well aware of the far-reaching consequences of such a message for the bourgeois churches of his day, and also for politics. The gospel, he suggested, aims to 'transform the socialism which rests on the basis of conflicting interests into the socialism which rests on the consciousness of spiritual unity'.[40] At the same time, he observed: 'The fallacious principle of the free play of forces, of the "live and let live" principle – a better name for it would be the "live and let die" – is entirely opposed to the gospel'.[41]

The gospel and the law
As far as the constituted authorities were concerned, Harnack acknowledged that Jesus was no political revolutionary; but Jesus showed 'emancipating and refreshing disrespect' for the unconstitutional power which political and ecclesiastical leaders exercised over people's lives. The vexed question of 'render to Caesar... and to God' is not to be solved by simply juxtaposing or positing an alliance of their two provinces, but by separating and divorcing them. A duty to Caesar is acknowledged, but the emperor has no power over the soul: that belongs to God. Mark 10.42, however, suggests a 'transvaluation of values': to be great means to serve. There is also a suggestion that authorities rely on force and therefore place themselves outside the moral sphere. The disciples were to build their community on moral grounds: not on compulsion, but on service.

What value may Christian ethics place on law or legal ordinance, since it also rests on compulsion? Was Tolstoy right in refusing, in the name of the gospel, to give any rights to the law? The experience of the Jewish nation underlined the fact that law was exercised by the dominant earthly powers in their own interests. By contrast, Jesus looked to the justice of God, which would prevail in the end. He linked it, without reservation, to the idea of recompense, and he suggested that, one day, the disciples would share in its administration. On that day, justice would indeed be done – to the poor and to their oppressors. Yet at an inter-personal level, disciples will waive their rights and co-operate in building a loving community in which justice is effected not through compulsion, but by willing assent to what is good and loving.

What then about groups and classes struggling for justice, in what would now be called liberation movements? At the beginning of the century, Harnack was aware of the possibility of socialist revolution and of Marxist objections to the gospel as a narcotic paralysing all real energy. For Harnack, the positive message of the gospel was clear. There is one inviolable goal – to be a child of God and a citizen of his kingdom, and to exercise love. We may well fight for justice and attempt to re-order the world in a better way, but let us not presume that the gospel will give us any direct help. Harnack fully accepted the priority of love to neighbour, and in his own way applied it in a radical sense. The gospel was always directly concerned 'with the souls of men'. When the option of revolution is under discussion, Harnack insists that we take account of the consequences of our actions and policies for the spiritual condition of humankind. He thereby leaves us in a dilemma: is this bourgeois ethics, involving a devious use of moralism to preserve the status quo? Or is it a genuine critique of revolution, springing from the essence of the gospel? Has he neutralised revolution – or neutralised the gospel?

The gospel and civilisation

To Strauss, a fundamental defect of the gospel was Jesus' apparent lack of interest in the importance of labour, the economic base of society and even civilisation itself. Harnack recognised that the gospel has no interest in prescribing how the affairs of the world are to be carried on, and so does not respond to 'the old and almost ineradicable tendency of mankind' to flee from its freedom and responsibility (an existentialist touch here) and to take refuge in the authority of law and regulation. He was prepared, however, to face the problem which Strauss raised, viz., Jesus' lack of sympathy with everyday business, and the fact that he was 'out of touch with the *humaniora* in the sense of science, art and civilization generally'.[42]

Harnack's reply is threefold. (i) Labour, art, science, the progress of civilisation are relative to the times in which they exist. The church has lost much by identifying with a particular culture, e.g., the Middle Ages. The gospel, on the other hand, 'sounded the notes of religion in mighty chords and banished every other melody'.[43] Harnack's rhetoric suggests dialogue between the gospel and the culture of each age, rather than the identification of the two. (ii) Labour is a most important aspect of most ages, but it possesses a decided ambivalence and does not comprise the highest ideal or convey the deepest satisfaction. In the same way, civilisation is a highly relative concept and must be evaluated in the light of the kingdom of God. It is to the kingdom that Jesus bore testimony. (iii) Jesus' message had an aggressive character: it summoned up the fire of judgment as well as the forces of love, and it aimed at the creation of a new humanity. Knowledge of God is the highest good, the condition of all edification and therefore the genesis of all true growth and progress. Jesus saw on the horizon a kingdom of justice, love and peace, coming from heaven, but destined for this earth. The gospel 'tells us of the real work which humanity has to accomplish, and we ought not to meet its message by entrenching ourselves behind our miserable "work of civilization"'.[44]

A brief assessment

Consider this observation by Dorothee Sölle:

Attractive and beautiful though Harnack's theology seems to me at first sight, it reveals nothing about the poor, those to whom the biblical message is really addressed. Harnack spoke about the infinite value of the human soul, but not about the colonialism of the German empire or about militarism. Indeed he was one of the many theologians and intellectuals who rejoiced at the outbreak of the First World War.[45]

Our brief review of Harnack might serve to question some aspects of this sweeping assessment, and to accept others. It is difficult not to endorse the attractiveness and quality of his thinking in the context of his day. In his view of the ethics of Jesus, which in liberal style he took as in some sense a model of values, he brought out clearly its individual and social aspects and illuminated the importance of motivation, disposition, intention, moral principle and, above all, the intrinsic relation between religion and morality. In all of this, he anticipated directions which Christian ethics itself would take much later. When Joseph Fletcher appealed to *agape* as the sole principle and criterion, he was – wittingly or otherwise – expressing a view which Harnack could have taken. When the intrinsic relation of belief or worship and ethics is expressed in modern philosophical discussion in terms of humility, Harnack has already seen the point clearly. When Käsemann declared, 'Jesus means freedom!', the sentiment is Harnack's. And, when modern liberationists agonise over the use of force *in extremis*, Harnack has faced the issue before them.

It is surprising that Dorothee Sölle singled out his attitude to the poor. It would seem from the above survey that he endorsed 'the option for the poor'. While he held fast to the notion of spiritual liberation as central, there is no reason to suppose that his concern for the plight of the poor and oppressed was other than genuine. To be sure, he refused to endorse any human revolution as an expression of the gospel, as Barth also did after him. Christians might commit themselves to such movements, but that was a matter of conscience. All human enterprises of this kind are, at best, morally ambivalent. But he criticised the established conventions of society in similar terms. In other words, he affirmed a critique in the name of the gospel. His standpoint was therefore much less bourgeois than that of many of his contemporaries. If his view was still 'top down', it was so in a modified way which allowed place for at least some alternative perspectives. In short, he was involved with society and culture as one bearing the message of the love of God in Christ. He sought dialogue with, not absorption into, the values of modern civilisation, and saw the gospel as a creative force.

But if it was truly to be a living force, the gospel must not be confounded with dogma. Indeed, the institutional churches, not unlike society in the wider sense, must continue to be reformed in the light of the gospel. For him, this was the only way to make sense of church history. Each age manifests something of permanent value, but the forms Christianity assumes vary from age to age. Church history therefore witnesses to one metamorphosis upon another.[46]

What is undoubtedly true is that Harnack was part of the German academic establishment. There was thus a large gap between his station in life and the lot of the poor for whom he evinced political and moral concern. This is true of most theologians! It is part of his tragedy, and that of many of his contemporaries across national boundaries, that in the hour of crisis he remained so loyal to that establishment and did not invoke the freedom which he so often professed. Here is the fault line, the debit side in Harnack's account. It has to do with his idealist philosophy and its weakness in relation to sociohistorical context. He sought to distinguish the essence of a phenomenon from the temporary form it adopted in a given age. Thus the principles he adduced from the ministry of Jesus are not to be identified with Jesus' teaching itself, which was an historical phenomenon in its own right. Indeed, for a historian, he paid remarkably little attention to the socio-historical context of Jesus' ministry. He treated the scriptures of Israel in purely historical fashion and would gladly have seen them removed from the canon of Christian scripture.[47] He recognised, but made too little of, the factor of eschatology, and he was so preoccupied with his challenge to the place of doctrine – Christology in particular – in the interests of doctrinal freedom that he lost sight of other forms of bondage. There was a blind spot in his self-understanding. Even the moral perspectives he offers lack the depth which a fuller treatment of the place of suffering and death in Jesus' ministry would have given. His view of Jesus is itself inadequate. It might be reasonable to suggest that Jesus 'lived in religion' and that 'his whole life, all his thoughts and feelings, were absorbed in the relation to God', but is it true that he never talked like an enthusiast ('I saw

Satan fall like lightning from heaven'), that he never used any
ecstatic language ('Amen, I say to you...'), and that 'the tone
of stirring prophecy is rare' ('My Father's house shall be a
house of prayer...')?[48] Harnack's Jesus, sensitively portrayed
though he is in many ways, is just too suggestive of a nineteenth-
century idealist to be convincing. Once again, the 'two
horizons' have been too easily reconciled. The liberal Protestant
was always inclined to mistake the reflection at the foot of the
well for objective reality, and that reflection was, like his
audience, 'bourgeois, educated, enlightened male'.[49]

Nevertheless, Harnack's contribution to the understanding of
the moral dimensions of Jesus' ministry is of too great importance to be lightly dismissed. As Rudolf Bultmann recognised, his work is by no means 'a lifeless residue of a vanished era
which no longer needs to be taken seriously', but 'contains
active impulses which...preserve their legitimacy and will
recover their validity'.[50]

THE ETHICS OF PAUL: A. B. D. ALEXANDER[51]

Paul and Jesus

The liberal historical view, expressed *par excellence* in Harnack,
combined pervasive idealist presuppositions with the rationality
of historical research and sensitivity to human experience and
spirituality. This combination attempted to ensure that the
study of Jesus' teaching opened up perspectives not only on the
ancient context (as in 'ancient ethics'), but also on fundamental
issues of modern life ('Christian ethics'). The two horizons were
differentiated, but also united by permanent truths and values.
The human sciences were gradually informing and challenging
the liberal approach. As we have seen, there was a persistent
tendency, evident in Luthardt as well as in the work of W.
Heitmüller among others,[52] to take personality not only as the
key to the interpretation of Jesus, but as the focus of significance
in all great religious teachers. This historical–psychological
view, which characterised a number of early twentieth-century
studies of Jesus, found even greater scope in the study of Paul. It
emerged clearly in Alexander's study of Pauline ethics.

Moreover, under the influence of the *Aufklärung*, dogmatics and dogmatism were equally suspect. Sometimes the 'simple religion of Jesus' was held up as an example of non-dogmatic religiosity; sometimes Jesus was castigated as an enemy of humanism and civilisation. In either case, Paul tended to be projected as the villain of the piece, enveloping the simplicity of Jesus' message in a web of theological speculation and dogma. There was a case to answer.

Alexander began by admitting that while, unlike the Synoptic Gospels, Paul's writing moved in the atmosphere of speculative theology, yet 'we cannot for a moment mistake its distinctively ethical character'.[53] Jesus' teaching and that of Paul are, *contra* Wrede, in fundamental accord. 'Both have an ethical purpose. Both lay the emphasis on character.'[54] Both point to the same source of the new life – receptiveness before God, the inmost spring of vital religion; to the same motivation – faith in God as Father and in the call to sonship; and to the same aim – the divine perfection, 'the prize of the high calling of God in Christ'. Alexander wrote: 'Surely no one can doubt that Christ's ethical ideal, which he looked for as the realization of the object of His mission, was a redeemed humanity, a complete renewal and re-establishment of human society – which he designated "the kingdom of God".'[55] Paul found the kingdom typified and realised in the risen Lord, whose coming 'will be itself the realization of the social ideal, the coming of God's kingdom on the earth'.[56]

The Psychology of Paul

Alexander began with a review of the influences which shaped Paul's teaching and which 'developed by contact and antagonism with the thought of the age'.[57] Major features were his 'encultivation' in the Hebrew tradition, the influence upon him of the Graeco-Roman world, including Greek language and Stoic philosophy, and above all Paul's unique personal contribution, fashioned by the influence of Christ: 'the unknown personal something we call genius'.[58]

Significantly, Alexander devoted a leading chapter to 'the

psychology' of Paul, although it is concerned with what is termed 'anthropology' by later scholarship. After reviewing seven key terms employed by Paul in reference to human nature,[59] and examining their interrelationship, he concludes that the human organism ('man') is a unity of body and soul: 'spirit' is not to be admitted as a third distinct element but simply as 'the soul viewed in its higher or Godward side'.[60] 'Spirit', in fact, is the new characteristic of the Christian, whereas 'flesh' describes man as a creature in his natural state apart from Christ. It follows that sin is essentially living to oneself, in selfishness and self-asserting independence, making oneself the sole object of concern. Yet, although sin is universal and as inescapable as heredity, it does not infringe 'the freedom and responsibility of every man before God'.[61]

Christian personality

Certain features of moral and spiritual development are selected by Alexander for special emphasis. He stressed 'ethical ideal', relating it to the will of God in Christ and to the brotherhood and unity of humankind. He underlined the dynamic of the new life as spiritual force or 'virtue making power'. The dynamic comes both from the side of God – the act of God in Christ and the power of the Holy Spirit working as 'an inner spirit of life' – and from the human side, for there is a subjective or personal element in the new life of faith. As for motive, there is a coincidence of aim and incentive – 'the love of God experienced in Christ is the deepest motive to Christian morality just because it is held forth as the chief good'[62] – but sanctions also play a part.[63] In Paul's words, 'Now that you have been set free from sin and have become the servants of God, the harvest you enjoy is the momentum to holiness and its end is eternal life' (Rom. 6.22). A central notion in Paul is that of vocation, which gives dignity and stability to the entire Christian life.[64]

With his interest in Christian personality, Alexander discussed 'the particular virtues of character in which the ideal is realized'[65] and ranged over Paul's concern with the classical virtues, the emphasis he placed on the amiable virtues, and the crowning glory of the theological virtues.[66] But growth and development in the moral life are central to Paul's ethics: the 'new man', Alexander observed, 'is not at the commencement a complete man'.[67] There is a gradual sanctification, a growth towards perfection, in which both God and the human agent are participants. God indeed energises both will and action, yet we must work out our own salvation with fear and trembling (cf. Phil. 2.12). Hence the Christian life can be compared to a battle, to a race or to a boxing match.[68] It is also supported by divine providence and discipline in which the struggle with temptation, as well as suffering and work, have a place, and it is nourished by scripture, church and sacraments together with self-examination, watchfulness and prayer.

Duties of the Christian life

Alexander's final task is 'to consider how the virtues of the Pauline ideal issue in their corresponding *duties* and cover the whole field of man's life'.[69] From his comprehensive discussion of these duties, we select three issues for comment here: duty to self (or the problem of self-love); the position of women; and duty to the state.

Duty to self

Alexander tried to demonstrate how the virtues of the Pauline ideal issued in corresponding duties covering the whole of life. He had considerable difficulty with duty to oneself. Why did Paul make so little of self-love and self-realisation? In the Hellenistic cultural milieu, Paul 'may have felt that not so much the virtue of self-regard as that of self-forgetfulness was what called for special emphasis'.[70] Even more important was the link he saw between self-realisation and self-surrender. This paradoxical notion is to be related to the interdependence of human beings. Alexander rejected Kierkegaard's notion of the individual as the only subject of ethics and moved towards an interactive view of personhood. 'I cannot make myself of no account even in my love for another. So inextricably are the individual and society bound together in the kingdom of love that neither can reach its goal without the other.'[71] Paul also emphasised stability or firmness of character, together with independence of judgment: 'Let every one be fully convinced in his own mind' (Rom. 14.5).

Christians are bodily part of the world, but they stand in a new relationship to earthly things. They are freed from bondage, whether to materialism, over-indulgence, asceticism, legalism or convention. They live in faith to God's glory. The human body itself is highly esteemed as the temple of God and organ of the Holy Spirit. Self-control is the guiding principle: not as a disparagement of the body, but as a mark of respect for it. Paul, one might think, was bound to endorse marriage, since it expressed so completely the interrelatedness of humankind – indeed even a deeper interrelatedness (cf. 1 Cor. 11.3; Eph. 5.32); yet he qualified his endorsement of it, particularly in the seventh chapter of 1 Corinthians. Alexander advanced a number of reasons for this peculiarity: a particularly strong vocation, such as Paul's own; the persistence of ascetic tendencies in Paul; the expectation of the end of the age; the distracting 'worldly troubles' that marriage involves; and the underlying assumption that marriage was a concession to weakness. What is lacking in Alexander's treatment is a thoroughly contextual study of 1 Corinthians 7.

Finally, Paul's complex attitude to 'worldly affairs' is reviewed: his insistence on being self-supporting while urging the claims for support and remuneration made by others; his advocacy of restraint, stewardship and generosity in relation to material goods; his recognition of the legitimacy of trade, coupled with a warning against excessive preoccupation with the affairs of this life (1 Thess. 4.11f.). Alexander expressed surprise that Paul did not offer direct counsel or warning on the Christian attitude to recreation, but made up for the omission with some reflections of his own on the subject. Finally, he discussed Paul's insistence on contentment with one's station in life. He carefully avoided the more notorious misinterpretations of this theme by relating the counsel to the context of the convert in 1 Cor. 7.17–24. To be sure, Paul was no revolutionary.

He did not conceive it to be his mission to denounce slavery, or in any way to meddle with the existing order of society. Nowhere does he, by word or deed, in the slightest degree, interfere with the externals of social life. He lets slavery, war, the tyranny of the Roman Empire, alone, not surely because he regarded them as satisfactory, but because he believed in first making the tree good and then the fruit would follow.'[72]

Yet in certain important respects Paul's teaching appears to contradict this remarkable respect for the status quo.[73]

Position of women

In spite of his apparent reinforcement of social convention, Paul's presentation of the Christian understanding of the nature and role of women is described by Alexander as part of a 'mighty revolution' which Paul advanced more than most. And the revolution was not only apparent when the practice of the Christian community was compared with Graeco-Roman conventions, but rested upon the recognition of equality in the sight of God. Paul becomes the focus of controversy in modern interpretation only in relation to the practical expression of this equality. In 1 Cor. 11.1–16, he was clearly bent on regulating excess. In an eastern context, Alexander explained, to lay aside the veil in order to come boldly forward in public was unbecoming and indelicate. But Alexander betrayed a greater degree of patriarchal naïvety than Paul when he concluded:

She is God's glory by being man's glory. She serves God by serving man, and helping him to realize his true self; and she never fulfils her destiny so faithfully as when she employs her womanly gifts according to the sphere and position allotted to her for the enrichment and elevation of manhood.[74]

The passage no longer reads as an expression of radical equality! In Paul's writing, there is a problem about the interrelation of principle and contingency, of theology and ethics. Alexander did not succeed in clarifying it, for his prejudices constrained his perception. The problem has to be tackled at a more radical level if the 'mighty revolution' is not to die with a whimper amid the strident reaffirmation of patriarchy.

Duty to the state

Augustine regarded the state as a response to human sin. Hegel took it as the highest form of moral society. Alexander adjudged Paul to be nearer to Hegel. The grounds for the claim are to be found in Rom. 13.1–7, a veritable *crux interpretum*. Here Paul appears to offer a theological justification of state power, to which the Christian submits with good conscience. Elsewhere in the New Testament, the question of the alienation of the authorities from God and obedience to God as the supreme duty (cf. Acts 4.19) is allowed to surface, but Paul does not pursue this line in his letters. Alexander, however, raises the issue in unequivocal terms:

> There are times when the Christian must employ more direct and active measures for righting wrong and achieving good. There is an ethic of revolt. There is a realm into which human law dare not intrude – the domain of conscience. When 'unrighteousness masquerades in the garb of legality', then the Christian man must take his stand and utter his protest.[75]

It is evident that Alexander did not reach this conclusion on exegetical grounds alone. Rather, his exegesis has been informed by the tradition to which he belongs. Not for nothing had Calvin agonised over the right of revolt against a tyrant, and Knox confronted Mary at Holyrood. But what connection is there between this kind of prophetic ministry and the discreet Paul who would never dare to meddle with the externals of social life?

A BRIEF ASSESSMENT

Transposition

A clue to the problem faced by Alexander is found in his observation that, for all their prominence in his study, the language of 'virtue' and 'duty' is essentially foreign to the New Testament. The same could, of course, be said of key words throughout his study: ideals and principles, personality and character, not to speak of progress and ethical ultimate. Why then does he use them? He had several aims in writing on the ethics of Paul. The subject was relatively neglected.[76] Paul's letters had strong implications for ethics, and there was a need, in face of widespread interest in the ethics of Christianity, 'to ascertain the attitude to the practical questions of life of one who was the first, as he was the greatest exponent of the mind of Christ'.[77] Here, then, is Alexander's answer to the problem of the relationship between Paul and Jesus. In liberal style, he recognised that his age was impatient with dogma, and accepted the need to translate Paul's meaning out of its theological terminology so that its 'deathless message for men of all times' might be understood. It is, however, impossible to miss his insistence that Paul's moral teaching is not a mere appendix to his doctrine, but flows directly from it and represents a vital part of it. Therefore, starting from a modern progressive stance, Alexander transposes the text into the modern idiom. Thus the horizons merged on Alexander's terms. With its contextual weaknesses, his study of Paul's ethics is somewhat removed from the world of Paul. A case in point is his reduction, translation and elimination of eschatology as a living issue for the apostle. Again in liberal fashion, he defended his resort to general principles. Precepts and commands, he argued, tended to be limited to particular situations, but principles by their very nature are applicable over a much wider spectrum. The result of such far-reaching, but conventional, transposition was that, apart from the achieving of these immediate aims, the nature and complexity of Paul's ethical insights were largely obscured.

Personality, equality and liberty

The bequest of Paul to the modern world, he maintained, includes the ideas of personality and human equality. 'In these two notions lie the seeds of that spirit of democracy and that sense of individual responsibility which are the features of the nobler social order of our times.'[78] The trouble with 'personality' is that it cannot easily be made a theme of enquiry, since it requires a reflexive move 'in which consciousness turns back upon itself and becomes self-consciousness'.[79] Besides, there is no counterpart for it in the New Testament or the

ancient world. E. F. Scott attempted to turn this to advantage
by the suggestion that the very novelty of Christianity out-
stripped the available linguistic and conceptual resources.[80]
Alexander represents only the early stage of the interplay
between biblical interpretation and social sciences such as
psychology.[81]

Other liberal values include equality, as noted above, and
also 'liberty'. The liberals often pointed out that Jesus had little
to say of civil liberty or political freedom or the reform of
outward conditions. By penetrating to the inner meaning of
freedom, Jesus proved himself the greatest of liberators, securing
for all their rightful place as human beings. But we need to go
beyond this point if we are to establish social relevance. Yet
another imperishable value is progress, a predominant concept
in liberal presentations from Luthardt to Scott but one foreign
to ancient society. It is a modern deduction from Christian
liberty and from the kingdom as goal: not a general good but
the fulfilment of spiritual being. Religion is about discovering
what is true and permanent, and this implies change and
progress.

Christian faith and culture

With what now seems incredible complacency, Alexander
implied that, while Paul was inhibited by the crass nature of
Roman imperium, he and his contemporaries in 1910 could give
much fuller expression to Pauline principles, since they lived in
a situation in which Christianity and the state were no longer
antagonistic and where the answers to contemporary social
problems were sought on moral principles and in terms of the
highest good. But not only has the course of twentieth-century
European history provided a devastating commentary on the
nature of its civilisation, but the economic and political realism
of the latter part of the century has undermined any naïve claim
to a high-principled base-line. One is bound to conclude that
Alexander, like the liberal school in general, had failed to realise
the essential nature of the interaction between Christianity and
culture, and the relativism involved in every social expression of
it, ancient and modern.

Beyond liberalism

Biblical interpretation in the hands of the liberals attempted not only to negotiate the hazards of reading an ancient text, but to highlight moral principles or lessons for today. A typical shortcoming was their lack of control over the differentiation of the horizons of text and interpreter and the subsequent synthesis of them. The result was the dominance of the liberal world view, which even the biblical characters were made to subserve. The characteristic interpretive procedure is illustrated by Jülicher on the parables. The Good Samaritan, for example, is a *Bild*, a portrayal of a universal truth, that an act of self-sacrificing love is of eternal value, and that – as so often in Jesus' teaching – the outcast and despised, the Samaritan in this case, practises what God requires more effectively than the staff of the institutional temple. The praxis of faith is thus enveloped in the trappings of a moralistic idealism and is presented as the unexceptional morality of cultural sophistication. It has become largely the story with a moral, ready to be attenuated even more in the moralism of pulpit or school.[82]

Liberalism is not without its paradoxes. In its championing of freedom, the historical critical method and personal value, it was liberating for many and helped to develop models of biblical interpretation which took account of the human factor in biblical formation and understanding, without denying divine inspiration and authority. Yet its inherent optimism was challenged to the core by events in Europe in the twentieth century, which in turn prompted a swing to dialectical theology and a much more critical relation between theology and culture. But not every sphere was equally affected by the European catastrophe, and liberalism continued to be influential in theology and ethics.[83] Perhaps, in spite of everything, its intellectualism and its bourgeois qualities appeal to policy-makers within Western churches. This has provoked a reaction against the academic or intellectual, and a clamour for experience, emotion and authority. In many non-Western churches, the liberal paradigm is neither liberating nor meaningful: in Dorothee Sölle's words, 'what was bread has become a stone'.[84] Yet it is remarkable how prominently liberal features figure in the work of a modern ethicist such as Hauerwas: Jesus as model, character, virtues, community, the social significance of the church, the church and democracy, and so on.[85] But Hauerwas also distinguishes his standpoint from that of the liberals, who failed to acknowledge that a society presupposed a specific kind of narrative as the source of its values. As we have argued here, the values of liberal theology are the product of the Enlightenment or a response to it; and as such they relate dangerously to the cultural values of the establishment, whose 'story', to use Hauerwas' term, draws from similar sources, but is geared to the maintenance of power. And it is *this story* or *these stories* (for there is a degree of pluralism) which make a takeover bid for the Christians' story in the name of liberal values. Thus Harnack, who did not lack awareness of the situation, finally endorsed the establishment line when the crisis came, and Alexander for all his Calvinist insight speaks as an educated Edwardian gentleman on matters of economic structure and gender roles. Hauerwas puts it rather differently, suggesting that liberalism persuades society that it has no common narrative.

As a result it tempts us to believe that freedom and rationality are independent of narrative – i.e., we are free to the extent that we have no story. Liberalism is, therefore, particularly pernicious to the extent it prevents us from understanding how deeply we are captured by its account of existence.[86]

CHAPTER 2

The principles of social ethics

Social ethics is historically relative, dealing with issues
which are appropriate to a time and situation, concerned
with universal imperatives but as they bear on particular
issues. This fact about social ethics makes the simple
application of historical examples to contemporary problems relatively meaningless, even when those examples
are drawn from holy texts.

(Gibson Winter)[1]

Liberal scholarship did not shrink from the challenge of social
ethics, which may be defined briefly as questions of 'moral
rightness and goodness in the shaping of human society'.[2]
Typically, it attempted a synthesis of Christian perspectives
with those derived from secular disciplines in a quest for the
highest corporate morality: hence appeal was made above all to
principles and ideals. But it could also sponsor a prophetic
dynamic much more closely related to the biblical tradition,
and transcending anything that could be described as 'the
simple application of historical examples to contemporary
problems'. Indeed, liberal scholars gradually absorbed perspectives from social science which enabled them to acquire some
understanding of the importance of context, although they did
not always recognise the extent to which their own views were
shaped by society and its intellectual traditions in particular:
witness their acceptance of the myth of progress, usually in the
form of a theological rationalization.[3]

The theological and philosophical background of social ethics
is impressive. Luther had always been concerned for civil order,
whether in his view of law (*usus civilis*) and the two kingdoms, or
in the attention he paid to the institutional structures (family,

state, calling and church).[4] Calvin recognised the *usus civilis*, and had a more positive view of government. *In extremis*, he also accepted a limited right of disobedience against the ungodly ruler.[5] Hegel had also been concerned with moral action within the basic social unities, such as family, civil society and state. While he took affection as well as duty to be the bond of family life, civil society provided a context for moral duty, although the whole structure was held together by mutual self-interest. He noted that, since one is born into the state, Kant's voluntarist principle did not apply, at least without severe qualification. Some moral choices are not universalisable: they are particular to the situation of the agents, or even to the agents themselves; and in some cases they have no choice at all.[6]

The liberals' understanding of social ethics was influenced by their recognition of the role of the church community, which was both separate from society as the people of God – through the daily avocations of its members – and also a bridgehead for the gospel in society.[7] At its best, it was a position which accepted the need for individual vocation and transformation, the fellowship, nurture and common life of the worshipping community, and the task of mission.

This kind of understanding was extended and modified by the pioneer sociologist, Max Weber, in interaction with the theologian Ernst Troeltsch. Weber posited the ideal distinction between church and sect types.[8] The former, with its broad, associational nature, is not rigidly marked off from society, and therefore tends to identify with cultural values, even if it would wish to modify them or view them 'in depth'. The latter, with its voluntarist and exclusive characteristics, expects its distinctive view of the world to be upheld by its members. While liberal practice did not always correspond precisely to this church/sect typology, which was in any case intended to be understood flexibly, the issue came up regularly in recognisable form.[9] In this chapter we shall sample cases from England, Germany and the USA, before looking at a leading theological interpreter of liberal social ethics.

SOCIAL ETHICS IN ENGLAND: THE ETHICS OF PRINCIPLED MEDIATION

In England, the fact that the industrial revolution coincided with the adoption of a *laissez-faire* policy in relation to trade and industry created a situation in which the social implications of Christianity came to be emphasised as a stimulus to alternative political initiatives.[10]

B. F. Westcott[11] provides an example of moral concern in an outstanding nineteenth-century exegete – although his exegetical work was academic and his social ethics popular. Disconcertingly, he tended simply to assume the exegetical basis of his ethics and to begin with the theological import of word studies.[12] One can discern, however, the holistic principle that the scriptures witness together to Christ: a position illumined by tradition and modern interpretation alike. Next, one moves towards engagement with society. A point of contact is found in the fact that society has assimilated ideas from Christianity, although these are impossible ideals without vital contact with the living Christ. Westcott therefore establishes a theological version of what would later be called 'middle axioms'. He describes them as 'historical certainties which answer to the manifold instincts, experiences, imaginings of all ages'.[13] The threefold foundational programme is stated thus:

If the Word became flesh, the brotherhood of man is a reality for us.

If the Son of God is crucified, the fall, and with it the redemption, are realities for us.

If the Son of man rose again from the dead, the eternal significance of our short space of labour is a reality for us.

By means of these three principles, he related the central doctrines of the faith to the transformation of human experience. The first, combining creation (Gen. 1.27) and incarnation (John 1.1, 14), affirms an 'energy of fellowship', encompassing God and humankind, and interrelates the traditional emphasis on natural law and an incarnational theology. The second affirms the dynamic of hope amid evil. 'No view of the human state is so inexpressibly sad as that which leaves out the Fall',[14] but his strong view of evil is set over against the power of forgiveness and the strength for the conflict with evil which comes through Christ. The third embraces the unity of what is and what will be: 'it shows us how we are shaping slowly out of things transitory that which will abide for ever'.[15] These axioms form 'the absolute law of our existence', and as such they form the basis of social ethics, not an appendage to it.

Westcott gave expression to these principles in relation to family, nation and state, race and church and society. The family represents the primary expressions of human fellowship (husband–wife, parent–child, brothers–sisters), which he calls 'the original sacraments of society'. Westcott's view of the family, however, is not only idealised, it is traditional and patriarchal, sociologically underdeveloped and notably lacking in critical edge. Like the family, the nation relates to 'the very constitution of man'. Its vitality is expressed in its language, law, government and religion. Government is to be seen as the necessarily incomplete reflection of an eternal order.[16] By 'race' Westcott meant the human race, rather than racial groups, and affirmed its oneness (Acts 17.26). Frankly acknowledging the dangers of imperialism, he traced the vicious circle of domination–imitation–indifference, and pointed to the need for a wider vision, such as the gospel provides (cf. Eph. 1.18), looking towards the kingdom of God.[17] The church is the realisation of human brotherhood whose pedigree reaches back to Abraham.[18]

While Westcott's ethics combines theological perspectives with insights from modern historical and even sociological approaches, there is a clear divide between his exegetical work, which reflects the limited type of hermeneutic that finds expression in text and commentary, and his social teaching, which tends to take the exegesis for granted, eliciting theological axioms as the foundation for policy and action and as expressions of the ultimate scenario within which all human action is set. His view of the church was strongly associational, although it enshrined a prophetic or kerygmatic element.

Westcott believed that his interactive view of humankind tended 'to counteract that spirit of isolating competition which is eating away the old repose and nobility of English life'.[19] Emphasising the social nature of *homo sapiens*, he tended to assume that society represents a kind of dormant fellowship, ineffectual and impotent until awakened to vital faith. He would draw all into the hermeneutical circle in which they would discover the ultimate law of their corporate being (he acknowledged a debt to Comte), and thus undergo transformation.

If Westcott grounded his social action on a combination of theological symbol and ethical principle, later attempts moved the encounter one step forward. J. H. Oldham saw the need for what he called 'middle axioms' between general statements of the ethical demands of the gospel and the decisions that have to be made in specific situations.[20] These were provisional statements designed to bring Christian values to bear on social reconstruction. William Temple exemplified them as freedom, fellowship and service, deriving from the great principles of love and justice and seeking expression in key areas of social and political life.[21] Temple was, of course, a considerable figure in English social ethics, drawing upon the idealist tradition in England and Germany, and placing much weight on the process of historical and societal development within which one identifies value and finds one's role in life. It is within this historical continuum that signals of the eternal are detected. He advocated the welfare state (perhaps even coining the term), but gradually moved away from collectivism. If in earlier phases of his thinking he allowed himself to express naïvely utopian views about progress towards perfection (made possible by the British Empire, or the United States, or Christendom!), his later views were in marked contrast, abandoning purposive notions of history, and even deserting the idea of fellowship as a key to the nature of society. This 'altogether bleaker and more pessimistic understanding of the social and political realm'[22] reflected the influence of Niebuhr and the dialectical theologians,[23] but surely also the grim circumstances of war and its commentary on the human situation.

How adequate are 'middle axioms'? Their intention and provisional nature must be emphasised: they make sense within the limitations of the purpose envisaged for them. While seeking to embody Christian values, they allow the agenda to be set largely by the worldly context. Hence there is an obligation on those who use them in public policy discussion to see them in the light of the gospel they so imperfectly embody. That is, they must be constantly related to and corrected by biblical interpretation if they are not to remain as reductions of biblical dynamics. There is a danger that the entire process is understood simply as applying principles to practice. Even Temple's idea of community lacks flesh and blood, and fails to generate a biblical or hermeneutical dynamic which would carry it into a much more participative mode. The process of interpretation must be fully contextualised – and here 'context' includes the empirical, problem laden situation, the biblical narrative as creative source and dynamic for change, and the interpreting community or agents. Principles have their limitations. As Duncan Forrester has observed, 'middle axiom thinking still operates at a far higher level of generality than many of its proponents wish to suggest, and offers remarkably little specific guidance either of a positive nature or by way of exclusion'.[24] There is also the problem of elitism: it is a kind of establishment thinking, a view from the top – very evident in Westcott.

It has been said that there are four stages in middle-axiom thinking: (i) the Christian faith; (ii) fundamental ethical principles; (iii) middle axioms; (iv) application in concrete decisions. There is, however, a problematic aspect to a term such as 'the Christian faith', which sweeps a multitude of questions – including hermeneutics – into a hold-all and encourages the liberal solecism that propositional understandings of the Christian faith are in all respects adequate representations of biblical dynamics. How far does this first base comprehend engagement with the biblical source, in which biblical symbols are contextualised in biblical story? Developing Temple's approach, Alan Suggate suggests a more comprehensive framework for Christian social ethics, having reference to (i) the dialectical method, (ii) a dramatic vision, embracing love and justice, (iii) persons, (iv) natural morality and Christian faith and (v) making decisions.[25] This represents a considerable advance, but it relates to the problem of biblical interpretation only by implication in 'dialectical method'.

At a personal level, one must confess that, in serving the church in social and secular contexts, one has frequently made at least implicit use of the 'middle-axiom' approach. In the late twentieth century, C. Villa-Vicencio still advocates it, at least as a contextual device to advance the Christian imperative.[26] This is not surprising, since he takes liberal theory as his point of entry to an interdisciplinary consideration of human rights.[27] It is an approach which can be effective within an academic community.

A final comment must, however, return to the limitations of this approach, with its recourse to the language of 'principle' and 'axiom', and its establishment or 'top-down' orientation. It spoke to the establishment, in the acceptable language of principle and policy, on behalf of the people – Temple made most effective use of it in this way; but it did not – and does not – in any sense empower the people. Since it is the Bible in particular which supplies the narrative quality essential to a Christian awareness of the flow of history, it is remarkable that scholars with the exegetical skills which Westcott and Temple both possessed should evince such apparent indifference to hermeneutics. The comment should probably be directed even more pointedly to the fragmented academic tradition which they represented.

PROPHETIC MINISTRY AND THE LIBERAL VISION IN GERMANY

A remarkable embodiment of prophetic ministry in nineteenth-century Europe is found in the two Blumhardts, father and son, who anticipated developments such as the importance of charisma and eschatology for social ethics, and also fore-shadowed in some ways the work of Rudolf Otto.[28] They do not accord precisely with Weber's typology, although they reflect

Württemberg pietism and thus, in some ways, relate to sect type. Yet the last description one would apply to them would be 'sectarian'.

The ministry of the elder Blumhardt (Johann Christoph) involved healing and exorcism.[29] On the occasion of a particularly memorable and dramatic exorcism in 1843, he interpreted the cries of the demon to mean, 'Jesus is victor'. This event not only underlined the dynamic and charismatic nature of his eschatology, it also moved both Blumhardts from pietistic individualism towards a social interpretation of the gospel. 'Jesus is victor' became their leading theme: victor over the devil, hell and death, over the flesh and over the whole world... The gospel proclaims hope and points to 'the future of Jesus Christ'. This dynamism carried over into the notion of the kingdom of God as expounded by Christoph Blumhardt (the son) in particular. Through Jesus, God has sown the seed of the kingdom in the midst of humanity, and eventually it will grow within humanity until its power is evident throughout the world. The transcendent kingdom is thus rooted in history. It works even through Jesus' enemies: when Jesus spoke of the kingdom as being 'in the midst of you' (Luke 17.21), he was addressing the opposition, viz., the Pharisees. The kingdom thus involves not only the establishing of the community of the faithful, but also the re-creation of all social and political structures.

The hermeneutics which the Blumhardts used interpreted the gospel in the light of present charismatic experience and present experience in the light of the gospel. A presupposition of this dialectic was awareness of what 'gospel' signified and a corresponding selection from biblical materials. The outcome was Christian social praxis. For the children of God, such an interpretation entailed involvement in historical processes, and identification with all those who work for their transformation. Hence one could commit oneself to the cause of social democracy in the spirit of Christ, and see in the aspirations of that movement a deeply significant sign of the times. Yet the kingdom comes by God's gift, not by human striving. Where does one look for the coming kingdom? Not, said Christoph

Blumhardt, to heaven, but rather 'there, where the multitudes of people perish in their misery...'[30] The Blumhardts marked the beginning of a line of development which included Kautsky and Bloch as well as Barth and Moltmann.[31] They made an impact on politics, and won the respect even of communists and atheists. They had an understanding of the structural nature of society and the necessity of involvement in its processes, and they inspired and operated with a community of disciples. They tend to coalesce the ideal types, whether church, sect or mystical. It is not easy, however, to express a prophetic ministry consistently while deeply exercised by political and institutional pressures – as George Macleod, for example, found to his cost.[32] A lack of consistency – theological and practical – in their position is sometimes cited to explain deviancy among some of their devotees: Johannes Müller, for example, ended up in national socialism. Even today, they are frequently charged with absorbing the facile optimism and belief in progress which came in the train of the *Aufklärung*. Yet something of Ritschl's ellipse remains. If one pole is rooted in history, the other is the transcendent kingdom whose mighty works are entirely in God's gift. The kingdom became a reality in the ministry of Jesus. Through his story we can discern the signs of our times. In consequence, transcendent power can be experienced here and now – in miracle, in new beginnings, in social transformation. The kingdom is experienced by the poor and needy. The rich – including many in the churches – reject it because they feel secure in their worldly existence. The Blumhardts therefore challenged conventional and establishment ideas in the name of the gospel, and called for obedience to God in social and corporate life. If they represent something of the 'view from above' in prophetic terms, they reflect something of the 'view from below' in social terms. The Bible is the source of the gospel criterion which they applied to social reality. Story and experience combine to illuminate the divine dynamic in society. Social reality is the interpreter's baseline. Whatever its shortcomings, there is a recognisable hermeneutic – at least *in nuce* – with an emphatic outcome in social ethics.

Needless to say, conventional interpretation in Germany took a very different line. In an essay – originally an address – on social mission, W. Herrmann considered the perennial problem of relating the Sermon on the Mount to the social sphere.[33] The nub of the issue was: in what sense are the imperatives of the Sermon to be understood? And what consequences follow from the view adopted? They are not to be understood legalistically, or as laws to be obeyed in every situation: that would be to impose a heavier burden on Jesus' followers than the legalism he opposed! It would also mean that certain social and political laws were enjoined by the gospel. Herrmann is clear that this is not so. Rather, the imperatives of the Sermon illustrate a new disposition, which depends upon inner spiritual transformation. 'It is when our inmost being is stirred and quickened by His Person that we are able to grasp something of the realities of which He speaks; and then, and not till then, His words become to us a gospel of power.'[34]

Herrmann, as a philosopher addressing the interpretation of the Sermon, wished to avoid the utopianism or anarchism of Tolstoy and the dismissiveness of Naumann.[35] Consistent with this emphasis are the means which the church has always used to make an impact on society: arousing the individual conscience, converting congregations into communities abounding in charity, and opposing what is altogether intolerable in society. While there is need for critical analysis of society, and for recognition of its inherent problems, it is not the task of the church to unravel all the difficulties, nor does it have a panacea for society's ills. The task of the church is to preach the gospel: it has to proclaim the living God and life eternal: sin is the root of the world's misery. The gospel gives freedom: spiritual transformation is the hub of the matter. As for the building up of congregational life, Herrmann comments: 'Next to the preaching of the Gospel, the reconstruction of congregational life is the chief evangelical–social task now before the Church.'[36] Here is a completely associational view which nevertheless preserves the distinction between church and society. The church should, of course, use its influence with the state to testify on questions of moral and social welfare. It should 'study and investigate the construction of the social organism, to examine which of its ills are inevitable, and which may be remedied by a spirit of self-sacrifice and energy'.[37] But, in complete contrast to the prophetic action of the Blumhardts, political alignment with social democracy is as alien to Herrmann as is the development of bureaucratic socialism. Three great tasks remain with the church: the defence of the evangelical faith; all possible action for the prevention of distress in society; and – not least – the encouragement of education and culture.

Herrmann's position, pedestrian by comparison with the Blumhardts, is that of a liberal theologian, for whom it was axiomatic that Jesus' teaching should embody universal truth or principle. The result is, as Windisch put it ironically: 'Jesus of Nazareth must have meant his commands to be taken exactly as the modern student of ethics who has read Kant, Tolstoy, Naumann, and others, interprets them.'[38] His emphasis on attitude takes much of the sting out of the imperatives. It was, after all, a matter of inner disposition, of cultivating the soul and doing charitable acts. Here is classic liberal reductionism. His insistence that the church must not pronounce on economic or political matters results in an astonishingly complacent and subservient acceptance of the status quo. 'A religion which aims at saving the soul and transforming the inner man, and which regards a change in outward circumstances as but a small matter in comparison with the power of evil, can only follow in the wake of earthly changes and exercise an after-influence.'[39] It is true that he acknowledged a Christian radicalism as a proper response to the perverted quietism which expressed a pious indifference to the poor and needy, but he wrote off the communism which 'has always clung to the Church like a shadow',[40] and had little to propose but philanthropy. In effect, he used the specialist nature of disciplines such as economics to prevent the church engaging actively with the structural and institutional problems which affect people's lives so markedly in modern societies. It may be that the outcome of his study accords well with the associational church and the priestly, rather than the prophetic, ministry. It is not surprising that, in the grim days that lay ahead, so many of Herrmann's contemporaries and successors were found wanting.[41]

The Social Gospel movement in the USA was far from being a transplantation of European social thinking. It was much more of an indigenous movement, with a spirit which accorded with the traditional pioneering outlook and was fed by American Puritanism, Methodist revivalism and a restated Calvinism, as well as by the scientific and cultural legacy of the Enlightenment.[42] Not that it was in any sense a simple aggregate of American church life. On the contrary, W. Rauschenbusch advanced its case against the prevailing individualism and introspection of much contemporary religiosity, and the tendency to use the terminology of 'crisis' pointed to the urgent need for change.[43] But its huge impact suggests that it tapped latent sources in American culture itself.

The general shape of its position may be sketched briefly. There was at its centre a basic hermeneutical claim, viz., that the true religion of Jesus had been distorted in the various epochs of Christian history and that Christianity had never yet been tried. Jesus was seen as the prophet and teacher of the new order. The central social concept was the kingdom of God: an ideal social order affirming the fatherhood of God and the brotherhood of men, and the universal dominion of love.[44] In so far as this position was broadly Ritschlian, it must be emphasised that the best of the Social Gospel movement recognised two poles: i.e., not only the immanentist, this-worldly view, but also that of the transcendent in history. The kingdom, as Rauschenbusch put it, 'is divine in origin, progress and consummation'.[45] Jesus was therefore more than a social reformer, but the religion of Jesus was thoroughly ethicised. One can serve God only through the service of one's fellows. In view of such solidarity, the cardinal sin is selfishness. The kingdom, as Jesus taught it, makes the world the theatre of action. Here and now the will of God receives dynamic expression to transform the existing order and foreshadow the new. Doing the will of God produces tangible results. The ultimate scenario is 'the social redemption of the entire life of the human race on earth'.[46]

The hermeneutical circle or spiral that emerges is something like this: first, there is an awareness, supported by a primary reading of the Gospels and by modern social science, that the individualistic view of human life is inadequate; next, there is a reading of the life of Jesus which highlights the social and this-worldly aspects of the kingdom as central to the religion of Jesus; then comes the commitment to the social gospel in modern society, fired by the dynamic of Jesus' message. This dynamic is translated into an ethic of principles: 'goodwill, love, fraternity, democracy, equality, service, reconciliation, sacrifice, cooperation'.[47] No aspect of life, least of all industry and politics, could be exempted from the sovereignty of Christ.

Shailer Mathews, in his book *The Social Teaching of Jesus* (subtitled *An Essay in Christian Sociology*) illustrates the central thrust of the programme. His concern was with 'the social philosophy and teachings of the historical person Jesus the Christ'.[48] He took the kingdom to denote 'an ideal (though progressively approximated) social order in which the relation of men to God is that of sons, and (therefore) to each other, that of brothers'.[49] With the ideal Jesus gave a kind of evolutionary dynamic, so that 'each generation could be trusted to transform the world in which it lived into a greater or lesser approximation to the kingdom'.[50] If one took seriously the renewing influence of the Divine Spirit and the love that springs from a sense of brotherhood, then one could speak confidently of the forces of human progress and the process of social regeneration.

There is much that is attractive and important in Social Gospel hermeneutics: not least the qualifying of principles by the story of Jesus' ministry and the attempt to express and embody the dynamics of the gospel. Nevertheless, its exegetical approach was characterised by contextual weakness. A social interpretation of the kingdom is read out of the New Testament without proper elucidation of its theological and socio-historical context in the Hebrew scriptures and Judaism or in the early Christian communities. Consequently, although the polarity

and antinomy it enshrines are recognised, the exegetical
imbalance is unmistakable. Furthermore, the emphasis upon
the religion of Jesus as fundamental to the hermeneutic strained
exegesis to breaking point, and fully deserved the trenchant
criticism bestowed on it by H. J. Cadbury in *The Peril of
Modernising Jesus.*[51]

The relationship between biblical interpretation and ethics is
critical. The basic assumption was that 'the religion of Jesus'
and the principles it enshrined could be applied directly to the
modern social and industrial scene, and so continue and
complete the process of Christianisation which had already
materially influenced other areas of society such as family and
church. Social sciences such as sociology and economics were
naïvely enlisted as partners in the process, and Christian ethics
made to collaborate in an ethic of progress, achievement, profit,
nationalism and the like. Nor was any element of compromise
admitted. 'It is so deeply convinced of the compatibility of
Christianity with social and industrial life that it does not see
any reason why it should so interpret itself.'[52] Here yet again is
contextual weakness.

A major part of this failure lay in the optimistic, evolutionary
view of human society – and, above all, of human nature –
which characterised the movement. Although it emphasised the
solidarity of humankind in a positive sense, it failed to come to
terms realistically with the negative side of this solidarity. The
fallenness of humanity, the notion of sin as inherent in the
human condition and in social and political structures and the
alienation of the human from the divine were brushed aside in
favour of an essentially individualistic interpretation of sin as
selfishness or an anti-social force occasioned largely by harsh
circumstances. Sin is a variable, rather than an invariable,
factor, and will diminish as the social order is transformed.[53] At
its best, such optimism could engender a powerful dynamic for
social reform, and the campaign to humanise industry, develop
education, extend family ethics to society as a whole and oppose
exploitation and militarism is notable. At several removes, this
kind of liberal ethics was given effective expression by Martin
Luther King and the human-rights campaign, although his

theological and contextual modifications of it are important. At worst, it confused the whole nature of Christian ethics, and reduced it to a naïvely optimistic human endeavour.

Finally, the social gospel took the teaching of Jesus, presented in the New Testament as an ethics of the disciples' group or the Christian community, and applied it to the life of society as a whole. Here is yet another contextual problem. Yet it was sufficiently in context with its cultural milieu to enable the prophetic voice to be heard within the associational churches and to be partly absorbed into church policy if not into society. Moreover, in a country where entrepreneurial mores have long enjoyed supremacy, this was the first sustained attempt to present a social ethics grounded in the interdependence and solidarity of humankind. As such, its significance should not be underestimated.

ERNST TROELTSCH: THEOLOGIAN OF SOCIAL ETHICS

With Troeltsch, we return to Europe (although he had a keen awareness of the American scene) and to a more advanced view both of hermeneutics and of social ethics. Troeltsch's method of interpretation was sociologically grounded, following Weber in presenting an analysis of church-type and sect-type, with enthusiasm or mysticism as yet a third sociological form.[54] The first celebrates the salvation embodied in the religious community and its ordinances; the second binds personally convinced Christians into the holy community, while the third is concerned with the immediacy of communion with God. Mixed types are possible, but each had a different way of coming to terms with the realities of existence in the world: the church-type offering a degree of accommodation to worldly structures, the sect-type rejecting cultural compromise and the mystical remaining indifferent to the worldly order. Broadly speaking, the Christian movement in its origins related to the sect-type and developed into the church-type, while a mystical strain permeated its life. Christian social ethics thus possesses a complex and changing character.

Troeltsch laid considerable emphasis on the prophetic tradition. Unlike some nineteenth-century liberals, he denied the adequacy of representing the prophets as giving principles for a just society. The prophetic demand was for action in obedience to the divine moral will, and carried with it a degree of hostility or at least indifference to cultural values. It was the former element which gave to the preaching of Jesus and the early Christian proclamation a universal application and final intensity, transcending the limitations of the ethnic and cultural context in which it was presented. The supreme summons is to surrender to the will of the sovereign and holy God, whose nature is love and whose purpose is to realise good. But, paradoxically, offsetting the other-worldly tendencies to cultural indifference was the prophetic insistence on creation, which validated this-worldly concern. The prophetic message thus stands in creative tension with society and culture, and a social ethics becomes possible.

Jesus proclaimed the kingdom of God and formed a community of eschatological hope. Its hope involved the total surrender of the will to God, and was marked by 'purity of intention and a greatly intensified reverence for all moral commands'.[55] Here is religious, rather than purely social, motivation, grounded in the religious heritage of Israel and the socio-historical scene to which it related. Jesus' message of the kingdom refocussed the mighty religious process which was already in operation. It set the idea of God in the centre of all moral purpose. From this flowed radical notions of the value of the individual soul, loving fellowship which involves 'the melting down of earthly smallness and worldliness in the Fire of the Divine Love'[56] and radical universalism. Jesus' ethic is heroic rather than ascetic; it inclines to the poor, yet is open to all. It is not a programme of social reform, but a summons to prepare for the kingdom, which is not to be reduced to the notion of a new social order, for it represents the victory of God over evil rather than reform of the state or society or the family. Yet, when a visible community was formed, a social order was bound to arise out of it as the community responded to the moral requirements of the gospel. In the early stages there was an attempt to express an ideal of *koinonia*.

It was a communism which regarded the pooling of possessions as a proof of love and of the religious spirit of sacrifice. It was a communism composed solely of consumers, a communism based on the assumption that its members will continue to earn their living by private enterprise, in order to be able to practise generosity and sacrifice. Above all, it has no theory of equality at all... All that matters is that all the members shall sacrifice something and that they all have to live; how this is carried out in practice does not matter.[57]

This 'communism of love', which was one of the notable features of the teaching of Jesus, did not last in the context of the church's world mission, in which the fundamental idea was the saving of souls. The fathers reverted at times to the love community as a fundamental of the faith, and it recurred in the monastic movement, medieval experiments, the Anabaptists and 'modern fanatics and idealists'.[58] But in contrast to this we find, particularly in Paul, the ethics of a new religious community. 'With the emphasis on the Church the principle of love seems to come very much to the fore',[59] and with it the principle of radical equality in the sight of God. But the Christian community is very cautious about transferring such notions into the realm of secular relations and institutions which lack the religious basis of such equality. Hence it tends first to regard them as alien, and then to see them as executing divinely given functions in the worldly order. It has also to recognise the inequalities in human life, which it does by affirming the organic unity and functional diversity of the faith community and, finally, by affirming conventional patriarchal structures. Thus there emerges 'a compact social system, with its various grades of authority and subordination, which are an inherent element in any sociological system.'[60] The sect ideal has given way to structured community which assumed associational characteristics as it was enlarged (for example, in the late second century) and eventually approximated even more thoroughly to the church type.

What we find in society itself, according to Troeltsch, are successive crystallisations of original or traditional values which are historically and culturally relative. Yet Troeltsch can speak of 'the Christian principle' or 'the prophetic principle', or sometimes 'the protestant principle', which implies a critical judgment about what is of fundamental importance in the tradition. While the identification and articulation of such a principle involves selection from the basic materials, Troeltsch believed that such compromises with historical tradition were inevitable and had characterised Christian practice in every epoch. It was a creative way of reading tradition, focussing on primary prophetic insight rather than selected moral ideals, but making full allowance for contextual factors.

Not surprisingly Troeltsch's approach offers a telling critique of absolutist claims, whether advanced on behalf of German militarism and expansionism in the 1914–18 era, British and American individualism, or socialist ideas of liberty and equality. Through the Christian prophetic ethical principle and the scrutiny of history, a new and ever more inclusive cultural synthesis can be created. Troeltsch thus took the study of Christian social ethics into a new dimension. Through his long association with Weber, he was able to harness sociological perspectives which enabled him to provide a map of the complex set of interactions which relate to faith and practice, especially as the latter impinges upon societal structures and institutions. Some have criticised what they saw as his bias towards the church viewpoint,[61] but what Troeltsch claimed was that *historically* it was the most influential type, and he emphasised the prophetic contribution to the sustaining of its life and witness. Religio-social context no doubt conditioned Troeltsch's judgment; it also conditions that of his critics! When all is said and done, Troeltsch's figure of successive crystallisations of the gospel, in terms of a social ethics that is also historically and culturally relative, persistently claims recognition by virtue of its recurring appositeness to Christian experience, and his influence is seen clearly in Tillich. Not the least valuable aspect of his work is his attempt to develop the link between biblical interpretation and Christian social ethics.

PART TWO

Eschatology and ethics

In the light of the ultimate, everything penultimate is brought into question and submerged in the 'sphere of relativity'.

(H. Zahrnt)[1]

ESCHATOLOGY AND THE CRITICAL METHOD

The liberal synthesis, which effectively merged the ancient and modern horizons of the text by its appeal to permanently valid principles and ideals, proved remarkably durable. The idealist tradition, which could claim an ancestry reaching back to Plato himself, had been firmly grounded in the work of Kant, and enhanced by the comprehensiveness of Hegel's system. The intellectual ferment of the nineteenth century was produced by, and largely contained within, this dominant world view: a feat all the more remarkable in view of the variety and complexity of the intellectual endeavours. As the twentieth century dawned, newer approaches rooted in the same Western intellectual tradition tended to disjoin ancient and modern horizons through their insistence that a given text be related closely to its historical milieu. When apocalyptic eschatology was pinpointed as the dominant feature of the world of Jesus, the disjunction was virtually inevitable, and the consequences for theology far-reaching.

To be sure, eschatology – Jewish and Christian – was open to a variety of interpretations, in the ancient as in the modern world. Eschatology literally denotes discourse about the end of time, and apocalyptic eschatology is concerned with visions of the end. For some ancients apocalypticism was dominant, with its attendant sense of urgency and imminent judgment, its stimulus to repentance and its sanctions of reward and penalty.[2] Others dissolved eschatology into pietism; some politicised it; for others it denoted the final, but remote, climax of the ages.

Some interpreted it in personal terms; others related it to national destiny. For some it went hand in hand with a prevailing pessimism and a devaluing of the material world. Revival movements emphasised the nearness of the final judgment in apocalyptic terms; prophetic intensity signified its present operation. E. Käsemann pointed to the creative role of primitive Christian apocalyptic in the birth of Christian theology.[3] The disappointment of eschatological expectation has been held to be an important factor in New Testament writings themselves, and in the formation of Christian doctrine.[4] At the same time, eschatology had a marked influence on the way people lived. It might sharpen the call to repentance, create a penitential or 'interim' ethic, concentrate the mind on the requirements of the *Torah*, radicalise moral teaching and colour prophetic utterance. It could also lead to antinomianism and worldly irresponsibility.

This plurality of view continued into modern interpretation, where consistent eschatology (Schweitzer, Bultmann), realised eschatology (Dodd) and inaugurated eschatology (Jeremias) are characteristic positions. Such diversity is not to be accounted for by reference to eschatology alone, but through the interplay of a number of critical and philosophical factors, some of which may be noted briefly here.

SOURCE CRITICISM AND BEYOND

Johannes Weiss, who foreshadowed Schweitzer's eschatological emphasis, not only employed source criticism, but also anticipated the procedure later termed *Redaktionsgeschichte* (redaction history or criticism). At this early point before form criticism had been formally developed, Weiss identified the creative role of the Christian redactor – as had Wrede in his study of Mark's Gospel.[5] An important consequence was that each evangelist – like each New Testament author – was seen to have his own perspective on ethics from within the Christian community. In general, however, Weiss anticipated Schweitzer's view that, for Jesus, the kingdom was an imminent reality. The ethics Jesus taught was essentially an ethics of preparation.[6]

By contrast, Schweitzer has been much criticised for his cavalier attitude to source criticism, illustrated particularly by the weight he gave to Matthew 10.23 – '... truly I say to you, you will not have gone through all the towns of Israel before the Son of man comes' – which source criticism would tend to identify as secondary, and redaction criticism assign to the evangelist Matthew and the circle he represented. Nor did Schweitzer anticipate to any extent the form critical emphasis on the *Sitz im Leben* of the tradition in the early faith communities. His interests tended to be historical and philosophical. Thus, factors other than the logic of biblical criticism were entering the equation; and each equation reshaped the understanding of New Testament ethics offered by the critic. It was with Bultmann, in company with K. L. Schmidt and M. Dibelius, that form criticism was given full rein; and it was not until the post-Bultmannian era that redaction criticism came into its own.

Formgeschichte expressed the importance of historical context in terms of the early Christian communities and their role in the shaping and transmission of the Jesus tradition. It focussed on the forms of tradition which underlay the gospel narratives and elucidated the creative role of the early Christian communicators. Attention was given to the variety of the contexts in which they worked – from Judaean groups, through various types of Hellenistic Jewish and mixed communities, to the Gentiles in the wider world. For all of them, ethos was important: an ethos shaped by their environment, by the traditions they received and interpreted and particularly by their understanding of 'the things concerning Jesus'. Here was to be found a world view – Bultmann used the singular, although we might be tempted to pluralise it – which in its fundamental assumptions was far removed from that of the modern interpreter. As Bultmann suggested, somewhat quaintly to modern ears, one cannot 'use electric light and the wireless' or avail oneself of modern medical and surgical discoveries and at the same time 'believe in the New Testament world of daemons and spirits'.[7] Still less can we expect others to do so. Here is disjunction indeed: the possibility that a biblically based Christian message is in itself unintelligible and un-acceptable to the modern world.

Like Schweitzer, Bultmann did not entirely relativise the message of the New Testament, even through his radical 'demythologising' programme.[8] As in Barth, its core was the *kerygma*, the Word, which found expression in all the different forms of communication.[9] The consequences for ethics were largely realised in community. The early church groups were *both* eschatological communities *and* communities of moral concern – not in the sense that they were actively developing a moral philosophy of their own, but in the sense that the ethos of each expressed responsive obedience to Christ, who was himself the centre of the 'eschatological event'. This kerygmatic centre of eschatology and its importance in modern interpretation is illustrated below in scholars as diverse as Bultmann, Otto, Dodd and W. D. Davies.

PHILOSOPHICAL CRITICISM

The interplay of philosophical presuppositions in the period under review had consequences for the interpretation of New Testament ethics. The idealist tradition continued in various forms: whether in Kantian categorical imperatives, or in Hegelian dialectic. Schweitzer's ethical thinking was indebted to Hegel for his concept of *Geist*, and to Kant for his insistence that the source of ethics must have a more objective source than moral sentiment.[10] But it also owed a debt to the German voluntarists and vitalists (particularly Schopenhauer and Nietz-sche) from whom Schweitzer derived the basic notion of the will to live or life affirmation; and to the French philosophers, Fouillée and Guyau, for 'a categorical imperative that is experienced inwardly'.[11] His affinity with Goethe is also readily acknowledged. His thought is thus deeply European and Western, whatever affinities he had with the East. Not for nothing did he describe himself as the child of the Enlight-enment. Indeed, he held that this development had helped Protestantism to develop a positive acceptance of the world and to understand the kingdom not in apocalyptic terms, but as something ethical and spiritual which was to be realised through human action. Historically, this is at variance with Jesus' position; religiously, it is completely legitimate.

However, other philosophical developments served to undermine the liberal consensus and proved influential for theology and ethics. Søren Kierkegaard, the apostle of personal, subjective truth, had no time for a philosophy which encompassed Absolute and finite within one all-embracing human system; nor for the kind of religion which simply affirmed cultural practice and world view. Properly understood, religion is disjunctive. One may attribute moral features to God, yet He never underwrites conventional morality: divine–human communication engenders surprise. To be sure, exegesis may impinge upon ethics and assist in its transformation, as his famous exegesis of the sacrifice of Isaac shows.[12] For Kierkegaard, 'ethical existence is a constant, self-critical activity by which one attains a deepening subjective individuation, an approximation to selfhood, that is not motivated by the pursuit of an illusory or imaginary happiness'.[13] The moral life itself operates at a lower level than the religious, and therefore cannot comprehend some of its major elements, such as penitence, which point beyond the moral plane. The value of systems of ethics is therefore called into question. Ethics in the New Testament, we deduce, should not be regarded as simply another variety of ethical system. It may contain material which operates at the moral level: conventional codes such as the *Haustafeln*, for example, or other moral topics. But it also comprises material which cannot be categorised in this way and which expresses the divine imperative. It is this transcendent element which occasions the element of surprise or astonishment in the reader or hearer and calls for decision.

It is fair comment that Kierkegaard fostered an unyielding pessimism about society and community, and that his notion of human existence underestimated the interrelatedness of humanity.[14] This fact limited the scope of his hermeneutic and inhibited its application to the field of social ethics. His demotion of the moral plane is also ambivalent. While his approach may highlight transcendence, it can also result in the impairment of the transcendent aspect of the moral. Is it not reasonable to suggest that Abraham's confidence in God arose precisely because he was aware of his moral nature? In God he could place his trust with confidence. 'Shall not the Judge of all the earth do right?' (Gen. 18.25)

Edmund Husserl developed the phenomenological approach to interpretation in an attempt to create a new theory of knowledge which gathered together all the variety of objects or phenomena into the unity of the subject. The subject is relational by nature. All thought is thought about something. Thus when one reads an ancient text, meaning is found only as the reader resonates to the text. This is not, as it tended to be in Schleiermacher, a question of psychological affinity, but of a deep resonance to the text which puts in question the self-understanding of the subject and thus enables the subject to discover his/her own being.[15]

Martin Heidegger, whose philosophic concerns were existential and ontological, was able to build on the method of Husserl. On the basis that human beings not only exist, but know that they exist, Heidegger believed it possible to make a descriptive analysis of the self-understanding which is given through human existence in the world. 'Ontic' events carry the message at the level of objective history, but existential concern is with the inner core, the ontological. This kind of knowledge, it is suggested, possesses an immediate certainty which is denied to scientific knowledge, with its range of assumptions and its constant necessity to adjust to the results of research. At the same time, it differs from speculative philosophy, since the latter is concerned to describe reality beyond or outside being-in-the-world. In other words, as Macquarrie has indicated,[16] Heidegger accepted that one can derive a fundamental existential analytic from 'the light of nature'. A feature of this analytic is the human reality of alienation, of estrangement from one's true being. Such 'inauthenticity' is characterised by a flight from freedom and responsibility, and an attempt to find the illusion of security in a variety of unproductive ways. But human existence also enshrines an awareness that life could be different;

that it has as yet unrealised possibilities of authentic living. Authentic existence remains life-in-the-world, i.e., historical, and it involves freedom, responsibility, openness to others, trust and community. It is entered upon, and lived out, in response to the call of true being, or Being itself, and requires decision and resolution on the part of human beings in their actual situation.[17]

Husserl and Heidegger made a notable contribution to identifying the complete cycle of interpretation, which involves not only respect for the text, but the participation of the interpreter in establishing meaning and significance. It was also important, as we shall see, in modifying the more positivistic forms of historicism. The theological application of this approach was explored by Bultmann in particular, its contribution to the theory of hermeneutics by Gadamer and Ricoeur.[18] Heidegger himself was much more concerned with his existential analytic than with either ethics or the contribution of the social sciences to the concept of 'being-in-the-world'; but, as Dilthey saw clearly, even though the social sciences proceed at an ontic rather than an ontological level, they supply important evidence about human life and conduct.

HISTORICAL CRITICISM

As we have seen, historical perspectives pertained to the critical approach almost since its inception – above all, in the emphasis it placed on sources. It was also responsible for underscoring the importance of contextualising ancient documents. Schweitzer took historical contextuality to a point at which its horizons were seen to be radically different from those of the modern reader. In consequence, there can be no easy transition to a modern biblical ethics. The moral teaching of Jesus was locked up within a strange world of intense eschatological expectation and crisis, thus rendering problematic the place of the Bible in modern ethical debate. But the emphasis on context, especially when linked to the phenomenological method, could produce positive results, as in the work of Davies, Ed Sanders and others who explored the Jewish context of the moral traditions of the

New Testament; and it also plays a notable role in the modern approaches which follow a more radical hermeneutics.[19]

It must be remembered that modern historical criticism was a product of the *Aufklärung* and became a powerful agent of secularisation. It represented 'a new total view of human life',[20] in which the Bible, the Christian faith and Christ are all seen as relative to their historical context, to the onward motion of history. No longer does religious or theological understanding relativise the historical or this-worldly scene. The reverse is happening! It could well be said that this is one of the severest tests the Christian faith has ever had to face.[21] It certainly focussed interpretive attention on the nature of historical understanding. The starting point for reconsideration was the realisation – though the penny was slow to drop at a more popular level – that history did not consist of 'brute facts', but was rather a process carried out by the historian as interpreter. There is thus a relative element in all history.

Collingwood is a key figure here.[22] History is properly the study of human affairs, and the historian participates in the object of his study. Collingwood accepted that historians are concerned with the data, the evidence, the 'outside' of the event, but they also of necessity attempt to think themselves into the action. By a kind of imaginative empathy, they recreate the action in their own minds while subjecting it to thorough criticism and re-evaluation. Thus, the aim or function of history may be described as primarily the deepening of one's understanding of human existence. As with Heidegger, we begin with our pre-understanding of human life, encounter the understanding of human existence in texts or sources from the given period of study and end with an enriched or modified self-understanding. Ethics, of course, is concerned – like faith itself – with present action and future possibility, but interpreting the moral teaching of the New Testament inevitably involves historical reflection. The implication of all this is that there is a continuity of human possibility binding past and present by a hidden but detectable thread: even when the picture of the past is as strange as consistent eschatology paints it.

This kind of reflection went far to illuminate not only

historical research, but also exegetical and interpretive procedures. Bultmann was one of the most self-aware of exegetes, and his historical understanding was a central part of his hermeneutics. Nevertheless, a crucial question is yet to be addressed. One may be greatly influenced – or changed – by reading certain texts, but what is the horizon of these texts? Is it simply further human reflection on the human lot? Is there even the possibility of a transcendent horizon – of encounter with the divine?

'KERYGMATIC' THEOLOGY

In 1892 Martin Kähler protested vigorously against the 'papal pretensions' of the historians whose method seemed to suggest that the claims of faith must be subjected to historical verification, and thus be at the mercy of the ebb and flow of historical debate. A theologically informed reading of the New Testament not only recognised that it enshrined the witness of the early Christians to the event of Christ, but also noted that its basic concern was not so much biographical as proclamatory. It had a message to proclaim: a *kerygma*. Thus, the historical significance of Jesus was the impact he had on his disciples and subsequent ages, and the confession of their faith in him as Lord. Hence, the primary concern of the interpreter is with the Christ to whom the whole New Testament bears witness. He it is who confronts the reader with an immediacy which has nothing to do with discerning the Jesus behind the gospels. 'The real Christ is the preached Christ, and the preached Christ is the Christ of faith.'[23]

Kähler himself, it should be said, did not doubt that there was historical substance to the recollections of the ministry and personality of Jesus, nor did he deny the propriety of historical research. His point was that faith did not rest upon it. And if faith does not rest upon it, then – we may deduce – neither does Christian ethics. For the biblical basis of ethics we must explore the relation of ethics to the *kerygma*, the message proclaimed and believed in the Christian communities: 'so we preach and so you believed' (1 Cor. 15.11).

Kähler's insights proved to be of great significance for the theological interpretation of the New Testament. Not only did he confirm the proclamatory strand in Ritschl's theology, but he anticipated the dialectical position of Barth and provided the groundwork for scholars and interpreters such as Gogarten and Bultmann. For our purposes, he indicates that the eschatological world view with which Schweitzer wrestled requires to be viewed, not as an ancient stereotype to be discarded, but as the proclamation of a reality to be faced.

CHAPTER 3

Interim ethics

Jesus' imminent expectation prompted the ethical teaching, and...the ethics cannot be discussed apart from the
eschatology.

(Jack Sanders)[1]

INTRODUCTION

While it was generally true that the 'interpretation of Jesus
during the nineteenth century had been almost completely de-
eschatologised',[2] an eschatological emphasis was present in
pietistic and millenarian circles and had begun to impinge on
scholarship.[3] Moreover, the historical and contextual work of E.
Schürer in particular gave a strong impetus to the trend,
already identifiable in Harnack and others, towards setting the
teaching of Jesus in its historical context and thus forming a
clearer understanding of the factor of eschatology in his
ministry. It was not altogether surprising, therefore, that
eschatology should emerge with such prominence in the work of
Johannes Weiss, and that Jesus' moral teaching should be
viewed in the light of it. The result was a form of 'interim ethics'
which Weiss described in penitential terms.

PENITENTIAL ETHICS: JOHANNES WEISS

If Johannes Weiss made the first influential statement of the
necessary disjunction between the position of Jesus and that of
the modern interpreter, he did so with profound respect for
those who had fashioned the synthesis he was apparently
undermining.[4] Thorough investigation of the historical founda-

75

tions would establish the centrality of Jesus' vision of the imminent kingdom.

Jesus and the ethics of the kingdom

Weiss approached the task through a critical evaluation of the sources. Critical studies had already identified secondary layers of interpretation in the gospels, and Weiss felt free to place aside the Gospel of John and distinguish primitive sources in the Synoptics from secondary overlay. Since Matthew in particular is adjudged to be 'of very late date', some of the parables of the kingdom – the redaction of the tares (Matt. 13.24–30, 36–43), the fishnet (13.47–50) and the last judgment (25.31–46) – are regarded as secondary.[5]

The genuinely ancient message is, 'Repent, for the kingdom of God is at hand.'[6] The kingdom of God has drawn so near that it 'stands at the door'. Extremely near – but not yet here! Weiss had considerable trouble with the notion of the presence, the actualisation or realisation of the kingdom, particularly as such views had been advanced by Ritschl, among others. But, he argued, paraphrastic interpretations of Matt. 21.31 and 11.11, suggesting that Jesus brought the kingdom to life within the community of his disciples, cannot appeal to a single un-equivocal passage in the gospels, in spite of the fact that the evangelists Mark and Matthew might have been expected to capitalise on any saying of Jesus which supported this meaning. The *coup de grâce* is administered by the Lord's Prayer: 'may thy kingdom come'. For the disciples, the kingdom is not yet present: it must be sought (Luke 12.31). 'This yearning and longing for its coming, this ardent prayer for it, and the constant hope that it will come – that it will come soon – this is their religion.'[7] Passages such as Matt. 12.28 and Luke 17.21, which suggest the presence of the kingdom, relate to Jesus' victories in warfare against Satan's kingdom: Satan's power is being broken. If Jesus speaks of the kingdom as present, it is only in 'moments of sublime prophetic enthusiasm, when an awareness of victory comes over him'.[8] The kingdom may be gaining ground, but it is not yet a full historical reality.

For Weiss, Jesus is – like John the Baptist – the proclaimer of
the kingdom. His ministry is preparatory. The kingdom will be
established solely by divine action. Jesus is presently rabbi and
prophet; Son of man he will become in the future. He has to
wait, like his disciples, for the coming act of God. Hence, Weiss
sees involvement in political revolution – the attempt to change
the world by the deployment of human force and cunning – as
alien to Jesus (cf. Mark 12.17), as is every attempt to force God's
hand (cf. Matt. 11.12). One's duty is to prepare oneself for the
coming of the kingdom by acquiring the righteousness which
God commands (cf. Matt. 6.33, 5.20). At the last supper, Jesus
speaks of drinking the cup anew in the kingdom of God (Mark
14.25), when the entire cosmos will be transformed and made
new (Matt. 19.28). This is the inheritance of the meek (Matt.
5.5). To be sure, the pictures of the End and of the judgment,
though sparingly used by Jesus, are conventional enough: he
followed the traditional scheme, but with a certain reserve. The
crucial issues, however, were what was genuinely religious in the
kingdom of God, and how one prepared morally for its
'coming'.

The moral concern of Jesus' teaching is therefore, for Weiss,
an ethics of preparation: a penitential ethics, in effect 'interim
ethics', although he did not use the term. The keynote is the
summons to repentance: a call addressed to all – whether tax
collectors and sinners or 'ordinary people' – to break with the
past, turn from worldly goals and prepare for the coming of the
kingdom. The focus is on developing that 'righteousness' which
follows from repentance, and is the condition for entering the
kingdom. Weiss tended to see the emphasis 'as a negative and
ascetic ideal rather than a really positive moral one'.[9] It is, says
Weiss, more of a new piety than a new morality in the modern
sense. The first object is to 'seek' the kingdom (Matt. 6.33,
Luke 12.31): 'passionate desire for the kingdom is to be the
mood that governs all else'.[10] It involves the true childlikeness,
the simplicity and singlemindedness, which for an adult is the
gift of God. The kingdom of God requires one's undivided
attention: one cannot serve God and mammon (Matt. 6.24).
Wealth is a particular distraction: 'ordinarily a rich man can be

saved for the kingdom of God only through a divine miracle (Mark 10.27)'.[11]

Weiss argues that Christianity has largely ignored the intensity of Jesus' summons or diluted it beyond recognition through compromise, evasion and casuistry. A much more honest approach, he suggests, is to view Jesus in historical perspective: i.e., to appreciate the eschatological context of his message. Here, the worldly goods of a permanent civilisation are but a fetter which ties one to the corrupt world that is passing away. 'The world has grown old, and human labour can no longer create anything really good or enduring upon it.'[12] Fidelity in one's worldly calling might be congruent with the righteousness that fits one for the kingdom, but the worldly demands of the calling itself suggest that it would be better to abandon it altogether, as the disciples did. So also with family life: it rests on a sacred bond (Matt. 19.41f.), but the demands of the kingdom take priority even over family life (Luke 14.26). Weiss is well aware that such interpretations cut across accepted lines of interpretation in the modern world. Commentators blunt the edge of Jesus' teaching by suggesting that he was using oriental exaggeration to point out that such blessings as vocation, family and wealth could give occasion for sin through abuse; or that his sayings had a particular limited purpose and reference, and that under no circumstances could Jesus have meant what he actually said! The truth is that Jesus was not legislating for the relatively permanent situation of the church. He was bringing to the crowds a sense of the immediacy of the kingdom. 'He summons them, therefore, to the frightful challenge, like the physician who confronts his patient with the choice between a perilous operation or letting things take their course. A half-remedy will not do.'[13]

Consequences for Christian ethics
It follows that Christian ethics today – Weiss speaks of 'our modern Protestant ethic' – cannot be a straightforward application of Jesus' teaching. We cannot expect to relive it in our every-day experience. To appropriate its meaning involves adaptation, but Weiss is clearly concerned about the nature of

the adaptation. Many theologians had attempted such a task, but in a confused and contradictory way. It is inadmissible to interpret the kingdom as the reign of moral righteousness in the world, or as the supreme ethical ideal for human emulation. The kingdom is transcendent; it comes at God's initiative; it is God's gift; it is objective and messianic. To enter it one must surrender to God and detach oneself from the world. The signs of such detachment are the love of one's enemy and the giving of oneself for God's sake. This may be described as the supreme ethical ideal, but there is an essential difference between Jesus' perspective and that of ourselves. His view sets the kingdom in antithesis to the world. The early Christians prayed, 'May grace come and this world pass away', while we assume that 'this world will evermore become the showplace of the people of God'.[14] It is only as we contemplate our own end that a note of eschatological urgency is imported into the modern situation.

That which is universally valid in Jesus' preaching, which should form the kernel of our systematic theology is not his idea of the Kingdom of God, but that of the religious and ethical fellowship of the children of God. This is not to say that one should no longer use the concept 'Kingdom of God' in the current manner. On the contrary, it seems to me…that it should be the proper watchword of modern theology. Only the admission must be demanded that we use it in a different sense from Jesus.[15]

Weiss subsequently clarified his interpretation of several features of Jesus' ethical teaching and its relevance for continuing Christian ethics. In the second edition of the *Predigt*, he admits that certain parables – the mustard seed, the seed growing secretly, the leaven – do have a connection with the kingdom, but denies any notion of growth or development in them. They are parables of contrast and presuppose the coming mighty act of God. He also makes the important concession that a number of Jesus' sayings did not come from an eschatological matrix. There were times when Jesus, captivated by the beauty and wonder of creation, simply reflected the goodness and love of God. When he spoke in this mood, there was none of the harsh asceticism that marked his prophetic utterances. Instead, he offered maxims of the purest and deepest wisdom, reflecting his

inward serenity as the child of God. Other sayings were
embedded in controversy with the Pharisees and others: sayings
upholding the permanence of marriage or the sanctity of
promises as against casuistical judgments. Finally, the 'double
love commandment' – often seen as pivotal – lacks an eschatological setting. Jesus was not its author, but gave his full assent
to this piece of scribal interpretation. Its detached nature allows
it to be used as it stands in Christian ethics in subsequent ages.
Yet Jesus did not envisage history as a continuing worldly
scenario: the notion of the imminent coming of the kingdom
was dominant, if not completely pervasive, in his outlook.[16]

Weiss in critical perspective

Weiss attempted to effect the disjunction between Jesus and his
followers which context and eschatology demanded. If he was
less thoroughgoing or consistent than Schweitzer, whom we
shall discuss shortly, his work was in some ways better grounded,
both in source criticism and in his anticipation of redaction
criticism. Yet he did not explore the *Sitz im Leben* of Jesus'
ministry – not even its eschatological setting – in any detail.
That task was left for his contemporary, E. Ehrhardt, to
attempt.[17] Weiss intended *die Predigt* to be no more than a
sketch, and his ideas are presented in bold outline.

One must reserve judgment on his treatment of those sayings
which suggest the presence or realisation of the kingdom. To
speak of 'moments of sublime prophetic enthusiasm, when an
awareness of victory comes over him' is to impart a subjective
element which he carefully excludes from Jesus' awareness of
the coming kingdom. He also minimises the relation of the
parables to the kingdom. The Archimedean point, established
by critical research, was the historical call to repentance in face
of the imminent coming of the kingdom. More recently, E. P.
Sanders has tried to demonstrate that the call to repentance
ascribed to Jesus is in fact secondary.[18] While this does not
necessarily refute Weiss' claim, it suggests that the case may not
be as straightforward as Weiss assumed.

Weiss' adoption of a mixed model in his second edition

undermined the consistency of his first picture. While he insisted that the morality which Jesus preached was thought of as the condition for entering the kingdom, the non-eschatological strands which he admits by the back door appear to have a different ethical quality. In moments of high prophetic drama, a negative, ascetic quality pervades Jesus' moral teaching; but when the dark clouds have rolled away – what a way to describe prophetic inspiration, and how different from Rudolf Otto, whose contribution is noted below – Jesus' message has all the love and joy of a child of God. His suggestion that Jesus performed more than one role in his ministry, and that his teaching must be related to its function within the particular role Jesus was executing, is important for interpretation, as is his highlighting of the role of the church as moral community.

Many liberal interpreters rejected Weiss' interpretation, mainly on the grounds that it emptied the person of Jesus of originality and universality. Accustomed to think in terms of eternal values, they could not countenance a view which seemed to ascribe to Jesus' teaching no more than a temporary and evanescent application.[19] Yet there is a curious ambivalence about the whole notion of eschatology. In one guise, it seems utterly other-worldly, standing in sharp antithesis to the present world scene. In another mood, it addresses the question of the transformation of the present world, so that even here and now people can order their lives through a dialectical relationship to it.

Whatever the theological merits of maintaining God's transcendence over against creation, there is little to suggest that the Jews of Jesus' day believed that the future reign of God would take place in any other world than this, nor is there any evidence to suggest that Jesus and his followers dissented from this view.[20]

The fact that Weiss ends up with a twofold current of thought may be related to this overlap, but his admission that the double love command is not eschatologically based offers the possibility of grounding Christian ethics on the command of Jesus, valid for all time: a position explored later. Whether this introduced a major inconsistency into his treatment of eschatology or represented a further insight into Jesus' position is open to debate.

The movement towards the disjunction of horizons reached its apogee in the celebrated work of Albert Schweitzer, who argued that the whole ministry of Jesus and the self-understanding it conveyed were to be set *unreservedly* in the context of the Jewish eschatology of his time. The visionary future was an imminent and urgent reality, to which everything else was subordinated. Through its immediacy Jesus found a powerful motive for detaching from the world's distorted values and the power to affirm freedom, peace and human integrity, whatever the odds against him.

Jesus and 'interim ethics'

There is no reason to detail here the familiar contours of Schweitzer's understanding of Jesus. For him, the hitherto accepted theological consensus had been finally undermined by the thoroughgoing historical scepticism of W. Wrede in relation to Mark's picture of Jesus, and by his own insistence on the dominance and pervasiveness of eschatology in Jesus' world view. Characteristic emphases include his understanding of the preaching of repentance, by John and Jesus, as the preparation which brings about the coming of the kingdom as the sowing of the seed brings about the harvest; and the disciples' urgent mission to Israel – they would not be able to complete their task 'before the Son of man comes' (Matt. 10.23). Other notable features were the 'eschatological sacraments', such as the feeding of the multitude, the baptism of John and the last supper; and the decisive nature of Peter's confession and the transfiguration. The disappointment of his original hopes led Jesus to revise his interpretation of the End and his own role in it. Now the pre-messianic tribulation was to be concentrated on himself alone. 'He must suffer for others... that the kingdom might come.'[21]

Nor is there any need to recapitulate the familiar criticisms of

Schweitzer's interpretation: his cavalier use of source criticism (his dialogue with Wrede notwithstanding); his one-sided emphasis on the eschatology of Matthew 10 and 11; his apparent blindness to the this-worldly, even political, implications of prophetic eschatology; his daring notion that Jesus attempted to force the coming of the kingdom; and, above all, the influence of his own philosophical presuppositions – particularly the Hegelian *tour de force* by which eschatology is totally affirmed through radically contextual exegesis and then nullified theologically.[22] Eschatology is, as it were, played out in this thoroughgoing eschatological drama. Henceforth, theology is free of its bonds. The disjunction of horizons is complete.

The concern of our study is with the consequences for ethics. Since Jesus' message was wholly informed by the perspective of imminent eschatology, the moral teaching of Jesus centred on repentance in expectation of the kingdom. In Schweitzer we find the classic statement of *Interims-Ethik*, denoting 'moral behaviour for the time being'. Strictly, one cannot speak of the ethics of the kingdom, for the kingdom, according to Schweitzer, presupposes a supernatural state of the world, involving an end to earthly mortality and a transfiguration into angelic perfection. Interim ethics describes the ethics of preparation, shaped by the eschatological crisis.[23]

The Sermon on the Mount is a prime example. Schweitzer related the Sermon to the motif of repentance in view of the imminence of the kingdom, and therefore described it as interim ethics.[24] Sharp contrasts are thus prompted within the Sermon itself. Entry to the kingdom requires more than the righteousness of the scribes and Pharisees (Matt. 5.20). As the antitheses show (cf. Matt. 5.21-48), the imminence of the kingdom reveals how inadequate scribal casuistry is for penetrating to the heart of the matter. By holding to the outward and literal statement of the law, the scribes accommodate its requirements to the continuing worldly scene. Illustration is found in the issues of sabbath labour (Matt. 12.1-14) or hand washing (Matt. 15.1-20). The radically eschatological perspective overturns all such worldly accommodations and human rationalisations – even when they occur in scripture, as in the question of divorce

(Matt. 19.3–12; cf. 5.31f.) or the *lex talionis* and the problem of retribution (Matt. 5.38–41). Jesus' quarrel with the Pharisees, whose piety and devotion to the *Torah* were beyond question, stemmed from their failure to recognise, and their determination to oppose, the radical challenge of the imminent kingdom. Schweitzer observes, 'We cannot but be deeply moved by the tragedy of this unavoidable conflict between two types of ethical piety.'[25]

How then does the Sermon penetrate to the heart of the matter? The qualities pin-pointed by the beatitudes (Matt. 5.3–12) provide 'an indication of inward membership of the kingdom'.[26] The kingdom will be given to 'the poor in spirit': described by Schweitzer as 'those who have retained the simplicity of heart which is necessary to understand the message of the coming of the kingdom, which is hidden from the wise and understanding and revealed to babes' (Matt. 11.25)[27] At its coming, the children of God will delight in God's presence: the peacemakers, the merciful, the meek... Those who long for righteousness will find satisfaction, and those broken by grief or persecution will have eternal consolation. They will enter the kingdom as the tribes of Israel entered the promised land. Faced with such a vision the righteous may indeed rejoice.[28]

Thus, for Schweitzer, the consistent eschatological perspective radicalises the demand for forgiveness (Matt. 18.21–35) and revalues temple offerings (Matt. 12.41–44): no hint of recognition is accorded, for example, to the economics of temple maintenance. Nor is Jesus concerned to determine his own or his followers' attitude to the state when he replies to the question about paying taxes to Caesar (Mark 12.13–17). Schweitzer wrote:

The state was simply earthly, therefore ungodly, domination. Its duration extended, therefore, only to the dawn of God's dominion. As this was near at hand, what need had one to decide if one would be tributary to the world-power or no? One might as well submit to it, its end was in fact near.[29]

Unlike Johannes Weiss, Schweitzer did not exempt the double commandment of love from eschatological conditioning. On the contrary, the notion of righteousness, when eschatologically intensified, demands not only neighbour-love, but also love of enemy (Matt. 5.43–45), as the wisdom tradition (coming at the issue by another route) suggested (cf. Prov. 24.17 and 25.21f.). Love for enemy is not found in the *Torah*, although love for the stranger who sojourns with you (Lev. 19.33f.) 'gives the Jewish Law its title to noble rank'.[30] The nearness of the kingdom focuses attention on, and gives priority to, doing God's will.

In presenting such a consistent thesis, Schweitzer cannot accept that any logia suggest the present actualisation of the kingdom. The present tense may be used as an intensive form of the future; or Jesus' mighty acts against the demons may suggest the action of God which will soon effect cosmic renewal. Jesus can envisage the fall of Satan so vividly that he sees it happening before his eyes! The kingdom is so close as to intimate its presence. But it remains essentially future: it is 'the coming kingdom'.

Yet consistent eschatology cannot avoid a qualitative dimension in relation to present action in the world. The coming kingdom will bring an end to the struggle with evil and death. In the 'interim', preparation for the kingdom involves the renewal of the moral quality of one's response to God, neighbour – and enemy. The scene here on earth is one where evil presses hard upon the faithful, who must reflect the righteousness of the future age in their response to their oppressors. They can do so without prudential care for the things of the world, for the world will soon be at an end. It is this eschatological factor, rather than the moral qualities involved, that differentiates the context of Jesus from that of his followers of later ages.

Paul and eschatological ethics

Paul the apostle provides an interesting further case study. By his time, the eschatological perspective has altered dramatically, although eschatological expectation is still intense, if variable. What consequences does this have for Paul's understanding of ethics?

'Ethics for Paul is not a matter of fruits of repentance but of fruits of the Spirit.'[31] With these words Schweitzer sharply distinguishes the standpoints of Paul and Jesus. For Paul, repentance is simply a preparation for baptism, in which the believer dies and rises again with Christ. Ethics, says Schweitzer, 'is included within the sphere of the mystical dying and rising again with Christ, and is to be interpreted from this point of view'.[32] In baptism the believer receives the Spirit of the glorified Christ, which bestows on him or her 'a new mind and a new heart'. Ethics, he maintains, springs from this mystical being-in-Christ and not from justification by faith, with its in-built defences against 'works of the law'. Indeed, justification by faith presents redemption and ethics as two roads on opposite sides of an unbridged ravine. Unlike the Reformers, Paul saw no reason to bridge it, for ethics proceeded naturally from Christ-mysticism. Conceived in a quasi-physical way, his position suggests that before redemption one is incapable of doing any good works, while afterwards Christ brings them forth in one's life. Paul's system brings together diverse elements to form 'a unity, unique in religious thinking, of cosmic philosophy, doctrine of redemption, and ethics'.[33]

What is the nature of Paul's 'ethics of the Spirit'? The Spirit of the Lord gives liberty (2 Cor. 3.17): a liberty which must be asserted in situations in which a law-ethics is being advanced, but otherwise should be tempered by expediency and concern for others, especially the 'weaker brethren'. If there is 'a touch of Gnosticism' in Paul's understanding of freedom, it is con-trolled by the fact that, for him, the true 'gnostic' is one who allows his knowledge to be ruled by love. Hence, although logically one who has been made new in Christ no longer sins, the believer is only in process of realising his/her new being by living according to 'the new life-principles of the Spirit'. If we live by the Spirit, we must walk by the Spirit and express the fruit of the Spirit in our living (cf. Gal. 5.16, 19–25). Love occupies the leading place and is made a reality through the Spirit (cf. 1 Cor. 12.31–13 *passim*). But as love is also the ground of the unity of God, Christ and the elect, Schweitzer can describe Paul's ethics as 'mystico-speculative'.[34] Like Jesus' ethics, it is born of eschatological expectation and 'derived from the special association, in a united whole, of God, the Messiah and the Elect, which is to realise itself in the Times of the End'.[35] Paul's great contribution was to bring ethics into connection with the Spirit, and to explain love as its highest expression. Schweitzer is not slow to point to 'ascetic tendencies' in Paul. In fact, these have to do largely with self-discipline and responsible action. The unmarried state is commended 'in view of the imminent distress' or 'because of the present crisis' (1 Cor. 7.26). Similarly one should attend to one's own business and avoid dependence on others (1 Thess. 4.11f.). The gathered community should restrain its more disorderly elements and 'let everything be done decently and in order' (1 Cor. 14.40). Moral conduct is well-ordered behaviour: the immoral shall not inherit the kingdom (Gal. 5.21). In view of the coming End, one should submit to worldly authorities: recognising both that their power is not ultimate and that in the interim they have a role to play within the divine economy (cf. Rom 13.1–7). Schweitzer admires the way Paul embodied his teaching in his own living. It is this encapsulation of faith-ethics in his life style that enables Paul to say, without arrogance: 'Imitate me as I imitate Christ.'

Schweitzer's verdict on Paul's ethics is unequivocal:

> By his eschatological mysticism Paul gives his ethics a relation to the Person of Christ, and makes the conception of the Spirit an ethical conception. By his eschatological thought he grasps ethics as life in the Spirit of Christ, and thereby creates a Christian ethic valid for all time to come.[36]

Schweitzer: a brief assessment

Schweitzer's 'mystical ethics'

If Schweitzer's study of Jesus and Paul represents the first two foci of ethical concern in his writings, the third is clearly his philosophy of existence or 'mystical ethics'. A full critique is impossible here, but some account must be offered, for his ethical concern and its cosmic rootedness are important aspects of his interpretation.[37]

Schweitzer's own commentary on the ethics of reverence for

life places to one side the 'façade problems' – for example, does the world really exist? – which have been a major preoccupation of philosophers and addressed the 'essential' problem of the relationship of human beings to the life of the universe. There is nothing sentimental in his recognition of a creative force which 'simultaneously creates and destroys'. But if ethics is not obviously reflected in the natural order, it may be more directly located in the will to live.

I do not say, 'I am life'; for life continues to be a mystery too great to understand. I only know that I cling to it. I fear its cessation – death. I dread its diminution – pain. I seek its enlargement – joy'.[38]

The will to live embraces instinct, thought and 'the capacity for divination'. Reverence for life involves freedom to choose, to find value and meaning in life, to accept life as a trust. It involves also an element of resignation: coming to terms with events beyond one's control. Schweitzer does not indicate here an absolute dependence. Our will to live engenders the possibility of transcending our dependence on events – of passing beyond the point of resignation. Yet 'resignation is the very basis of ethics', for the acceptance of one's will to live involves being sincere with oneself; it involves fidelity to one's own nature or integrity. Evil is 'what annihilates, hampers, or hinders life'.

Schweitzer describes this position as rational – the result of thought upon life ('to be truly rational is to become ethical'); as absolute – in the sense that it is not capable of complete achievement; as universal – because its remit is boundless; and as spiritual – seeking harmony with the Spirit of the Universe: an active rather than a passive harmony, expressed in co-operation with the universe itself. This, Schweitzer believes, is the fullest expression of what Kant meant by 'practical reason'. 'Only by serving every kind of life do I enter the service of that Creative Will where all life emanates.' Herein lies 'the mystical significance of ethics'.[39] It was a significance which Jesus grasped through the immediacy of the eschatological vision, and Paul found in his Christ-mysticism. The horizons converge in their several perceptions of the life force which permeates all.

Schweitzer's interpretation of ethics
The abiding significance of Schweitzer's interpretive work cannot be gainsaid. The verdict of Amos Wilder is worthy of note:

A lot of water has passed under the bridge since Schweitzer first published his views of Jesus and the Gospels. No informed scholarship since has been able to undercut the major contribution here, namely, that Jesus, an alien to our modern ideas and rooted in his own time and place, saw history and the world in terms of the late Jewish apocalyptic eschatology of his background, though he gave this outlook his own creative interpretation.[40]

The inadequacies of Schweitzer's exegetical approach have also been widely recognised and need only be noted here in passing. E. P. Sanders summed them up thus:

he used the material in the Gospels too arbitrarily, his hypothesis does not arise naturally from the study of the texts but seems to be imposed upon them, and the dogma which he ascribes to Jesus may not in fact even be thoroughly grounded in the contemporary Jewish expectation.[41]

An element of caution in assessment is therefore proper. Here we concentrate on the implications of his interpretation for ethics.

Interim ethics Schweitzer's much criticised notion of 'interim ethics' has the merit of emphasising the strange visionary dynamic of Jesus' ministry as opposed to the domesticating attempts of liberal idealogues. It relativised all accommodations to the interpreter's world (including religious and moral accommodations) and underlined the force that empowered his ministry. Nevertheless, it has always seemed to emphasise an eleventh hour in Israel's religious experience at the expense of the deeper intent of divine teaching. 'Interim ethics...clashes irreconcilably with characteristic veins of Jesus' teaching.'[42] Weiss' change of mind about the presence of non-eschatological material in the gospels is not without its significance. Not all parables are consistently eschatological, and scholars such as Windisch and Wilder indicated that not all types of teaching ascribed to Jesus have an eschatological root.[43] There is also danger in emphasising the eschatological to the exclusion of the theological. It is important to focus on the coming of *God's reign*, on the conception of the will and purpose of God and its implications for his people. For Bultmann, there is no overt appeal to 'interim ethics' in Jesus' condemnation of legalistic piety, nor in his rebuking of hypocrisy, nor in the radical ethics of the Sermon on the Mount. The intrinsic connection between eschatology and ethics lies in the fact that the 'Now' of the demand for obedience is always seen as the decisive hour.[44] Even if we do not opt for existential interpretation, the basic criticism stands that interim ethics works within an emergency situation which distorts, rather than enhances, the under-standing of the relationship of God to his people.

Paul's ethics Schweitzer's treatment of Paul's ethics is par-ticularly interesting, for in developing an effective balance of eschatology and ethics he breaks with the dominance of justification by faith, develops a Christological base and points to the importance of the Spirit for ethics. As we shall see later, some influential exegesis has subsequently confirmed his basic insight without endorsing his particular form of 'Christ mys-ticism'. But there are occasions on which Paul *does* link ethics and justification, and Schweitzer's depiction of justification and ethics as separated by a great chasm is not entirely true to Paul. Schweitzer corrects extremely one-sided exegeses which focus on this one element, but he introduces other elements of imbalance, including his particular understanding of 'mysticism' and sacramentalism. There are, in fact, several other bases of ethics in Paul which are passed over by Schweitzer. These will be discussed later. But it is easy to parody consistent eschatology, and we must not miss the force of Wilder's observation that, for Schweitzer, 'Paul had a realistic idea of world transformation here and now, all linked up with the believer's own redemp-tion.'[45]

Ethics and changing moral paradigms Schweitzer paid attention to the fact that eschatological paradigms change, and moral paradigms respond. With Jesus, it was a matter of imminent eschatology and interim ethics. The failure of this expectation was a crisis for his followers, resolved in the resurrection faith. Paul represents a second eschatological paradigm: Christ mysticism. The moral paradigm is the ethics of the Spirit, who is described as the earnest of salvation and who produces in the believing community the moral 'fruits of the Spirit'. Here, faith works through love. But Paul is acutely aware, not least in his moral teaching, of the imminent end of the era. The expectation was again disappointed, leading to another complex paradigm shift. In the organised church of later times, the kingdom is a far-off event, and eschatology one item of faith among others. The consequences for moral attitudes and ethical stances were considerable: a lack of hope for the world, ascetic tendencies and an introspective concern for individual salvation, among other features, led to a loss of outgoing social concern as well as legalism and rigorism in ethics. There is thus a direct relationship between ethics and eschatology, but the nature of that relationship changes with the variables of context. Schweitzer himself, reviewing a long series of liberal lives of Jesus and embracing still a European idealism, located ultimacy in the affirmation of life force: a stance freed from the overt trappings of eschatology. Ethics is therefore not unrelated to problems of cognitive dissonance and disequilibrium. This kind of reading has been challenged, but obstinately refuses complete refutation, and in recent studies it has come to the fore once again.[46]

Ethical presuppositions Schweitzer's position is by no means as naïve as his 'elemental' presentation tends to suggest. He had weighed leading ethical theories in the balance and found them wanting: whether the appeal to duty, or the natural ethics which, he claimed, amounted to a negative quietism, or altruism as a sublimated egoism, or the primacy of societal ethics. He recognised the possibilities of relating ethics to sympathy, as did Hume and Adam Smith: 'if they had properly explored sympathy, they would have reached the universal ethic of reverence for life'.[47] But, while his radical philosophy stands in the Enlightenment tradition, there is no question about its Christian foundations. Much is derived from his understanding of ethics in the New Testament. Implicit is an approach to interpretation which is thoroughly contextual, even if its execution can be questioned. The interpretive movement operates within its own contextual world, whether of Jesus, Paul or Schweitzer. What is less clear is the historical and analogical connection between these worlds: a connection inadequately affirmed by the liberals in terms of permanent or eternal values. For Schweitzer, the central feature seems to be the ability to respond in one's own context to life in its totality, and to do so with courage and integrity. By doing precisely this, at great personal cost, Jesus achieved a victory for human integrity, and lives on in spirit in all human struggles for the same end. Paul encountered this spirit in 'Christ mysticism', as well as in his ministry as apostle to the Gentiles, and his ethic expresses and realises it. Schweitzer's reverence for life is its modern secular, yet intensely religious, expression. If these correspondences were more fully developed, it would be possible to sketch an integrated and defensible hermeneutical position.

By highlighting the issue of eschatology and exploring it so single-mindedly, Schweitzer performed a notable service – to theology, interpretation and ethics alike. Jack Sanders is right to protest against appeals to the moral teaching of Jesus which ignore this dimension, just as one should distrust accounts of 'the founder of Christianity' which do not come to terms with it. Schweitzer placed eschatology firmly on the agenda of scholarship, and his uncompromising approach challenged entrenched liberal and dogmatic stereotypes.

It is the way of a kind of salutary violence. So an equinoctial storm sweeps away dead limbs and branches and prepares the way for spring. It carries the blessing of needed one-sided emphasis and hyperbole.'[48]

Consistent eschatology and social ethics   For Schweitzer, reverence for life is the ethic of love widened into universality: it is the ethic of Jesus, now recognised as a logical consequence of thought. Ethics has thus lost its 'interim' nature: we can discern its universal significance. Within the totality of human experience, he suggested, an awareness of God could emerge in 'the dictates of the spirit': a conception which was capable of universal application. Indeed, one of his singular achievements was to present a Christian view of ethics which is capable of multi-cultural expression.[49] He could also evince an affinity with later theological trends in eschatology, particularly the 'theology of hope' associated with Moltmann and Metz. Eschatology is wrongly interpreted if, like some types of theology, it appears like a body from a strange world. It symbolises completion, goal, *telos*, and thus relates to social ethics in its teleological aspect.

More particularly, Schweitzer anticipated the enormously influential ethics of non-violence, whether in the Indian *satyagraha* form espoused by Gandhi or the *agape*-based ethics of Martin Luther King. By developing an holistic paradigm, he was anticipating a cultural shift which Europe had not yet fully recognised. He could thus be described as a forerunner of modern eschatological ethics, of protest movements against the exploitation of animals and nature, and of peace movements. Schweitzer's insight is that such concerns spring from an inner necessity of the will to live: they are cosmically rooted, not merely subjective or reactionary stances. Indeed, his engagement with the inner meaning of Jesus' teaching for the life of the world contrasts sharply with Herrmann's careful social neutrality. As Amos Wilder put it: 'Schweitzer can best be honoured by action in the line of his own commitments.'[50]

CHARISMATIC ETHICS: RUDOLF OTTO

A short note may be entered here about the work of Otto: short not because he is of minor importance, but because he never developed the ethical implications of his position.

Otto's study of religion focussed on the 'numinous' or non-rational factor, the *mysterium tremendum ac fascinans*, the sense of the awefulness, the overpowering and fascinating energy of the 'Wholly Other'.[51] The transcendent presses upon us with dynamic urgency yet remains attractive, even magnetic, in its effect. Otto came to the study of eschatology in the New

Testament by way of its Iranian and Near Eastern ante-cedents.[52] He could thus demonstrate that the proclamation of the kingdom was much more than a call to preparation. It involved the vanquishing of Satan. It signified a *dynamis*, a dynamic power already released in the world – vanquishing evil, healing and working miracles, restoring the lost and bringing the salvation which the pure in heart were awaiting. Jesus' person and work were part of a comprehensive re-demptive event which saw Satan fall from heaven like lightning. It was not so much that Jesus brought the kingdom as that the kingdom brought him with it!

For Otto, consistent eschatology left no time for any ethic other than instant repentance, or a cry for mercy. Jesus' call for righteousness was 'full of content' presupposing life and time and duration. The eschatological tension engendered forgiving love, humble service, watchfulness, trustful confidence, lack of anxiety, the abandonment of materialism. In short, for hu-mankind there is a new 'ideal' implicit in the kingdom: a new obedience to the will of God, a veritable call to perfection, a radical repentance, a decision that goes to the depth of the soul. The goal it sets is beyond human capacity. The kingdom grows of itself, it is a surprising blessing and treasure when found. A blessing, Otto insists, does not work through command, but awakens and evokes the strongest interest and search and self-surrender. The kingdom is not the *summum bonum* of the philosophers, but is the blessing which can only be received as a gift. And if one protests at the inconsistency between intense imminent eschatology and moral teaching which presupposes continuity of the present scene, Otto points to 'the irrationality of the genuine and typically eschatological attitude'.[53] The natural *ratio* cannot comprehend it, but the inner logic of religion suggests that the two poles must be held together. Here is 'a theology of *mirum*, in which opposites unite'.[54]

Otto combined contextual strength in his comparative method (although he pushed his case too far, thus incurring much criticism)[55] with exegetical skills and genuine insight into religious experience. Had he developed his perceptions of ethics, there would have been no easy compromise with moral philosophy. He presupposed a dynamic interaction between ethics and religion which precluded any autonomous or quasi-autonomous system of Christian ethics. Yet his ethical and theological insights debarred any interpretation which simply revolved around personal feeling or excitement. The kingdom entailed the encounter with a dynamic reality, a field of power, whose source transcended this world and whose operation was on a cosmic scale. Something of the possibilities of Otto's position had been anticipated by the Blumhardts. Christian ethics developed on this basis would involve community, experience, a sense of moral power, turbulence and joy.

CHAPTER 4

Existential ethics

> And *this* burden is just what Jesus puts upon human
> beings; he teaches them to see themselves as called to
> *decision* – decision between good and evil, decision for
> God's will or for their own will.
>
> (Rudolf Bultmann)[1]

DIALECTICAL THEOLOGY

Rudolf Bultmann was a many-sided figure. His adherence to
consistent eschatology indicated an affinity with Schweitzer.
His emphasis on the religio-historical context of primitive
Christianity denoted sympathy with the 'history of religions'
school. In his concern to communicate the gospel to 'modern
man', he evinced similarities to the liberal concerns of such as
Harnack, whom he admired. His programme of existential
interpretation and his hermeneutical understanding were indebted to Heidegger and others, while his 'dialectical' approach
to scripture (as well as his emphasis on form criticism) made
common cause with Barth, whose philosophical progenitor –
among others – was Kierkegaard.

Barth's dialectical method operated on the basis that we can
never speak of God except in terms of statement and counter-
statement. All human language about God is inadequate. Every
positive must be balanced by a negative. If we are under God's
grace, we are also under his judgment. Indeed, as far as humans
are concerned, the negative has leading force. There is no way
forward from human ideals or the religious experience of
humankind. 'Nothing in my hand I bring...' Ethics is viewed in
a similar light. There is no human goodness except in submission

to God, no endorsement of Christian civilisation, no unqualified recognition of human achievement. There may be a bias towards the poor, the victims of oppression, the peacemakers, for they relate in a special way to God's negative. But that is all! They too are under the judgment of God.[2]

Thus when Barth comes to discuss Romans 13.1–7, with its apparent endorsement of the powers that be as the instruments of God, he again places the 'great minus sign outside the bracket'.[3] There can be no endorsement of an unqualified Christian doctrine of state power, just as there can be no unequivocal endorsement of revolution (from whatever source). Only God can effect true revolution. The Christian can therefore get on with the business of doing right and avoiding wrong-doing, knowing that these judgments are not of an ultimate order, and all fall under the grace and judgment of God. If the worldly order becomes intolerably hostile to God, then with the confessing community one professes one's single-minded loyalty to Christ, thus giving a coded message to his enemies and to the compromisers.

In his *Commentary on Romans*, Barth had the avowed intention of refusing to be confined within the circularity of critical studies and attempting real engagement with the text. The resultant conversation with it can give the impression of a monologue in which Barth pursues his own theological reflections, albeit with the text as basic reference. But eschatology is more than a latter-day scenario impressing itself on creation: it issues in the Final Word of God in Christ to his creation. Barth's hermeneutic is thus theological and dialectical: the Word stands over against us, qualifying all our thoughts and actions. It never assumes the form of a hermeneutical system, for such would incur the same negation as applies elsewhere, although there is certainly a theology of the Word. The outcome, however, is unpredictable and puzzling for exegesis and ethics – and even for theology.[4] Henceforth there are negatives outside every human bracket, to be ignored at the cost of getting the calculations completely wrong!

The development of dialectical hermeneutics was left to Rudolf Bultmann, exegete and hermeneut *par excellence*.

ESCHATOLOGY AND ETHICS IN JESUS' MINISTRY

The work of Rudolf Bultmann has an important bearing on ethics and eschatology. Although he accorded a secondary place to the historical Jesus (at least in comparison with the 'kerygma': he would not allow interest in the historical Jesus to undermine its centrality), he addressed the question of the relation between the coming kingdom (eschatology) and the will of God (ethics) in the ministry of Jesus.[5] The key to grasping the unity of eschatology and moral demand lies in understanding their final decisive sense. Obstacles to understanding are often raised by modern presuppositions. If we think of ethics as the systematic study of moral action in the world, we cannot see how moral teaching of this kind can be reconciled with the preaching of the imminent end of this world. But Jesus did not presuppose such a view of ethics: indeed, his eschatology expressly denied it.

> Every ideal of personality or of society, every ethic of values and goods was repudiated. The one concern in this teaching was that man should conceive his immediate concrete situation as the decision to which he is constrained, and should decide in this moment for God and surrender his natural will.[6]

The message of the coming kingdom and the question of doing the will of God form a necessary unity as they bring one 'now' to decision as in the final hour. In this way the future exercises a controlling influence on the present, and obedience to the will of God opens up a new future for oneself.

For Bultmann, Christian ethics, like the moral teaching of Jesus, is never an independent or autonomous system. It remains eschatological ethics: moral teaching integrally related to the kingdom of God. But while the inherent unity of eschatology and ethics is seen to be a leading feature of Jesus' ministry, 'interim ethics' is excluded. Moralism and legalism – including an ethics of principles – are also ruled out by the narrowness of their horizons. For Bultmann, the moral decision is inseparable from the decision of faith in the moment of encounter with God.

Eschatology and ethics are thus viewed primarily in a

theological sense. For Bultmann, however, context was always important, and he therefore attempted to relate Jesus' message to the Jewish tradition within which he ministered: in particular, to God as sovereign Will, the Creator who wills that his people freely respond to him in their historical existence.[7] He is the sovereign who instructs his people – 'I am the Lord' – through his *torah*, and is therefore also judge of their actions. He is known from the past – in recital or story, moral demand and liturgy – yet his work reaches its climax in the future, when his kingdom comes. In the present time the righteous are always conscious of their sinfulness in God's sight, and strive to fulfil his law, but the people as a whole is described as disobedient. 'Woe is me... for I dwell in the midst of a people of unclean lips' (Isa. 6). Indeed – according to Bultmann – the danger into which Judaism, under foreign cultural influence, tended to fall was that of dualism: of dividing the present unfulfilled, and therefore evil, age from the age to come. To be sure, this dichotomy between present and future could be bridged by belief in God as the future judge of the present, but this promoted a tendency to orient obedience to the future judgment and to emphasise God's remoteness. The sense of living before God in the present, of the nearness of God, was progressively lost.

As far as Judaism is concerned, Bultmann may well be charged with a prejudicial reading, brought about by viewing the material in theological and eschatological perspective.[8] The hazard arises because Bultmann is not content to give a descriptive account of Judaism, but to interpret the religious scene from within. His strictures would apply equally to the way eschatology has been neutralised in the later Christian tradition. His central point is that, for Jesus, God is personal, holy and gracious will: the transcendent God who is also the God near at hand ('Father'). He is encountered not through some escape mechanism, but precisely in one's historical situation. Bultmann sweeps aside doctrinal or general philosophic understandings of God, as well as sacramental and mystical notions, and focusses on how God deals with people. Jesus does not offer a new concept of God nor make a new revelation of his nature. He presents the message of the coming kingdom and of God's holy and gracious will; and, since that message is existential in its import, the horizons merge and the challenge is heard by us today.

God's claim upon us is a claim on our responsive moral obedience. The Great Commandment interprets the 'duty' of love to God in terms of neighbour love. In each concrete situation our obedience to God is tested through our attitude to our neighbour. This demand to show love transcends every legal demand and every boundary or limit, encompassing even our enemy (Matt. 5.43–48). There can be no computing the number of times one may be called upon to show forgiveness (Matt. 18.21–2). Love requires no formal stipulations nor prescriptions: one knows what to do when the cry for help is heard. The lack of formulated principles indicates, according to Bultmann, that Jesus' teaching is not an ethic of world reform nor does it offer a blueprint for the better ordering of human life. It simply brings one into the last hour of decision ('now') and makes the individual responsible to his or her God.

Thus Bultmann advances a distinctive view of eschatology, springing, he believed, from Jewish roots and encompassing the kingdom as the final marvellous work of God. Bultmann accepts that obedience to God's will is *in some sense* the condition for participating in the coming kingdom: namely, it denotes true readiness. If this sounds like 'interim ethics' (which has a preparatory nature), Bultmann protests that to speak of the 'interim' is a reduction of the moral demand to the status of an exceptional measure valid only for a short interval until the end comes. His case is that the demand for obedience is total and unqualified. Neither the Sermon on the Mount nor Jesus' criticism of casuistry, he suggests, is based on the imminence of the end of the world. Rather, to recognise the nearness of God is to be made to face the future – a future when Satan's sway is finally broken (Jesus can 'see' it happening now) and God's will is done on earth as in heaven. It is to regain one's freedom from the dominion of Satan and to live for God the creator. The ethical and the eschatological are thus united in Jesus' message.

In relation to ethics, Bultmann was fighting on at least three fronts. While he was at one with the liberals in rejecting the strait-jacket of dogma, he was concerned to repudiate their notions of eternal values and highest good, with the concomitant emphasis on personality, natural development, self-realisation, and the language of natural process. At the same time, while absorbing Schweitzer's emphasis on eschatology and giving due weight to contextual considerations, he implicitly distanced himself from Schweitzer by his emphasis on existential interpretation (including the demythologising of apocalyptic) and by rejecting the thesis of interim ethics. Further, he wished to repudiate any notion that Jesus constructed or presupposed a system of ethics: 'Jesus teaches no ethics at all'![9] His moral teaching is related to his proclamation and interpretation of the will of God. When Bultmann's approach is thus related to his own context, his *Sitz im Leben*, it is possible to evaluate it in a positive way. He tried to renew the authentic focus of the moral teaching of the New Testament. All of the features noted above were important correctives in the earlier part of the twentieth century.

To set Jesus in the religious and moral tradition of Israel raises the question of the authority of the *Torah*. What is critical in assessing a teacher, however, 'is not his acceptance of an authoritative mass of tradition, but the way in which he interprets it'.[10] Bultmann allows himself to speak of the 'intention' of Jesus and to contrast it with the consequences of his procedure. In his polemical teaching, he *intended* to attack selected scribal interpretations of the *Torah*; the *result* was the (unintentional?) undermining of the law as formal legal authority.[11] The grounds for both assertions are open to question. Perhaps the most that can be argued for is the rhetorical purpose or tendency of given passages.[12] Jesus may well have demanded that the will of God in the *Torah* be given full expression, and that it be understood, without reservation, as impinging on the whole person and the total community. In relation to current interpretation, Jesus may be said to have employed the 'hermeneutics of suspicion'. Personal evasions and institutional defensiveness are then shown in a true light, and the need for change vigorously pressed. Tensions with the establishment were inevitable. But polemics must not be mistaken for definitive statements. It is one thing to argue, from a Christian perspective, that Jesus can be seen to 'fulfil' the *Torah* – which, after all, was Matthew's verdict – and that division occurred over precisely such a claim. It is another to allow such disagreements to distort the Jewish religion or to present a theological reading of Judaism which has the same effect.[13]

A feature of Bultmann's approach is that he differentiated Jesus' teaching not only from ancient Hellenism, but also from modern ideologies such as humanism. Jesus' teaching cannot be reduced to humanistic idealism, where value resides in the ideal self and where love is the universal love of mankind; nor can Jesus be recognised as a kind of high watermark in humanity's developing consciousness of God. Nor may *agape* be dissolved into sentiment. Like Dodd,[14] Bultmann denied that the love which God commands is an emotion. Indeed, he goes on:

the love which is based on emotions of sympathy, on affection, is self-love; for it is a love of preference, of choice, and the standard of preference and choice is self. Friendship and family love are expressions of the natural self; they are as such neither good nor bad; they are bad when the will of man is bad.[15]

Humanistic notions of self-love are thus eliminated, and the command to love is related to situations, so that a general theory of ethics cannot be built on it. But there are dangers in this approach. While the importance of the will – like the distinctive nature of *agape* – cannot be gainsaid, emotions are also part of 'the whole person' and are involved in our response to situations, persons – and God!

In his existential interpretation, Bultmann derived from Heidegger a powerful hermeneutical tool: indeed, one so powerful that it almost overwhelms the material. True, it jells with the radical nature of Jesus' moral imperatives. It also enables Bultmann, through his 'demythologizing' programme, to relate to both ancient and modern contexts. It is capable of further expansion: for example, in understanding self-deception. But it has its limitations.[16] Was Jesus' message really so 'momentary'? To be sure, Bultmann manages to affirm future eschatology without emptying it of present significance or dissolving it into apocalypticism, and to affirm present significance without reducing eschatology to realised dimensions. His interpretation, however, may limit the understanding of Jesus' teaching to a highly personal faith ethics. The question deserves fuller scrutiny.

AN INDIVIDUALISTIC FAITH ETHICS?

We select different areas of the New Testament to test the hypothesis, taking account of notable contributions from the *formgeschichtliche Schule*. We begin with the Sermon on the Mount, to which reference has already been made in several contexts.[17]

The Sermon on the Mount

M. Dibelius accepted the eschatological orientation of Jesus' teaching, but did not endorse interim ethics. For him, eschatological expectation provided the occasion for the proclamation of the divine will, without regard to the changing circumstances of daily life. But the Sermon was not to be understood as presenting 'commands': a notion which Dibelius describes as 'probably the most serious misconception that encumbers the tradition of Jesus'.[18] Viewed in *formgeschichtliche* perspective, the material of the Sermon has been understood by redactors and the faith communities as a disciple's catechism. Beyond that, the language of command, with its startling requirements and vivid stimulation, is entirely related to the kingdom and prompts a consistent ethos into which Jesus wished to induct and confirm his hearers. This ethos is really a new state of being, far exceeding the literal fulfilment of formal commands. The demand of Jesus is not 'So must thou *act* but rather, So must thou *be!*'[19] But since Jesus viewed his world as perishing, the application of the Sermon to continuing history turns on adaptation to the modern world and seeks to express the ethos Jesus commended. In this situation, one can understand the eschatological element as preserving Christian ethics from degenerating into the patriarchal conservatism which endorses the status quo or social activism based on human illusion.[20] It relates to, and prescribes, the distinctive ethos of disciple communities rather than to an individual faith ethics.

Bultmann, who was critical of a number of Dibelius' assumptions, faulted in particular his refusal to countenance the imperatives of the Sermon as commands, since it was of the nature of Jesus' teaching to express the unconditional demand of God. This did not mean that the imperatives of the Sermon should be read as concrete ethical demands or as generally valid regulations. The rhetoric of the Sermon offers vivid, even extreme, examples of what it means to obey God unconditionally, but to take these examples as rules or to build them into a system of ethics is, in fact, to reduce their value as statements of the unconditioned will of God. In this, Dibelius and Bultmann were in accord. But to insist on such a sharp distinction between acting and being was to risk an even greater distortion of the thrust of the Sermon.[21] Yet Dibelius appears the more consistent form critic here, and his emphasis on community ethos was one which would recur both in subsequent exegesis and in Christian ethics.[22]

G. Bornkamm approached the interpretation of the Sermon from a wider angle. He contrasted the 'new righteousness' of the Sermon on the Mount with fanatical revolutionary movements, such as Marxism or Bolshevism, which replaced the will of God with a picture of the future world that was for them the only valid law. Against all such fanaticism Jesus affirmed his goal of 'fulfilling' God's law. Bornkamm further emphasised Jesus' radicalising of the divine demand in the antitheses (Matt. 5.21–48) in order to demonstrate the righteousness which exceeds that of the scribes and Pharisees (Matt. 5.20). The question was not of a kind of super Phariseeism, but of something qualitatively different. In spite of all the insights of the rabbis, casuistry entailed a formalising both of the *Torah* and of the obedience due to it, and thus helped create 'the traditions of men'. Jesus therefore 'liberates the will of God from its petrification in tables of stone and reaches for the heart of man...'[23] Conciseness, vividness, even simplicity, are the hallmarks of his 'wisdom sayings'.[24] The primary question is not about practicability, but about truth: the acknowledgement of the reality of God's will in its wholeness (Matt. 5.48). One finds here no programme for the shaping of the world nor for legislative and social reform. Rather, there is a call for the faithful to be the salt of the earth and the light of the world (Matt. 5.13f.).

The pervasive problem in the above examples is the relation of eschatological material to continuing history, not least social history. The Sermon is distanced from the world of praxis. The writers thus reflect their own *Sitz im Leben*, in which Europe was wracked by Marxist utopianism, while the churches were too often seen as a merely conservative force. Eschatology presented a powerful critique of both: the effect of Jesus' eschatological urgency was to radicalise its message, to transcend the human concessions and accommodations of law and to confront his audience with the demand of God in its entirety. This demand certainly had the effect of raising the critical consciousness, but it did not translate into a specific programme of Christian action. Is social ethics impossible to contemplate?

Dibelius probably over-reacted to the danger of legalism in the language of command, and his solution (which is not without its attraction) risks dissolving the Sermon's teaching into mere ethos and attitude. For all three interpreters, the end has drawn near in Jesus, and his call to obedience is unequivocal – in this world. But if this unequivocal call is a call not only to have faith, but to act, the refusal to link with praxis is surely a conspicuous failure of interpretation: especially if it is noted that Jesus' 'illustrations' are related to practice in specific situations, such as encountering the violence of occupying forces. Hence, if one were to challenge Bornkamm, it would not be on the grounds of his alleged mistreatment of eschatology, but on his failure to consider that, if the eschaton represents the divine transformation of creation, the radical obedience for which Jesus calls *anticipates action in the direction of that transformation*. It is therefore not sufficient simply to distance the Sermon from the European revolutionary tradition (a stance which could readily be confused with 'bourgeois' detachment), but one must also consider whether the ethos of the church community should not properly enshrine a different type of revolutionary tradition representing the radical obedience for which Jesus called, and that as a disciple community the church is charged with living out the messianic teaching. This is quite different from suggesting that one is building the kingdom on earth: one takes to heart Barth's warning about the unsatisfactory nature of all worldly revolutions.[25] One must certainly endure the conflict between the kingdom and existence on earth, but other responses may also be called for: in particular, a steady witness to the direction in which the will of God points, and the implementation of his will in and through the faith community as far as the situation allows. In fact E. Fuchs and G. Ebeling, post-Bultmannians both, made more of this community base than Bultmann.[26] Their emphasis on the performative function of language – a phrase which recalls the English philosopher, J. L. Austin[27] – was termed 'language event' by Fuchs. It constitutes a remarkable correction to the older critical notion of the scholar interpreting the text. Now the text is seen also to interpret the interpreter! Both Fuchs and Ebeling (the latter preferred to speak of 'word event') related this type of understanding to preaching and, therefore, to the dynamics of the community at worship. The Sermon itself implies a disciple community base and the decision of the individual to affirm its ethos. The qualities reflected in the beatitudes characterise both the ethos of the community and the qualities of the individual disciple.

Finally, one must note the tendency in all three interpreters to differentiate too sharply and unfairly between Jesus' treatment of the law and that of the rabbis. Legalism was not a special preserve of the rabbis, any more than spiritual insight was an exclusive attribute of Christians. The exegetical heritage from Bousset and Harnack was counter-productive in this respect.[28]

Paul, ethics and authentic human existence

Bultmann – like Bornkamm after him – began his study of Paul by setting him in his religio-historical context.[29] Bultmann claimed that Paul's theology was a new structure, reflecting his place in Hellenistic Christianity. What then are we to make of Paul's ethics?

Paul's crisis of faith is reflected in his theology and, through it, in his understanding of ethics. Bultmann, therefore, makes a careful analysis of 'man prior to faith': that is, of the anthropological base-line. The rhetoric of 'new creation' cannot disguise the fact that there is a continuity in the life of the individual: for example, between Saul of Tarsus and Paul the apostle; but there is also a radical break. The gospel of Christ crucified is an invitation to understand oneself anew – as a sinner to whom God in his grace offers the gift of life. No longer can one boast that one is 'righteous under the law', even if one is proud to have been born an Israelite. There has been a recentring, a shift of focus. It is Christ's death and resurrection which are now seen as 'salvation-occurrence', 'God's eschatological deed', and the gift of 'God's righteousness'. Faith has a double action: belief in the act of God in Christ, and self-surrender to the grace of God in Christ. Faith comes through hearing the gospel message (the *kerygma*) and involves free decision, obedience, confession, hope and confidence for the future. Thus the faithful are committed to obedience as they live out the grace of God moment by moment. Particularly, they identify with the death and resurrection of Christ. Those who belong to Christ 'have crucified the old nature with its passions and desires' (Gal. 5.24) and open themselves to 'the power of his resurrection' (Phil. 3.10).

In spite of Paul's characterisation of the law as 'the power of sin' (1 Cor. 15.56), Paul is by no means wholly negative towards it. Bultmann tends to cling to the classic Galatians/Romans view. For sinful humankind 'law' articulates the demand of God for righteousness, which may be summed up as 'you shall love your neighbour as yourself'; even the Gentiles are not unaware of such a moral requirement (Rom. 2.14–5). For Jews, the *Torah* comprehensively confronts them with God's demand, and, because of failure to keep it in all its particularity, one is condemned by it as a sinner – and by God as judge. And this remains true even if one desires to obey it. Indeed, the very attempt to keep it is, in a sense, an act of presumption designed to establish a personally attained righteousness of which one may 'boast'. Sin, it must be realised, is not isolated failure to fulfil God's demand but the human condition itself. The total obedience which one owes to God means that one must realise one's absolute dependence on God's forgiving grace. The law can therefore be seen as a taskmaster to bring us to Christ (Gal. 3.24) and as finding its end in him (Rom. 10.4). Forgiveness is the transforming factor. Through it one passes from bondage to freedom, from anxiety to joy, from alienation to obedience. To go back to the law as the way to salvation is therefore to regress, to put oneself again under the bondage of sin; but positively, to know the power of God's forgiveness is to recognise that God's will encounters humankind both as law and grace.

Freedom is the keynote of the way of faith: freedom from the bondage of self-will and the compulsion of sin; freedom from death; above all, freedom consequent upon surrendering all to Christ the Lord (cf. Rom. 14.7–8). It is not freedom from all binding norms. One has surrendered not to the flesh but to Christ. The indicative – 'we are saved by God's grace' – coexists with the imperative, 'walk according to the Spirit'. Here we come to Bultmann's characteristic portrayal of the centre of Paul's ethics. The imperative coheres with the indicative and follows from it. The indicative expresses the grace of God – the fact that one is no longer 'under law' but 'under grace' (Rom. 6.14). It expresses the breaking of the power of sin (Rom. 6.14), the washing and consecration of baptism (1 Cor. 6.11), the gift of the Spirit. But the indicative sponsors the imperative: 'If the Spirit is the source of our life, let the Spirit also direct its course' (Gal. 5.25; *REB*). The force of the imperative is to deny a purely sacramental view of baptism and a merely ecstatic or speculative view of the Spirit. Christians become what they are by constantly appropriating grace through faith and obedience. This is the secret of their freedom. They no longer 'walk according to the flesh', which Bultmann describes as the quintessence of the worldly, visible, controllable and fleeting, and which therefore ties one to the transitory, to the past, to death. 'Freedom is nothing else than being open for the genuine future, letting oneself be determined by the future. So Spirit may be called the power of futurity'.[30]

This slightly strange language indicates how Bultmann interprets Paul's eschatology. As human beings we are 'between the times'. The future – the eschaton – has entered into the present in Christ, or through the gift of the Spirit. The Spirit is therefore the 'first fruit' or 'guarantee' (2 Cor. 1.22; 2.5) of that glorious future which now determines the life of the believer as motivating power and norm, and which is the ground of hope. The believer continues to live in this world (1 Cor. 5.10), often in unchanged circumstances (1 Cor. 7.17–24), but in the knowledge that it is passing away (1 Cor. 7.31). It is in this 'as though not' that the believer finds freedom from the world. The only motive for action which lacks ambiguity is love, and with it is associated action for the glory of God (1 Cor. 10.31). This paradoxical detachment is reflected in a few other early Christian traditions (e.g. 1 Peter 2.16), but sometimes the paradox is dissolved either into civic duty and moral exhortations such as the *Haustafeln*, which are almost indistinguishable from pagan teaching, or into an unqualified flight from the world.

The Christian life of faith, as Bultmann interprets Paul, is buoyant with the vitality of hope and positive even towards suffering. There is an apparently circular movement: from hope through suffering and endurance to strength of character and strengthened hope. The heart of the matter is that faith makes room for God – in suffering as in death – so that his life-giving power becomes effective. In short Bultmann claims that, for Paul, Christian freedom consists of liberation from sin and death. 'Dying with Christ' involves 'the crucifixion of passions and desires' (cf. Gal. 5.24); it involves 'being dead to sin and alive to God' in obedience (cf. Rom. 6.11ff.). However, through awareness of 'the death that is at work in one's mortal body' in the experience of suffering one may experience God's life-giving power and share in the resurrection life of Christ.

In the above sketch, the organic relations established in Paul's thinking between eschatology and ethics, indicative and imperative, and theology and practice, render it impossible to view Paul's ethics as an autonomous system. Yet, in spite of Bultmann's determined efforts, it has been suggested that Paul's position is not as coherent as such an account implies. In relation to ethics, three areas may be queried.

(a) Eschatology is broader in scope than is often allowed in descriptions of the Pauline *kerygma* which centre on justification. Paul, as apostle to the Gentiles, believed that he was a participant in the divine event of salvation. That is why his message is no carried tale, and why its basis is incontrovertible. For this reason, the table fellowship which expresses the unity of Jews and Gentiles in Christ must not be compromised (cf. Gal. 2). Similarly, the giving of the Spirit is part of the mighty work of God; hence, all must live 'in accordance with the Spirit'. While such aspects of the divine action may be related in Paul's mind to justification by faith (as in Gal. 2), Paul's ethics can relate to any part of the divine event. Eschatology embraces a number of motifs, and should not be defined in such a way as to exclude important elements which may have a bearing on ethics.[31]

(b) The place Paul gives to the *Torah*, his theological interpretation of it and its relation to ethics are notably controversial. What did Paul mean by describing Christ as the 'end' of the law?[32] Was it the end of the law as the justification of Jewish exclusivism – a feature unacceptable to the apostle to the Gentiles? Certainly, for Paul, the law is no longer the means of salvation, but Israel has gained 'much in every way' from it, and no Jew could discount its revelatory importance. E. P. Sanders and others would propose the term 'covenantal nomism' to describe Judaism,[33] but this does not solve the problem, since Paul clearly diverged from it. The crux of the matter is precisely how Paul's 'covenantal' thought redefined his nomism. In Paul's ethics the law is broadly affirmed as divine guidance in so far as it interprets *agape* as its chief head, and thus clarifies the way of Christ. However, in his struggle both to revalue the *Torah* in the light of Christ, and to describe the basis of the Christian way, Paul did not evince a single invariable attitude. His material should therefore not be forced into an alien mould in the interests of a theory of consistency.

(c) Taking up the issue of 'nomism', is Paul's ethics a rules-ethics or does it have a different character? In so far as it centres on justification by grace, it can hardly be other than relational, responsive and personalist within the *koinonia* of the church, the body of Christ. In content, it can absorb many influences, and subject them all to the service of Christ. Such service is carried out to the glory of God and in love to one's neighbour in the world. This loving praxis stands in sharp contrast to legalism and antinomianism, to asceticism and hedonism, to pneumatic excess and apocalyptic irresponsibility. Even if it has some other focus – e.g., the Spirit – Paul's ethics is capable of retaining its relational nature. But if the law remains operative (with whatever qualifications) for the ethics of the Christian community, then his ethics follows at best a mixed model or takes a deontological form, at least in some of its aspects.[34] Hence one may note that ethics reacts markedly to changes of emphases in the study of Paul himself.

Problems in Johannine ethics

For Bultmann, John is even more effective than Paul in expressing the dialectic of indicative and imperative on which ethics depends. At its core is God's forgiveness, not simply as a once for all act, but as the divine grace under which one's entire life is lived out. Freedom from sin and walking in the light are both related to confession of sin. 'If we confess our sins, he is faithful and just, and will forgive our sins.' (1 John 1.9) By the same token, indicative and imperative are both comprehended in Christ, whose commands are inseparable from his person. In the discourse about the vine, believers *are* clean (John 15.3) but they *must* remain united with Christ the vine in order to bear fruit (15.4–5). Barren branches are cut away (15.2, 6); to belong to Christ is to bear fruit. Jesus is the light of the world, the source of the light of life for his disciples (8.12), but they also must 'walk in the light'. To say that one walks in the light while hating one's brother is to remain in darkness and fail to 'do the truth' (cf. 1 John 1.6, 2.9). The imperative is the command for brotherly love which, Bultmann comments, is a new command because it finds its basis in the love of God for humankind bestowed in Jesus.[35]

This central command in John, expressed as it is with sublime simplicity, has become something of a storm centre in modern debate. Because the command is given to the community of the faithful – 'brothers' is used instead of 'neighbour' – the question is raised whether John has delimited the scope of love. Bultmann, and at least some of the post-Bultmannians, adopt different stances here. The former held that no such delimitation was involved. The command was addressed by the departing Revealer to the intimate circle of 'his own' who have received his love and it is to be the rule within the community, but this is no closed group. Indeed, its task is to bear witness to the world and draw it into this circle of mutual love. Moreover, Bultmann insists, when 1 John speaks about brotherly love (e.g. 1 John 3.17), it does not seem to be restricted to one's Christian brother.[36] Besides, John was certainly aware of synoptic tradition and affirmed it.

However, while Bultmann argued that love for one another did not exclude love of neighbour, Käsemann argued that love for brother did not expressly include it.[37] God's love was for the world in the sense that he sent his Son to summon the world to faith and to proclaim deliverance from death. But the practice of love was within the fellowship of the faithful: a brotherly rather than an unconditional love. In more extreme tones J. Sanders, alive to the dangers of the 'new fundamentalism' of today with its rejection of social responsibility in the world, castigated the 'weakness and moral bankruptcy of the Johannine ethics'.[38]

This is the kind of issue which can well give rise to special pleading, and critics like Käsemann and Jack Sanders are certainly guilty of overstating the case. Let Sanders speak for himself. After contrasting Johannine ethics unfavourably with

Paul's notion of love as fulfilling the law and with the parable of the Good Samaritan in Luke with its concern for the victim of violence, he goes on:

Johannine Christianity is interested only in whether he believes. 'Are you saved, brother?' the Johannine Christian asks the man bleeding to death on the side of the road. 'Are you concerned about your soul?' 'Do you believe that Jesus is the one who came down from God?' 'If you believe, you will have eternal life', promises the Johannine Christian, while the dying man's blood stains the ground.[39]

Impassioned rhetoric, but a gross exaggeration of the tension within Johannine ethics.

With Bultmann, one recognises that it is difficult to overlook the moral significance of John 3.16, which speaks of God's love for the cosmos. The notion that the ethics of the community – the ethics taught by the Lord, not simply community practice – expressly contradicts this legitimation of mission (and even Käsemann comes very near this), is inherently improbable. To be sure, the community is to love the Father, not the world (1 John 2.15), but this clearly refers to worldly desire and is a commonplace of early Christian ethics. There is no hatred of enemies, as in Qumran. On the other hand, love of enemies is not found explicitly in the Johannine literature. There *is* a limitation or narrowing of perspective – in practice if not in theory. Two factors may be cited in explanation. One is the eschatological. It is the last hour. The world in its alienation from God is darkness. Evil has been defeated (John 2.12–14) but the Antichrist is still active in the world (5.19). The world is therefore hostile to believers; they are 'hated' by the world (John 15, 1 John 3.13). The community of believers is sustained by God's love, which finds expression in loving one another. As J. L. Houlden put it, 'Love seems almost like a huddling together for warmth and safety in the face of the world.'[40] The second factor looks more directly towards historical factors rather than theological considerations: to the conflict of the Christians with Judaism, for example, or to paganism and Gnosticism within the churches themselves and similar tensions, resulting in the narrowing of perspective noted above.

Nevertheless, the fundamental significance of Jesus for Johannine ethics must never be forgotten. In the memorable pericope of the washing of the disciples' feet, an early interpretation (13.12–20) emphasises the example of Jesus. 'If I, your Lord and Teacher, have washed your feet, you also ought to wash one another's feet. I have set you an example: you are to do as I have done for you.' (13.14–15) As Bultmann emphasises, here we have a symbolic anticipation of the exposition of the love command (cf. 13.34, 15.12). But a consequence, ignored by those scholars who complain of a double standard in John, is that, while the believing community is, *par excellence*, the community of love, the faithful in their mission to the world also follow the example of Jesus. He laid down his life – and in this respect too the disciple is called to follow him – in order that the world might not perish but have life.

Does Bultmann's existential interpretation leave any space for social ethics? His interpretive work relates well to the faith community and is expressly differentiated from an individualist stance. He faced up to the question of social ethics through the fact that in the religion of Israel justice is understood as the requirement of God.[41] Indeed, by identifying justice and righteousness as the will of God, the prophets took these principles (*sic*) to be a check on human self-will and a bonding of the community against oppression of any of its members. Law in the formal sense, while establishing parameters, makes concessions ('you *may* divorce...') and leaves room for self-will. Hence 'law' as a category is inadequate to comprehend the totality of God's will. For this reason, Jesus' 'but I say to you...' is set over against formal justice. Law and the ordinances of justice are essentially instruments of coercion, dependent upon sanctions and force and necessary in the human community where evil is at work. They belong to what Bonhoeffer termed the 'penultimate' age; only when the kingdom is realised will they cease to be required. Hence the state's ordinances of justice have a provisional nature. True human community, Bultmann observes, grows out of a deeper ground than the ordinances of justice.

Yet however ambivalent the concept of formal justice may be, the demand for justice as such does not contradict God's will. If one appeals to law and justice merely to further one's own interests against one's neighbour or for retaliation or revenge, then the law and the notion of justice it enshrines at this point *do* contradict God's will. There is also an implication in the Sermon that justice has a legitimate meaning when it expresses love or when it serves the community in practical terms. Indeed, Bultmann sees here a critique for developing a more positive and creative view of justice, even though Jesus did not develop his teaching in this way: a project carried out well by P. Tillich.[42] At any rate, any appeal to justice must be in dialectical terms.

Perhaps the most obvious weakness in Bultmann's position is that he does not pursue the issues into the realm of practice (or 'praxis') but is content to remain within the world of ideas. He also limits his frame of reference mainly to the inter-personal, in spite of his understanding of history as resting upon study of the efficient forces which connect historical phenomena, such as economic needs, social exigencies and the politics of power, as well as individual purposes.[43] For this reason, Dorothee Sölle has faulted his 'bourgeois and presociological' thinking. 'There can be no place in this pre-democratic way of thinking for participation in decision making, constructive criticism, and political change, not to mention revolutionary transformation of existing structures.'[44] In other words, Bultmann's understanding of social morality was irretrievably 'top down'. This was true also of Schweitzer, but his particular type of praxis presented an alternative to bourgeois conventions which mitigated its otherwise patriarchal features.

For whom then are theology and social ethics intended? When Bultmann interprets the Word as opening up the future, we must ask, for whom? When he thus implies a praxis made clear by the Word, to whom is it open? Only in the latter part of the twentieth century, with attention being forcibly drawn to global perspectives, has Western thinking in the Enlightenment tradition been jolted into recognising its own cultural relativity. Who might be our dialogue partner? Granted, the question is not as simple as it seems. It is legitimate to write for restricted markets, such as students and scholars: the 'interested general reader' or 'lay person' is often an understandable fiction beloved of publishers! A serious book itself demands a restricted market! Perhaps we should ask, what kind of people are we presupposing as we write? Whose interests do we bear in mind? For whom are we ultimately concerned? In the past, the answer (when it was not simply 'in house' discussion) has presupposed readers who were predominantly Western, white, male, bourgeois (they would characteristically deny the validity of this term), and for theological purposes, church oriented or questioning agnostic. These comprise Bultmann's 'modern man', which in global terms excludes the vast majority of the world's population. The readjustment required before we are likely to break through into meaningful dialogue with wider constituencies is therefore immense.[45]

CHAPTER 5

The ethics of covenant and command

The ethics determined by the new situation can best be
characterized not as interim ethics but as ethics of the time
of salvation or new-covenant ethics.

(Amos N. Wilder)[1]

INTRODUCTION

As well as liberal idealism, dialectical theology and existential
interpretation, there emerged a broad and varied approach to
eschatology and ethics which centred on the idea of the people
of God, the covenant community. It emphasised historical
context and religious – especially prophetic – experience, and it
could evince 'realised', 'inaugurated' or 'futurist' views of
eschatology. It also allowed scholars to focus on the rediscovered
centre of New Testament concern: the *kerygma* or apostolic
preaching, and the moral imperatives of Jesus and the apostles.
But underlying all this varied activity was the understanding
and reinterpretation of the moral tradition of the Hebrew
scriptures. It is here that we find the roots of covenantal ethics.

James Muilenburg has observed that even to speak of the
ethics of ancient Israel means using the terms with considerable
latitude.

Here we find no unified and coherent body of ethical principles, no
autonomous values or ideals which one can possess and make one's
own, no norms which have independent status in and of themselves.
The Old Testament contains no treatises on the nature of goodness,
truth and justice. No Hebrew ever thought of writing a dissertation *de
natura bonitatis* or *de natura veritatis*.[2]

117

But Israel recognised that she had been addressed by One who stood in a special relationship to her, and who required that the justice and right which reflected his nature be expressed in her historical and social practice.

A review of ethics in Israel is not possible here,[3] but some indication of the moral ethos of Judaism is required. Ancient Judaism was a reshaping of the religion of Israel in the light of traumatic historical experiences such as the Assyrian conquest of North Israel and the later Samaritan schism, exile in Babylon and the return to an impoverished and hapless land of Judah, life under successive empires – Persian, Hellenistic and Roman – and the struggle for religious freedom, national identity and a distinctive ethos or way of life. This ethos was fostered by temple, priest and cult; by pilgrimage and festival; by the study and reading of scripture, to which the emerging synagogue movement was dedicated; by the expositions, teaching and disputations of the scribes and rabbis; by the devotions of Israel, family based and, when possible, communally expressed.

Complex but coherent as this ethos was, it proved resilient against threats from outside and from within. Hellenism was a predatory force and found rich pickings in the cultural elite of Jerusalem. Rome was the mailed fist which eventually brought destruction. Within Israel, there were those at the top who compromised for political and material ends; and there were those at the bottom who failed, for a variety of reasons, to maintain purity of practice and observance. In the dark days, some found consolation in apocalypticism, with its visions of renewal and the vindication of elect Israel. Some became politically active and sought martyrdom. Such groups tended to an ethic of loyalty to the *Torah*, perseverance and other-worldly hope. But loyalty and obedience could be predicated of Judaism in general. This general ethos E. P. Sanders describes in terms of 'covenantal nomism', which he regards as pervasive in Palestine before AD 70. He enumerates its main features thus:

(1) God has chosen Israel and (2) given the law. The law implies both (3) God's promise to maintain the election and (4) the requirement to obey. (5) God rewards obedience and punishes transgression. (6) The law provides for means of atonement, and atonement results in (7)

maintenance or re-establishment of the covenantal relationship. (8) All those who are maintained in the covenant by obedience, atonement and God's mercy belong to the group which will be saved. An important interpretation of the first and last points is that election and ultimately salvation are considered to be by God's mercy rather than human achievement.[4]

As a general summary this may serve, although it reflects an element of abstraction. The term 'nomism' is a twentieth-century neologism which denotes adherence to law. A preferable term in ethics is 'deontology' (a nineteenth-century neologism!), which denotes obligation in a more flexible way, and is more appropriate to the ethics of Israel as a whole, especially if the qualifier 'covenantal' is used. More of this later! In this chapter we shall consider the importance of the notion of covenant community, with its norms and life style, for the understanding of the moral teaching of Jesus and for Christian ethics; and we shall reflect in passing on the presuppositions which govern the reading of the material.

THE ETHICS OF 'CREATIVE FULFILMENT': T. W. MANSON[5]

In his celebrated work, *The Teaching of Jesus* (1931), Manson noted that critical opinion about the kingdom of God tended to bifurcate unsatisfactorily into the liberal and the apocalyptic views.[6] Since these views brought scholarship to an *impasse*, he suggested that there was a *prima facie* case for a fresh review, particularly in the light of the Semitic contribution to the content of the New Testament and to its subsequent interpretation.

The eschatological setting of the ethics of Jesus

Manson begins by noting that, in the first part of his ministry, Jesus speaks of the kingdom as coming, while in the latter part he speaks of people entering the kingdom: hence, for Jesus the kingdom had actually come at some point in his ministry. The key passage is Peter's confession at Caesarea Philippi – the recognition of Jesus as one divinely anointed and thus of the kingdom in the person of Jesus. From this point onwards, Manson argues, Jesus speaks of people 'entering the kingdom' and of himself as 'Son of man'.

The term 'kingdom' denotes the sovereignty of God, and entails a personal relation between God as king and the individual as subject, but it is not to be interpreted in individualistic terms. After Caesarea Philippi in particular, the kingdom comes to be manifested in the society of those united in a common allegiance to the king: that is, the people of God. But this society is never to be identified with the kingdom itself. The kingdom always transcends it, even as it finds expression in it. However, there is another important strand in the development of the latter part of Jesus' ministry. The Son of man – a term which embodies a long Old Testament pedigree that includes the notion of the faithful remnant, the servant of Yahweh and Danielic usage[7] – is identified not only with Jesus, but with the faithful remnant who acknowledge God's kingship. The latter part of his ministry sees Jesus increasingly isolated until, on the cross, he alone is the Son of man. Through his death the Son of man comes into being as the church, the body of Christ, the incarnation of the kingdom on earth.

For Manson, therefore, the debate about whether the kingdom is present or future, and whether it is to be thought of as a gradual religio-moral evolution or a catastrophic divine act, is fundamentally confused. There are different strands which must be carefully distinguished. The eternal sovereignty of God embraces both present and future aspects. The kingdom becomes a present reality in the course of Jesus' own ministry, but its final consummation is a future event, as is the 'coming of the Son of man'. These aspects of the kingdom are in fact clearly discernible also in the Hebrew scriptures, in rabbinic teaching and in early Christian discourse.

The consequences for ethics are immediate. Manson found the essence of Jesus' preaching in the words 'Thy will be done': all the rest, he observed, is commentary. Jesus had an intense awareness of God's sovereignty over the natural world, and this is reflected in many of his sayings and parables, but, in the personal sphere where freedom operates, the sovereignty of God is challenged by the power of evil, the kingdom of Satan. Hence human beings are summoned to decide, and the stakes are high: life or destruction. 'The final destiny of man lies in the disposition of his own will – for or against God'.[8] The decision should be made in the knowledge that the kingdom will prevail in the end. Satan is signally defeated in Jesus' ministry. Jesus is conscious of being the vehicle of irresistible power, which he imparts to his disciples. Hence, to put one's trust in Jesus is to be delivered from worldly care and to find strength for the day of trial.

The imaginative side of Jesus' presentation of ethics is seen in his parables. For Manson, they are much more than sermon illustrations, designed to state some abstract principle in pictorial form for the unlearned. They are derived from the Hebrew *mashal*, which embraced two parabolic types: one is directed *ad rem* (for example, sentences of popular wisdom relating to some aspect of the human crisis and aimed at awakening religious insight), and the other the *ad hominem* form designed to arouse the conscience.[9] In the latter aspect they are 'quick and powerful and sharper than any two-edged sword'; they 'make God real' to human beings. The true parable, according to Manson, is virtually sacramental. Its purpose is 'to show, directly and indirectly, what God is and what man may become, and to show these things in a way that will reach men's hearts...'[10]

Religion and morality

For Manson, Jesus' moral teaching requires to be set in its religious context: that is, of 'the prophets and psalmists and sages of Israel'. *Torah*, the revealed will of God, is therefore a central concept. Its moral requirements were seen to be prescribed by God, revealed through his servants and laid upon God's people as an unconditional obligation.[11] Jesus' life and teaching reflect these characteristics: in his 'Thy will be done'; his 'I say unto you...' (which Manson consistently regards as prophetic), and his invitation to enter into the community of the kingdom of God. Here is no independent ethic nor even an 'interim' ethic. It is rather the ethics of the kingdom, a setting forth of the way in which God's will may be done on earth as in heaven.

Manson draws a sharp distinction between the prophetic and the legal approaches, emphasising that the prophets insisted on 'the radical transformation of the human heart'.[12] The goodness that Jesus calls for is the fruit of such change, the spontaneous response of a transformed character. Jesus' moral teaching is not a new law nor a code of rules to replace the law of Moses. It attempts to illustrate the relation between the springs of conduct and conduct itself. Thus, Manson maintains, moral questions are 'brought before the bar of the conscience of the responsible person'.[13] Nevertheless, in his later work particularly, he laid emphasis on messianic law and covenant, and characterised the Sermon on the Mount as containing the new law (Matt. 5.17–48), the new standard of worship (6.1–34) and the new standard of corporate solidarity (7.1–12).[14] He emphasised the call to perfection – another example of the close relation of ethics and eschatology – but 'to follow Christ is not to go in pursuit of an ideal but to share in the results of an achievement'.[15]

Paul's ethics is also rooted in his religious faith, which focussed on the significance of the Cross. Rejecting theories of the atonement which suggest that God required an inducement to justify the sinner, Manson emphasised the grace of God in justification (cf. Rom. 3.24, 4.2–8). The solution to the problem of how God can justify 'apart from law' (Rom. 3.21) while still maintaining law is found in the fact that 'in the Christian dispensation God's dealing with the sinner is removed from the law court into the throne-room'.[16] Manson stresses the place of repentance, as in Israel: the justified sinner must be a repentant sinner, but such repentance is made possible by response to the grace of God in Christ. It comes as a gift, creating confidence to approach God and breaking the power of evil in human life. It is comprehended not only cognitively, but also through the feelings and the will. As in Judaism, moral obligation is inseparable from religious benefit. Salvation is deliverance from the power of evil into the glorious liberty of the children of God who cry, 'Abba, Father'. And this freedom has its own dynamic: if we live by the Spirit, we must also walk by the Spirit and bring forth the corresponding fruit in our living (Gal. 5.22–25).

Christian ethics

What kind of picture of Christian ethics emerges from this discussion? Manson rules out any return to legalism as incompatible with Christian roots. Nor will mechanical imitation of Christ serve: each situation is unique and demands a distinctive response. What is indicated is 'a creative initiative, based on the Law and the Prophets, instructed by the words and deeds of Jesus, and able, with him as guide, to deal constructively and imaginatively with the problems of our time.'[17]

Manson saw a strong affinity with the ethics of Judaism. In going beyond the requirement of the Hebrew–Jewish code, Jesus' teaching on love does not abrogate the old standards, but 'fulfils' them. 'Jesus shows what is really involved in love of neighbour; and shows it in thought, word, and deed.'[18] In *The Teaching of Jesus*, Manson argued that the essential difference was that, for Jesus, the notion of the 'good heart' was carried to its logical conclusion, while in Judaism 'the whole apparatus of Law and Tradition is still maintained beside the moral principle which renders it obsolete'.[19] But in *Ethics and the Gospel*, he emphasised that it was quite wrong to suggest that, while Jesus stressed the inward springs of action, Judaism did not.[20] Both were concerned for right action and good will. Manson also distinguished Jesus' teaching from the understanding of sin and forgiveness found in the Westminster Calvinist tradition, which is much too narrowly legalistic and tends to treat the symptoms rather than the disease. Sin is not a matter of omission and commission, but a condition of the soul. Repentance (*metanoia*: 'change of character' is Manson's definition) is therefore fundamental, as is Paul's teaching on 'justification by faith'. To receive forgiveness one must become forgiving. Manson puts it more daringly: 'a forgiving spirit in man is an essential condition of his receiving God's forgiveness'.[21] In a nutshell, Christian morality requires that we have 'the same mind which was also in Christ Jesus' (Phil. 2.5).

Manson's work: a brief appraisal

(i) There are many positive features in Manson's work. These include a highly developed awareness of the critical tradition in which he was working; a determination to distance himself from the dominant philosophical presuppositions of liberalism, which served to distort the study of the ministry and teaching of Jesus; a desire to come to terms with the thoroughgoing eschatology which had been advanced with such single-mindedness by Schweitzer, but which provided an unbalanced account of Jesus and his teaching; and an awareness of the importance of religio-historical context for the study of Jesus which brought Manson to explore the Aramaic background of Jesus' teaching and the dialogue with Judaism which it implied throughout. To these might be added a theological sensitivity which enabled him to distance his biblical interpretation from traditional dogmatic patterns, and a willingness to relate the teaching of Jesus to the wider question of religion and ethics.

(ii) There are also limitations. Manson's devotion to the source critical method[22] prompts an attempt to discern a definitive pattern in Jesus' ministry which may owe more to Mark's arrangement of the material than to historical veri-similitude. It also leads him to relate conflicting emphases in Jesus' presentation of the kingdom to chronological development rather than to inherently religious and prophetic factors. His lack of sensitivity to form criticism, at least in his earlier work, reduced his awareness of the role of the early Christian communities in interpreting the teaching of Jesus. He tended to think of the earliest Christian community as the milieu or environment in which Christians were called to obey the law of Christ.[23]

(iii) The theological factor in Manson's work is problematical. It militated against his making as full a contribution as might otherwise have been possible to Jewish–Christian debate. It led him to take a strongly Christocentric view of the Hebrew scriptures,[24] to the detriment of other perspectives important for dialogue and probably for other purposes. A similar point could be made about his ecclesiological interest.

There are at least two influences from theology and philo-sophy which enter the equation. Manson was deeply influenced by English incarnational theology, which coloured his notion of the person of Jesus and the authority of his teaching, and enabled him to connect Jesus, the incarnation of the kingdom, with the church which in Pauline terms is his body. Thus the creative or synthetic elements in his biblical theology influenced his exegetical results. The other influence upon his ethical understanding in particular was that of Kant. While he did not impose Kantian categories on Jesus' teaching, he treated them as a foil to Christian ethics.[25]

(iv) It is possible to see development in Manson's work. He seemed to be much bolder in his later work in using terms such as messianic law, new law and new Moses, and he was clearly influenced in some of this work by Dodd and Jeremias.[26] His exposition of justification in Paul and its bearing on ethics was a corrective to common misunderstandings of the doctrine, but it afforded Pauline ethics a very limited basis. He was always clear that Christian ethics was not a matter of rules and regulations, but 'active living' with 'the power to go to the heart of every ethical situation as it arises'.[27] With his propensity to draw images from the aesthetic realm, he described Christian ethics as a work of art. It embodied a sensitive response to the situation in the light of obedience to Christ, and an imaginative application of the teaching of Christ and the apostles.

DIVINE COMMAND: C. H. DODD[28]

Eschatology, ethics and kerygma

Dodd's approach to the question of eschatology is totally different from that of Schweitzer, has rather more affinities with Weiss and Otto, but reminds one most of all of Harnack. In effect, he emphasises the criterion of differentiation.[29]

In relation to Jesus, Dodd focusses on some of the key texts to which Weiss, Otto and Harnack gave attention. Jesus calls his hearers to repentance in view of the arrival of the kingdom. He interprets his own ministry as signifying the invasiveness, and therefore the real presence, of the kingdom: if he casts out demons by the 'finger' of God or by the Spirit of God, 'then the kingdom of God has come upon you' (a 'Q' saying: cf. Matt. 12.28/Luke 11.20). Dodd endorses Otto's view that in some way the Kingdom of God has come with Jesus Himself'.[30] 'blessed are the eyes that see what you see...': for Dodd the 'plain meaning' of such passages is that, with Jesus, the kingdom 'is not merely imminent; it is here'.[31] John the Baptist is the dividing line between the law and the prophets before him and the kingdom of God after him. Dodd saw so-called consistent or thoroughgoing eschatology as in effect a compromise. Faced with the dilemma of present and future eschatology, it opted for the notion of 'very, very soon'. 'Whatever we make of them, the sayings which declare the Kingdom of God to have come are explicit and unequivocal'.[32] In them we find the *differentia* of the teaching of Jesus on the kingdom of God.

The early Christians recognised that the kingdom 'had been inaugurated on earth in an act which was both God's judgment on the iniquities of men and the supreme opportunity afforded by His mercy for forgiveness and a fresh start'.[33] This meant that the Christians had a story to tell, and Dodd presented his earlier account of the *kerygma* as a recital, in propositional form, of the mighty acts of God in Christ.[34] But with the 'mighty acts' tradition there are dominical sayings – a preliterary tradition of the teaching of Jesus – which are also key points of reference in the moral teaching of the church. Dodd's characteristic position is that *kerygma* and *didache* – proclamation and teaching – are closely related, but the teaching is secondary to the proclamation.[35] Ethics arises as a response to the gospel. We must never lose sight of the fact that with Christ 'the zero hour in which decisive action is called for' has come. As Mark put it, 'The time is fulfilled and the kingdom of God is upon you.'

Jesus' use of parables relates to this crisis. In Dodd's view, parables are not moralistic stories nor are they completely other-worldly.[36] Parables are designed to bring things to a head, to depict the arrival of a zero hour, to confront the hearers with the kingdom of God. Dodd notes that Jesus never defined the kingdom. Some understood him to say that it was a mystery which few understood. Jesus showed his hearers what it is *like*.[37] The kingdom could be pictured as, or compared to, known experience. The event which showed affinity to the kingdom might be unexpected or disconcerting, but it always called for decisive action. Thus Jesus' teaching

contemplates human conduct in the most concrete way possible, as related to a real situation in which the one overriding fact is the fact of God Himself; a situation, therefore, in which the whole seriousness of the predicament of man is laid bare and in which endless possibilities of fulfilment and satisfaction are opened.[38]

To be involved in such a crisis of decision tends to engender a sense of impending catastrophe which reduces all worldly concern to transience and impermanence. All human ties are relativised. In particular, one should not tie oneself to the world by a continuing indebtedness to it: hence, one should discharge one's duties to the state, remembering how critical the time is (cf. Rom. 13.1–8).[39] Attention must be focussed on the things which are worth caring about; in short, on the will of God. Dodd cities 1 John 2.17: 'The world is passing away, and the world's desire, but he who does God's will abides for ever.'

The paradox highlighted by the Fourth Gospel – 'The hour is coming, and *is now*' – signals that 'what was essential in the great expectation was already realized. God was confronting men in a new way.'[40] In view of Christ's work, what Dodd calls the moral possibilities of human nature were revealed as never before. 'Within the workaday precepts which the church put forth, there lay the potentiality of immensely more exigent demands and more efficacious moral resources than men had thought of before':[41] not, Dodd hastens to add, mere idealism nor perfectionism, but the recognition that all stand under the judgment of God, that the divine judgment carries forgiveness with it, and that such forgiveness affords 'new, originating power'.

Eschatology, grace and obligation

In relation to Paul, Dodd neither endorsed the classical Lutheran *cum* liberal view of 'justification by faith' as the sole ground of Pauline faith and ethics, nor did he embrace *simpliciter* Schweitzer's focus on the Spirit in the context of Christ mysticism. True, he emphasised our self-abandonment to the will of God ('faith' or 'trust'), and God's gracious action in 'justifying' us. Paul's faith centres on what God has done for us (the eschatological action of God in Christ), not on what we do (as in legalism). 'The immense energy of the religious life is rooted in a moment of passivity in which God acts'.[42] But does this leave a problem in Paul in relation to ethics? Dodd acknowledged the difficulty.[43] He agreed that Paul wrote of justification as if it were an accomplished event, without qualification (Rom. 5.2, 9; 8.3; 1 Cor. 6.11) – perhaps because of the suddenness and completeness of his own conversion. But Paul also emphasised 'the tremendous moral endeavour to live out the righteousness of God'.[44] Dodd points to Paul's understanding of 'sanctification', and to the transition from the 'backward looking' to the 'forward looking' aspect of Christ's work expressed in baptism: if one dies with Christ, one begins to live in the power of his resurrection. 'That positive doctrine of the resurrection-life in Christ was an even greater thing to Paul than the doctrine of justification.'[45] Baptism is 'in the Spirit'. The Spirit and the living Christ are all but identical, and the moral life and eternal life are the products of the Spirit. 'The moral demand of letting Christ's Spirit rule you in everything is far more searching than the demand of any code, and at the same time it carries with it the promise of indefinite growth and development.'[46] It means moral discernment and moral power, and freedom to obey the inner law of the Spirit.

Eschatology and the ethics of community

Dodd emphasises the organic nature of the community as the context for the ethics of the early church. Paul apparently coined the phrase 'the body of Christ'. John spoke of the vine and its branches. 1 Peter used the metaphor of building. To place the moral life of Christians within such a social organism has consequences for the understanding of ethics. As opposed to modern trends, neither the individual nor the community is absolutised. Both live not for themselves nor for the church, but for Christ. 'Rightly understood', Dodd wrote, 'the church is the one society which can make total demands upon its members without being totalitarian, because it is not, and never claims to be, a self-determining sovereign power'.[47] In other words, it has a transcendent horizon and exists for the glory of God.

Thus when Paul speaks of being 'in Christ', his language denotes not a 'Christ-mysticism', as Schweitzer argued, but membership of the church as Christ's body. Here, Dodd believes, Paul identified the transforming factor in ethics. Within the Christian society, family and household relationships, like marriage itself, are transformed. The church therefore finds in Christ, the head of the body, 'an objective standard of ethical conduct'.[48] For Paul as for others, Christ is example or model: whether in his suffering (cf. 1 Pet. 2.21) or in his gentleness and forbearance (cf. 2 Cor. 10.1) or in his self-giving (cf. 2 Cor. 8.9; Phil. 2.5–8). Instead of referring to the gospel story, Dodd characteristically points to the 'hard core of historical fact': the human action of Jesus giving expression to 'the divine act of self-giving beyond space and time, eternal in its significance, revealing the character of God Himself'.[49] To imitate God is, of course, a dangerous pursuit for a mere mortal. The New Testament, therefore, makes clear in what sense it is intended. In copying the love which Christ showed to humankind, one is following the divine pattern in so far as God can be a model to his creatures. Thus the *imitatio Christi*, in Dodd's words, 'becomes a mode of absolute ethics'.[50]

Law and love

Love (*agape*) is clearly a principal motive of Christian ethics. As a concept it requires clarification, and receives it in a number of memorable passages in the New Testament. Indeed, it can be understood only from the gospel. It is neither soft sentiment nor cold charity. It is, Dodd emphasises, 'not primarily an emotion or affection' but 'an active determination of the will'. 'That is why it can be commanded, as feelings cannot.'[51] Taken in isolation, this might be seen as a forbidding formula, but in fairness to Dodd he relates it directly to the New Testament. It is not a virtue for human aspiration but 'is that total attitude which is brought about by exposure to the love of God as it is expressed in Christ's self-sacrifice'.[52] As 1 John puts it so clearly, we are enabled to love only because we first experience love.

Here then is a paradoxical picture. On the one hand, *agape* relates primarily to the will; on the other, it is evoked, it is deeply personal and relational. The paradox is heightened when we see that Paul, the determined opponent of 'justification by works of the law', is not similarly opposed to law as such. He stands within Christ's law (1 Cor. 9.21) and urges his followers to fulfil the law of Christ (Gal. 6.2). The paradox is explained in terms of covenantal logic. 'Covenant', whether of Sinai or Christ, suggests divine initiative and human responsiveness and obligation. The new covenant reflects the character and purpose of God in Christ. It is his law that is to be internalised, 'written on the heart'. This, however, is not to be reduced to some notion of 'inner light'. It affirms God as sovereign and his people as his subjects. The focus of the new covenant is God's action in Christ. Its quality is that of *agape*. Its direction is towards the perfecting of life in God's creation: eternal life. One is under obligation 'to reproduce in human action the *quality* and the *direction* of the act of God by which we are saved'.[53] This is the law of Christ. It stirs the imagination, arouses conscience, provokes us to ethical thought, impels the will and prompts us to action. Thus is the law 'written on the heart'.

But Paul also appealed to the law written on the hearts of pagans (Rom. 2.14–15). Dodd points out that Jesus appealed to the created order as pointing to the law of God: his teaching on marriage and divorce is a case in point (cf. Mark 10.2–9). The church, therefore, is concerned not only with the moral practice of its own members, but also with the life of the world. There is a quality and direction which must be affirmed of all human action. Thus the law of Christ, Dodd concludes, 'affirms the principles upon which His world is built and which men ignore at their peril'.[54]

An assessment of Dodd's position

Dodd demonstrated that there is an integral relation between faith and ethics, proclamation and ethics, and eschatology and ethics. Moreover, there is a sensitivity to moral concerns and ethical discourse, and a lucidity in handling them which adds an extra dimension to his theological and exegetical work. As his work has been widely discussed, only selected criticisms are offered here – and in brief compass.[55]

(i) Dodd claims to derive the theological framework within which ethics is set from the New Testament. But he was also – inevitably – a modern thinker, conditioned by his times.[56] Indeed, there are several noticeable phases in his development. The early Dodd related freely to the language and conceptuality of liberalism. He connected the authority of the Bible with the religious genius of those who spoke in it, and appealed to religious experiences, to the 'personality' of Jesus and to notions such as progress and progressive revelation.[57] Here is the anthropocentrism of Western liberalism, tempered by theological insight, religious commitment and classical scholarship of the highest order. In his middle period (to speak generally), his kerygmatic emphasis reflected the influence of dialectical theology, modified as always by his independent exegetical efforts: hence his emphasis on crisis, zero hour, the call to decision. The theological framework, however, remained idealist. He can speak of the kingdom as 'timeless reality', of history becoming the vehicle of the eternal, and the absolute being clothed in flesh and blood.[58] The components of his idealism are various: the Platonist tradition that so influenced English universities; a particular philosophy of history (sometimes Dodd sounds positivistic in his appeal to 'the facts'); and English incarnational theology. Some of these notes were perhaps more muted in his later works. Similar constraints affect his interpretation of ethics. Though less obviously than T. W. Manson, for example, his ethics is influenced by Kant and his notion of categorical imperative. Once again, interpretation and exegesis merge, so that his idea of covenantal law claims biblical warrant. It is a salutary demonstration of the subtle ways in which presupposition and exegesis blend.

(ii) Note should be taken of a series of interpretive problems for ethics in realised eschatology.

(a) *Divine command*   Dodd's description of the nature of ethics in the New Testament is open to question. First, he relegates the affective aspect of *agape* to a subordinate position and elevates the conative aspect in order to make sense of the language of command. But if *agape* is drained of emotion, then compassion and feeling for others are likewise removed. Could it be that we find here the residue of Kantian formalism and intellectualism? He also describes Christian ethics in effect as a type of covenantal nomism. To that extent, it belongs to the same realm of discourse as the ethics of rabbinic Judaism. Major considerations include the apparent centrality of 'new covenant' thinking in the New Testament, allied to the retention of the language of law, even in Paul. But, even if the logic of covenant is accepted as normative, if not universal, in ethical discourse in Israel and the early church, the language of 'law' or 'command' is polyvalent rather than monolithic, as Jesus' insistence on the 'intention' of the language indicates; and when an eschatological dimension is introduced, the situation becomes even more complex. Jeremiah, for instance, speaks not only of the 'internalising' of the law, but of the cessation of teaching in favour of the immediacy of understanding (Jer. 31.31–5). This seems a far cry from covenantal nomism with its accompanying casuistry in which the teacher's role is paramount.

(b) *Impossible goal*   On the basis of realised eschatology, the divine command is inescapable yet unattainable (cf. Matt. 5.48). Hence there can be no easy compromise with conventional morality, no concession to human weakness in our statement of ultimate demand. As J. Knox has argued, Jesus' followers seem obligated to do the impossible.[59] But they are taught to pray: 'Forgive us our debts, as we herewith forgive our debtors' (Matt. 6.12). The *imitatio Dei*, therefore operates not only in terms of goal, but also in terms of acceptance of the other. It is thus to be contextualised within the realm of human penitence and divine forgiveness. It cannot be equated *simpliciter* with divine demand or the call to repentance. The divine acceptance receives radical expression in Jesus' ministry: for example, in his table fellowship with sinners. To interpret such actions of Jesus as a lowering of standards is to miss the point. Rather, there is given with the kingdom – and with Jesus as its agent – a dynamic of righteousness, truth and acceptance which provides the context in which the total demand of God can be set. The impossible goal becomes possible only within the realm of being which was made real – 'realised' – in the ministry and teaching of Jesus.

(c) *Antinomianism*　By the time Paul was writing Romans, his teaching about justification by grace through faith had already earned him the charge of antinomianism (Rom. 6.1). Such an accusation is credible only if the term is used, not in the broad sense of rejecting all norms (which would be an outrageous allegation to put to Paul), but in the specific sense of undermining the righteous demand of God. In other words, his understanding of the great eschatological event by which God in Christ brought the Gentiles into the people of God led him to emphasise the notion of divine grace – experienced as a deep reality in his own life – and thus to create the apprehension, in the minds of some, that the basis of divine law was being stripped away from the Christian life style. Some modern scholars have tended to agree, particularly on the grounds that Paul has unintentionally polarised the justice and the mercy of God so that they cannot interact within a logical and coherent process.[60]

The problem, though long canvassed, is worthy of note here, since it arises out of Paul's notion of realised eschatology, and is an issue in ethics and interpretation. Futurist eschatology provides a relatively simple convergence with ethics, whether interim, penitential or preparatory to judgment. The divine law or demand is located at its centre. But an eschatology realised in a supreme act of grace? Why should we not sin all the more, so that the grace may be all the greater! Paul rejects the notion, but has to appeal to a wide range of differing yet converging lines of thinking: a relational view permeated by divine grace; a participative view of being 'in Christ' and therefore divorced from contrary realms of living; a dynamic view of the Spirit and the fruits it creates in living; church discipline and apostolic teaching; and even appeals to the final judgment. These motifs stand in tension with one another, though not, perhaps, in contradiction. Nevertheless, this plurality of approach is probably required to counter the difficulty of the problem.

MESSIANIC LAW AND COVENANTAL NOMISM: W. D. DAVIES AND E. P. SANDERS

The ethics of Jesus

The relation of eschatology to ethics is a central theme in Davies' work.[61] Understanding Jesus as both accepting and transcending the ethical tradition of the people in which he was nurtured, Davies took the kingdom to be central to Jesus' moral teaching. The active rule of God was already present or in process of realisation in his ministry. Jesus' moral teaching is therefore best understood as the demands placed upon those who have accepted God's rule as he proclaimed it. Prudential considerations were set aside as at best secondary, and moral issues viewed with utter radicalism. 'He places men immediately under the gracious and demanding will of God, relentless and uncompromising, untouched by the relativities and contingencies of "the world", as it is unlimited by human sin.'[62] However, eschatology is also related in Jesus' ethics to the renewal of the cosmos: 'it was the ethics of a new creation, of a new heart and spirit, of a new covenant, of a new people – a new Israel that had responded to Jesus' call to repentance and received the rule of God'.[63] Thus the apprehension of the will of God is contextualised in covenantal language. Jesus, even as the 'new Moses', is viewed, not as the giver of a new law code (Davies rejected the view of Christian ethics which would follow from such a position) but as the revealer of the will of God and 'the quality and direction of the good life' which God requires.[64]

Since ethics and eschatology alike were such central concerns of Jesus, those closely associated with him in this crisis of the ages had a particularly acute experience of the absolute demand of God.

In view of his general approach, it is not surprising that Davies showed particular interest in the Sermon on the Mount. In its setting in Matthew, it is messianic *Torah*: suggestive of the law of a new Moses, but transcending Mosaic categories. Thus, the force of the law is not annulled by the so-called antitheses (Matt. 5.21–48) but carried to completion in its ultimate meaning. Hence, in the eschatological perspective of the new age, the old law is denied at one level, but affirmed and fulfilled on another; and the authority for such definitive exposition derives from Jesus himself as messiah. The unmistakable prominence given in Matthew's gospel to the teaching of Jesus – Davies speaks of 'the truly majestic deliberateness with which Matthew prepared his great manifesto'[65] – may be a response to incipient Gnostic laxity or the infiltration of sectarian legalism or the resurgent Judaism of Jamnia. The risk Matthew took, according to Davies, was the isolating of the demand of God from the notion of divine gift, as might be the case if the Sermon was read on its own. Davies believed it characteristic of Jesus – and Matthew – to balance demand and gift or grace. But the Sermon has its own point to make: 'It is the penetrating precepts of Jesus that are the astringent protection against any interpretation of that life, death and resurrection in other than moral terms.'[66]

Davies and Sanders agree that Jesus could not have done other than accept the *Torah* as fundamental and unitary. Given by God through Moses, it was the basis of covenant and promises and therefore of Israel's relation to God. Sanders emphasised restoration eschatology – eschatological expectation involving the restoration of Israel: one need only indicate the mission of John the Baptist, the calling of the 'twelve' (with all the symbolism it implied), the expectation of the coming of Elijah who would first restore all things (Matt. 17.11 par.), and the apostolic hope of the restoration of the kingdom to Israel (Acts 1.6). The inner logic of Jesus' ministry – what Sanders calls the 'facts' – establishes Jesus' concern for the hope of Jewish restoration. More problematically, his teaching is individual in tone and does not characteristically address 'all Israel'. Instead, Jesus invites people – not least, 'sinners' and outsiders – simply to accept him and his message of the coming kingdom.[67] Thus would Israel be restored.

Did Jesus' eschatological orientation lead to his questioning the adequacy of the Mosaic dispensation? To this question, critical for ethical understanding, Sanders gives several responses. Since the temple rites were based on the *Torah*, Jesus' sayings and actions in relation to the temple indicate that, for him, the current dispensation was not final.[68] Some other cases are less certain. Concerning divorce, Jesus discounts Moses' concession – which is not the same thing as overruling a Mosaic commandment; and he contextualises his teaching in scripture (not unlike the Covenant Document of Qumran in this respect). His motive may have been eschatological (like Paul's), but Sanders recognises that this is open to question. In relation to sinners, Jesus may have allowed eschatological urgency to override the need for the prescribed expressions of repentance. It is his saying, 'Let the dead bury their dead' (Matt. 8.21f., Luke 9.59f.), which shows that, when necessary, Jesus was prepared to overrule the Mosaic requirement on eschatological grounds.[69] But while all this shows that Jesus was aware of the critical nature of the times, there is no evidence – for example, from his disciples' practice – that the Mosaic dispensation was emptied of value, nor that the law was no longer to be obeyed. His general life style was one of obedience to the law: like his co-religionists, he lived within the 'covenantal nomism' of the Judaism of his times.

Paul's ethics

Davies read Paul's ethics in the light of its origins in rabbinic Judaism. Paul's divergence from it is accounted for by the fact that the apostle was 'a rabbi become Christian',[70] who recognised 'the advent of the true and final form of Judaism, the advent of the Messianic Age of Jewish expectation'.[71] Faith in

Christ (the messiah) replaces obedience to the law as the way of salvation, but the law is not simply jettisoned: it is understood in relation to the new covenant, involving spontaneous obedience (cf. Jer. 31.31–4) and universal significance. The cosmic range of Christ's salvation is brought out particularly in the contrast of the first and second Adam.[72]

The setting for Paul's ethics is, of course, the early church, with its resurrection faith, its ethos of *koinonia*, its baptismal practice, its rootage in the Christ event. From such a setting Paul's ethics derived norms and motives. And as Paul was graciously called by Christ to his apostleship, so all Christians called by divine grace shared in the work of salvation and shaped their moral life accordingly. Hence, the Christian life is life in the Spirit, which is the eschatological gift which is also the source of Christian morality (Gal. 5.22–3). Since the chief gift of grace (or fruit of the Spirit) is love (*agape*), the Christian moral life is one of community or solidarity with Christ the Lord and with one another in the body of Christ.

For Sanders, the centre of Paul's position is the saving action of God in Jesus Christ and what it meant for believers to participate in that mighty action.[73] Thus, as Paul was commissioned to be apostle to the Gentiles by the risen Christ, he himself became a participant in the glorious end-game in which God in Christ effected the salvation of all humankind.[74] All his thinking is consequently geared to this new aeon. The law of Moses related to the old aeon and therefore, in spite of its many positive features, did not apply to the new aeon without severe qualification. Christ stands in radical contrast to Adam: a new Adam rather than a new Moses! Hence care needs to be exercised in reapplying the typology of the Mosaic dispensation – Moses, exodus, law, even covenant – to the new aeon. The term 'messiah', with its roots in Israel's kingship, also needs to be treated with caution: it has a specific denotation in Judaism, while the connotation of the Greek translation, 'Christ', comes to include the notion of 'Lordship' of the entire cosmos. Any appreciation of Paul's position must therefore begin, not with attempts to ground it in Diaspora Judaism nor to characterise it as some kind of reduction of Judaic views of the law, but with his acceptance of, and participation in, the eschatological event of Christ. For Paul, this was the essential point. 'It is the Gentile question and the exclusivism of Paul's soteriology which dethrone the law, not a misunderstanding of it or a view determined by his background.'[75]

Even in the new aeon, however, the language of covenant has currency (1 Cor. 11.25, 2 Cor. 3.6). From the point of view of ethics, it is particularly important not to import with it – as Davies does – a concept such as the new *Torah*. Not only is it more Pauline to speak of a 'new creation' – in itself a transcending of covenantal categories – but the roots of Paul's ethics are different. Sanders acknowledges – somewhat minimally – the basic element of covenantal logic in Paul, and observes that obedience is sometimes required to a 'word of the Lord' or the apostles' instructions, but not to a written code. Paul seems to find a self-evident quality in ethics (cf. Gal. 5.9; Rom. 2.14f.). Sanders goes on:

One may observe that the self-evident proper behaviour, the fruit of the Spirit, coincides materially with the ethical elements of the Old Testament. That is, Paul seems *de facto* to accept the Jewish 'commandments between man and man', although he does not accept them as being commandments.[76]

Thus, in spite of the inadequacies of covenantal categories (particularly in relation to Paul's 'participationist transfer terms', such as the believer's 'dying with Christ'), Sanders finds evidence in Paul that 'Christianity is going to become a new form of covenantal nomism'.[77]

There can be no doubt about the requirement to act morally. 'It is not the hearers of the law who are righteous before God, but the doers of the law who will be justified' (Rom. 2.13). There is no question here of 'salvation by works': through faith in Christ, believers *have been* (Sanders' italics) justified by God through faith. In Romans 2.13, Sanders insists, the righteousness terminology refers not to salvation, but to punishment for misdeeds, and this applied alike to Jews and Gentiles. Paul himself must give account of his stewardship at the final judgment (1 Cor. 4.2–5). Such a view was in line with rabbinic teaching: as Sanders puts it, 'good deeds are the *condition* of remaining "in", but they do not *earn* salvation'.[78] A corollary of this is that the element of judgment remains part of Paul's understanding of ethics: not, indeed, its foundation, but an inalienable part of the superstructure.

Issues for ethics

Davies and Sanders oblige us to take full account of the Jewish context of New Testament ethics. What matters of direct consequence for ethics emerge from their work?

Messianic law or covenantal nomism
Davies is inclined to the former, but adumbrates the latter; Sanders is unequivocally for 'covenantal nomism'. Davies recognises that Jesus does not speak as the new Moses (Adam is a more appropriate correlative, at least in Pauline terms), and that similar terminology – new Sinai, messianic law, covenant rule – is seldom explicit in the New Testament; yet one sometimes gets the impression that Davies treats it as if it were. It is important to note that even when the formula 'but I say unto you...' is employed (as in the fifth chapter of Matthew), the operation in question is not so much the giving of a messianic rule as an interpretative dialogue with the *Torah* in which the teacher underlines certain fundamental orientations as against others which have been given. Since this dialogue takes place within the logic of 'covenant', it is reasonable to affirm a term such as 'covenantal ethics' or – with certain safeguards – 'covenantal nomism'. In certain contexts, 'new covenant' does occur in the New Testament: a feature which underlines the fact that even 'covenant' comes under eschatological review.

The adequacy of 'covenantal nomism'
This term is frequently used by biblical scholars in a theological or exegetical context without close attention to its bearing on ethics. Both components require close scrutiny. If 'nomism' is used in its root sense – 'adherence to a law (*nomos*) or laws as a

primary exercise of religion'[79] – its propriety may be questioned both in relation to Jesus and Paul. In practice it is used more loosely to denote some kind of norm at the heart of religious ethics: whether principle, prescription or law. Its proponents are usually at pains to exclude 'code'. As we have already indicated, the more appropriate term in ethics is 'deontology', denoting that which is necessary, fitting or required. With nomism goes the apparatus of casuistry; beyond it lies the hypothesis of natural law: the moral order at the heart of cosmic reality. The term can thus embrace what Davies calls the 'absolute' dimension – the will of God – as well as secondary or paraenetic functions. The difficulty is that, while biblical ethics resonates in part to deontology, it also resists its embrace. Typically, ethics in the Bible contextualises deontological features within a wider realm of discourse. God is not simply the Absolute: he enters into relationship with his people. This relational aspect is picked up by the qualifier 'covenantal'.[80] Yet, while this concept is typical of biblical discourse and the world it reflects, it is not universal within it: the earlier wisdom tradition is relatively independent of it; while in the New Testament it is transformed in various ways by the Christ event (what H. Marshall calls the *sensus plenior*).[81] The denotation of 'covenant' has therefore to be established in any given context. Nevertheless, the term is useful in denoting both the relational context in which obligation is expressed, and its grounding in the divine will or nature. The obligation itself, however, can be expressed in a variety of ways: some deontological (commands, rules, principles, maxims or gnomic sayings, exhortations, warnings), some teleological (aims or goals – both immediate and 'perfectionist' – and consequences of action), and some relational or 'personalist' (where motive is linked strongly with action). This procedural polyvalence may be compromised by terms such as 'covenantal nomism', and it might be better simply to speak of 'covenantal ethics'.

Theology and interpretation

For all his sensitivity to Judaism, Davies' work is informed by Christian theology of a 'biblical' variety; and this influences his understanding of Christology, eschatology and ethics. Against this Sanders launches a protest. His purpose has been 'to free history and exegesis from the control of theology', by which he means 'from being obligated to come to certain conclusions which are pre-determined by theological commitment'.[82] Mistakenly, he assumes this to be a simple task. The question for us is not how Sanders squares his historical approach with his ecclesiastical allegiance, but whether his deeper theological convictions have, in spite of his best efforts, coloured his work. In his implicit emphasis on divine grace and on individualistic response, one may suspect that they have. Nevertheless, one may applaud his attempt at *epochē* and eidetic vision (especially in relation to Paul) but note that the interpreter is never wholly absent from the picture. What remains is a critical reading of the gospels or of Paul: a late twentieth-century interpretation of the evidence from a distinctive viewpoint. Beyond this, Sanders' attempt to resist theological dictates in contextual evaluation is undoubtedly correct.

The validity of New Testament ethics

The question of the validity of New Testament ethics – whether of Jesus or Paul or another – demonstrates how theological questions simply will not go away. If Jesus geared his proclamation of the kingdom to Jewish restoration eschatology, what evaluation are we to make of his message? If Paul bids his hearers be transformed by Christ, specifically through sharing in his death and resurrection, what are we to make of the truth of his position? Or, to put it in Davies' terms: if New Testament ethics – like Christian ethics itself – involves the recognition of 'absolute' or unconditioned demand as well as contingent duties, the 'absolute' claim in particular is inescapably theological. Sanders seems to give partial recognition to the point. 'Christianity, in assigning Jesus a high role, was apparently being true to him. As long as we stay just with this point... we are on safe historical ground.'[83] The nub of the issue, however, is whether we are prepared to give our lives for being true to Jesus. The key question for ethics is not totally contained within the historical: it is theological and existential. As Davies put it: 'Here is the peculiarity of Christian moral teaching: that it places us not in the presence of the normal moral virtues, but under the judgment of absolute demands.'[84] This remains a key issue in biblical interpretation, not least in its interaction with Christian ethics.

CHAPTER 6

The problem of Christian social ethics

> The religion of Jesus is prophetic religion in which the
> moral ideal of love and vicarious suffering, elaborated by
> second Isaiah, achieves such a purity that the possibility of
> its realization in history becomes remote.
>
> (Reinhold Niebuhr)[1]

If we set aside Schweitzer's idiosyncratic solution to the
challenge of social ethics (without devaluing it), do the positions
surveyed above represent a retreat into the ghetto? Context was
a major concern. Can one be wholly contextualised in today's
world and still be true to the gospel? Eschatology, one of the
strongest features to emerge from a contextual understanding of
the New Testament, tended to be resolved, at least partly, into
the summons to ultimate decision. This implies personal
commitment to God and neighbour: hence the emphasis on the
interpersonal and interactive, and on 'personalism' in ethics.
Does eschatology mean the abandonment of social ethics? The
proposition can be resisted on a variety of grounds. M. Keeling,
observing that 'in the twentieth century, Christian ethics has
become concentrated on the question of social justice',[2] pointed
to the question of global survival and the necessity to connect
our understanding of God with our perception of human need.
Eschatology also has an intrinsic link with creation and the
fulfilment of the creator's purpose, as in the theology of
Pannenberg and Moltmann.[3]

But how has Christian ethics come to terms with this
dilemma, which has become more obvious with the collapse of
the liberal synthesis? The problem is the gulf which divides the
confessing communities and the structures of power, gospel

culture and worldly culture, ideal possibilities and historical practicabilities. Its very existence testifies to the reality of fragmentation, to a loss of wholeness; and many Christians, bestriding both worlds in their daily avocations, either feel the division keenly or simply assent to a divided existence. There is, of course, a differentiation implicit in the gospel itself, concerned as it is with 'authentic' as opposed to 'inauthentic' existence, with alienation and atonement, and with 'salvation' which implies defect in the existing organism; but, as Tillich has emphasised, the justice of God strives for the recovery of the alienated parts.[4] If then the gospel speaks to God's world, the 'real' world which all inhabit and constitute, then social ethics implies the need for communication and reconciliation. But can it do it without reducing its links with its biblical roots to very general terms? Must it become a quasi-autonomous discipline itself?

ESCHATOLOGY, CONTEXT AND SOCIAL ETHICS

Command and contingency: W. D. Davies

Without denying that the first duty of the church is to be the church, Davies held that the moral perspectives of the New Testament were considerably wider. Eschatology has to be understood contextually: that is, in relation to the world of the Old Testament and Jewish eschatology. When this is done, eschatological hope, as well as judgment, is seen to pertain to the whole world: it is the kingdoms of this world that are to become the kingdoms of God in Christ. Thus eschatology lends to ethics a social and cosmic dimension.

Davies followed this up by emphasising the intimate relation between the moral teaching of the New Testament and creation itself. On this basis, the church could borrow material from a number of sources for use in its own moral teaching: a clear enough indication of an affinity between Christian and non-Christian moral understanding reflecting a common concern for creation. He pointed to the affinity between the natural and moral in Jesus' teaching: 'a kind of "natural law" in the "spiritual world"', as Dodd had effectively demonstrated with reference to the parables.[5] And Paul also, at a number of points, evinced a similar type of thinking.[6] Even more important is the fact that for Paul and other New Testament writers Christ the Redeemer is also the agent of creation (John 1.1–14; Col. 1.15ff.; Heb. 1.1ff.).

Thus the ethics of the New Testament, rooted as it is in the gospel, is not only of relevance to the Church but also to the world in so far as it affirms and confirms what is truly natural for all men in virtue of their creation... The Christian moral life is the 'natural' life and the teaching of the Church does not annul the virtues of the natural man: rather it confirms them and even depends on them.[7]

Although statements of this kind undoubtedly require fine tuning, they represent a valuable response to the basic questions we raised above.

But even if creation is mirrored in New Testament ethics, does the latter have positive guidance to offer the world today? Or is it merely judgmental, as its more extreme exponents tend to make it? Clearly there cannot be an immediate – that is, an unmediated – application of first-century New Testament social teaching to the modern age, limited as it was by its own context. Allowance must be made for the churches' minority position in the Graeco-Roman world and for the eschatological fore-shortening of time perspectives: hence the undeniable motif of community ethics in its teaching. But Davies refused to stop there. The very existence of the church as the people of God was a challenge to the world.[8] It is from this feature that Davies argues for relevance to the modern – and every – age. Thus, in the interpretation of the basic moral situation of humankind, and in the symbolic being of the church, Davies finds universals which serve in some measure to fuse the horizons of ancient and modern times.

Since the focus of New Testament moral teaching was new covenant and messianic law, two levels of operation are suggested: one is absolute, inescapable and impossible of fulfilment; the other is paraenetic and prescriptive. The former proclaims the gracious, demanding, uncompromising will of

God, unlimited by human sin. The latter contained specific rules for conduct: rules (or principles, prescriptions, laws – Davies does not opt for a particular type of deontology) which express the structure of *agape* and an important part of the church's moral awareness.[9] For later ages, this is the deposit of tradition, which can neither be lightly dismissed nor rigidly implemented (for context affects practice), but which is to be interpreted by a process of casuistry akin to what is discernible in, for example, the Sermon on the Mount itself.[10] For this operation, Christians today must avail themselves of all the resources of the contemporary world – including the social sciences – as did their predecessors, even if prescriptive casuistry in the early Church was not highly developed (as a comparison with the Mishnah shows). Yet, Davies admits, the 'peculiar genius' of the Christian moral life does not lie here. This is to be found in the living tension between 'the absolutes of Jesus' and the moral rules and duties which need to be patiently observed in a world in which the parousia has not yet dawned.

However, this limited casuistry recognises a core, a summation, in the demand of *agape*, which found its supreme expression in the Cross. 'All response to the demands of the Gospel, expressed in prescriptions, is to be informed by *agape*, which is translatable as openness to suffering and moral sensitivity.'[11] If this appears too general, Davies reiterates the community base of Christian ethics and the characteristics of its 'way'. In relation to the state, it involved a policy of recognition and civic obedience but, like Judaism, denied any overweening claims. 'I know of few things more relevant to our present situation than the demand urged upon us in the New Testament to honour the State but not to divinize or absolutize it.'[12] Again, the Christian way transcended cultural, economic and sexual differences: reconciling Jew and Greek, and inaugurating the eschatological unity which corresponded to the primaeval unity in creation.[13] Another feature is the realm of sexual practice, where *agape* indicates quality and direction.[14] Economic relations should evince the same quality. *Agape* 'demands a realistic, earthly recognition of the economic rights of all at which all social legislation and political action should aim'.[15] In thus justifying the 'social Gospel', Davies supplied a much firmer base for 'middle axioms' than Bennett and others normally did;[16] but he thought of them as guidelines only. Reference to the 'way' and 'Spirit' of the early Christian practice will give guidance in new situations, rather than prescriptions.

Davies' emphasis on the 'relevance' of the moral teaching of the New Testament connects with the work of ethicists such as Ramsey, Lehmann and Sittler, and comes close to offering, in general terms, the basis of a strategy for Christian social ethics. It links biblical interpretation to ethics as effectively as the resources of traditional critical scholarship will allow. The 'two level' hypothesis may be a useful approach to Christian social ethics: *agape* is the overriding principle, anchored in the gospel or Christian story, and embodying eschatological or covenantal command. Rules, principles or whatever are means of expressing it in social context. More critically, Davies' awareness of the hermeneutical process is limited. The horizons merge too readily, to the detriment both of the ancient context (as Sanders indicates) and the modern.[17] The most serious criticism, however, is that Davies' understanding of context is not nearly radical enough and avoids the notion that social problems are governed by the particularity of their contexts, within which questions are shaped and solutions engendered. The demands of institutional life seem to have largely escaped his attention. Davies still reflects more than an element of idealism.

Justice and social ethics: Paul Ramsey

In his earlier work, *Basic Christian Ethics*, Paul Ramsey made direct appeal to the biblical themes of the righteousness of God (*tsedeq*) and his mercy or covenant love (*chesed*).[18] The covenant was central to Ramsey's thinking at this stage in his career, influenced as he was by biblical theology (he cites Snaith, Baab, Burrows). The covenant 'promulgates the justice of God on earth'.[19] Indeed, human justice (*mishpat*) is completely parallel with God's righteousness in judgment (*tsedeq*). Thus, he notes, the justice which obtains on earth – including the justice of institutions – has been invaded and permeated, within the experience of God's covenanted people, by the righteousness of God,[20] which comprehends concern for neighbour and alien, for the poor, the orphan, the widow and the helpless. This creative or redemptive form of justice is sharply distinguished from that of Aristotle in that it does not depend on one's stake in the community, but decisively links justice with benevolence. Indeed, the Sermon on the Mount simply continues this line of interpretation, not least in the perfectionism of Matthew 5.48, which Ramsey takes to mean, 'Be all-including (in your goodwill) ...' Your love must search the neighbour out and meet his or her need. The Christocentrism of the early church continued the theme, and this has consequences for ethics. 'Jesus Christ must be kept at the heart of all Christian thinking about justice – and precisely that sort of justice which should prevail in the "world of systems", in this world and not some other.'[21]

At first sight, Ramsey has moved rather too quickly from the biblical to the modern worlds. We are therefore justified in interrogating his position in relation to eschatology and context, both of which have a disjunctive element.

Like Schweitzer, Ramsey accepted that neighbour love was engendered by apocalyptic eschatology. Precisely because it had this setting, 'Jesus' ethic gained an absolute validity transcending limitation to this or that place or time or civilization'.[22] But if it is to be applied to 'this or that place or time or civilization', it is not so much a question of our transposing it to fit new circumstances (where there will always be competing claims upon us) as of our being transformed by it. That is the first requirement, and it could well lead into considerations of the contextual importance of the 'eschatological' community of faith. The disciples' vocation is to practise the way of love, although that way is not guaranteed to overthrow every form of evil. Such an outcome was dependent on God's action in bringing the evil world to an end. Ramsey has thus established the ethos of the faith community, which knows nothing of legalism or code morality. '*Absolutely everything is permitted which love permits*' is Ramsey's summary of Paul's position.[23] Impelled by *agape*, Christian faith is always in search of a social policy.

As far as social context is concerned, Ramsey recognised that social ethics itself entailed certain distinctive functions. He identified four responsibilities relating to (i) the restraint of sin; (ii) Christian 'obedient love' as a social policy; (iii) the relation between Christian love and social policies; and (iv) the question of human rights.

Under the first heading he affirmed traditional views of social policy as entailing the restraint and, to some extent, the remedy of sin; and he combined this with an endorsement of the perspective of Niebuhr's Christian realism.[24] He granted that Christians might have to assent to the use of force in certain circumstances, even though it flew in the face of Jesus' strenuous commands. Under the second, he had to face the question as to whether the ethics of love lacked determinate content: 'always in search of a social policy yet never completely identifiable with any current program with which it happens to make common cause'. He insisted, as against Kierkegaard and intuitionism generally, that Christian love defined obedience to God and therefore no law or command, however 'divine' or 'absolute', could be allowed to override it or the claims of conscience. Equally, while Christian love might use the insights of natural law, the latter 'cannot occupy the ground floor of Christian ethics'.[25] Indeed, Christian love itself, Ramsey argued, gave more direction to social ethics than intuitively based natural law, and offered an indeterminate but liberating norm. As for social policy – the third of Ramsey's points – he rejected any coalition at the ground level, where the righteousness of God and *agape* must not be compromised. In its quest for effective social ethics, Christian love would seek congruent tactical alliances, relevant understanding of the situation, and the promotion of neighbourly concern. As to human rights, Ramsey sought to shift the emphasis from rights to duties, from claiming to giving.

The tensions in Ramsey's position are plain to see. In his earlier work, he attempted to hold together biblical norms, eschatological setting, covenantal community, social ethics and practical policy. He did not have a highly developed notion of biblical interpretation, but, in the theological climate of his earlier writings, he focussed on the eschatological action of God in Christ and the divine commands which proceeded from it. As an ethicist, however, he was aware that the biblical material had to be related to moral action in this world, and that there was a necessary tension between eschatology and ethics. He held that while *agape*, though eschatologically conceived in the New Testament, retained an unqualified validity in ethics, other principles were subject to situational constraints. Indeed, as we have seen, provided one was true to *agape*, one might even, as in the question of war and peace, go against the apparent direction of Jesus' strenuous command. Is he justified in isolating *agape* from other commands with which it is closely – perhaps organically – related in the New Testament? It is hard to assent. To suggest that a social stance based ultimately on *agape* prompts one to restrain sin, but that in doing so one may use means which are the denial of *agape*, is stretching paradox too far. Yet Ramsey based his version of the 'just war' theory on precisely these grounds: an approach which led him to defend nuclear deterrence.[26]

What a hornet's nest is raised when one tries to relate biblical interpretation and ethics!

SOCIAL ETHICS AND THE POWER STRUCTURES

The personal and the corporate: Emil Brunner

Brunner represents the high point of the impact of dialectical theology on Christian ethics. Natural morality is shot through with contradiction, which Christian theology identifies as sin. The focus is put on revelation, and particularly justification by grace alone. With the divine gift is given the divine imperative – Bultmann's 'indicative and imperative' – positing the will of God as the basis and norm of the good. Thus there comes about 'the new man', created and claimed by God. Brunner's position is personalistic, but comes to terms with the orders of society as reflected in the New Testament (especially the *Haustafeln*) and in the Lutheran tradition. It is here that the tensions of

Christian social ethics emerge clearly. In discussing the Christian relationship to the economic order, Brunner wrote thus:

> It is unfair and absurd to require a Christian business man to conduct his business 'according to the laws of the Sermon on the Mount'. No one has ever conducted business on these lines or ever will; it is against all the rules of business itself. The 'office' of a business man belongs to a specific order which is not that of the relation between one person and another ... But ... the seriousness of his Christian life must manifest itself in the fact that he fights with all his power against the evil autonomy of his official work, and that he tries again and again to break through it, which means that he treats the people with whom he has to do in business as his neighbours, to whom he owes love, and that he conducts his business as a service to the community.[27]

Here is a frank recognition that the business world has its own symbolic system which the business man must follow or perish. Eschatological visions do not make company policy! The Christian, like any other, is at the mercy of this ruthless, impersonal system, but any opportunity of expressing human value should be gratefully accepted! Brunner's observation that one does not act *merely* as a member of an institution, but always as a person who can find room for love not in the work of the institution itself but 'between the lines',[28] sounds like relegating the gospel to the coffee break! Paul Ramsey faulted Brunner's conception of justice. 'What man nurtured in the Bible can be content with love effective only through the interstitial spaces? What prophetic voice announced that "justice" need not flow down like a mighty stream but only as a gentle spray?'[29] Brunner was also criticised by J. A. T. Robinson for the inadequacy of his understanding of institutional life, and his failure to contemplate the recovery of truly corporate life symbolised by the biblical image of 'the Body'.[30]

At a more pragmatic level, the dynamics of institutional life would repay study. Brunner's approach pragmatically assumes that one must adjust to the demands of the institution; and at one level he is correct. But Christian ethics has the right to enquire in what ways institutions must change if they are to harness the *personal* resources in their corporate body and overcome depersonalising tendencies. Management may speak hopefully of all being members of a team ('team spirit' is a favourite cliché!), without pausing to think about the conditions which must be created within the institutions before anything approaching an inclusive team becomes possible. 'Team' is a corporate concept (as is 'the body' in the New Testament) which presupposes interdependence and combines the constraints of the overall enterprise with the freedom of each member to contribute creatively. It involves a sharing of responsibility, which in turn implies the encouragement of critical awareness and the securing of channels of communication. It is important that creative ideas, especially those emerging from the people actively engaged on the 'shop floor', be listened to and evaluated. This has much to do with motivation, with a sense of worth and of achievement, and with the attaining of goals (personal and corporate). Doubtless there are other important elements: conflict resolution in the organisation or dealing with grievances is one example; harm reduction in relation to working conditions (or the product, if there is one) is another. Doubtless also one must live with a degree of tension, with compromise and with double effect. But all this is not effected in the interstices: it is an organic process which requires to be fostered within an institution that is open to change. The dynamics of Christian social ethics thus takes one to the heart of corporate life. Its radical questioning must not allow itself to be confined to the margins, however entrenched the opposition may be.

Impossible possibility: Reinhold Niebuhr

A more negative assessment emerges in the work of Reinhold Niebuhr. For him the ethics of Jesus was the perfect fruit of prophetic religion.[31] It did not relate directly to the mundane problems of everyday life, as a prudential ethic might do. Jesus' rigorist teaching made few concessions to self-love or the forms of self-assertion to which social and moral approval is readily or tacitly given in most societies. Rather, it enjoined love to enemies, unlimited forgiveness, non-resistance to evil...It is an ethic in which the reference points are vertical rather than horizontal, a purely religious ethic, unconditioned and universal. Yet, Niebuhr insists, it is not 'interim ethics' in the sense that the end is imminent and the world consequently devalued. Paul, rather than Jesus, tended to strike such notes, for example in his treatment of the family or marriage. In Jesus' teaching the kingdom of God is always coming, and this means that his teaching cannot be fulfilled in present time, but only 'when God transmutes the present chaos of the world into its final unity'.[32]

Prophetic religion uses apocalypticism to express mythically what cannot be stated rationally, namely that the eternal will find fulfilment in the temporal. It is precisely at this point that Niebuhr sees myth as generating historical illusions, from which Jesus may not have been entirely free. But the apocalyptic myth serves an important purpose, namely to give expression to the impossible possibility under which all human life stands.[33]

What does Niebuhr mean by 'impossible possibility'? In the deep perspective which prophetic religion provides, a transcendent possibility – the ideal of *agape* – always stands above every historical actuality and human experience. In the light of it, human actions are weighed and found wanting. It highlights the reality of sin and the human need for repentance and forgiveness. But, although Jesus' teaching does not itself provide a blueprint for action in a sinful world, we may find within it valuable insights and criticism towards a prudential social ethic geared to present circumstances. Further, it provides not simply a principle of indiscriminate criticism directed at all proximate notions of human justice, but also a principle of discriminate criticism between forms of justice.[34] Thus equal justice – over against the inequalities capitalism creates, or disadvantage because of sex, class or race – is an approximation to *agape* in an imperfect world, for it is affirmed in a cut-and-thrust world. It does not belong to the transcendent order, yet points towards it. The fact that all human ideals are proximate or relative does not absolve us from the duty of choosing between them. But there is no way in which human beings can transcend their own finitude, and no social ethic can be derived directly from religious teaching as such. The lesson of history is that those who have claimed to act on an absolute basis without taking due account of their human limitations have increased evil. 'Therefore', Niebuhr observed, 'it is as important to know what is impossible as what is possible in the moral demands under which all human beings stand'.[35]

This 'moral realism' greatly reduces the scope of the theological visionary without declaring the prophet completely redundant! Indeed, Niebuhr grants that prophetic religion should place political opportunism under a religious perspective, but makes a plea that its exponents 'know the kind of world we are living in and learn how to place every type of statesmanship under the divine condemnation'.[36] Similarly, Duncan Forrester speaks of the need to appreciate the complexity of the issues and of 'confronting the powers without necessarily denouncing or damning the people who work the system, or suggesting that they have more freedom, responsibility or ability to change things than is in fact the case'.[37] In fact, Niebuhr's approach to social ethics represents a thoroughly contextualised, feet-on-the-ground view which accepts that one is part of the corruptions of power, tells one to get on with the job even if one is compromised left, right and centre ('sin boldly', in other words) but suggests that one strives to contain the damage. It is a scenario many business men and politicians recognise, as do many who find very limited scope for creative justice within institutional life.

But does this interpretation express the scope of the 'prophetic principle' in social ethics – or does it spell its death? Amos certainly experienced in his context the institutional resistance which neutralised his moral teaching. The power brokers dismissed his teaching as impractical because it would have undermined their power base. That does not mean that it *was* impractical. Amos was not putting forward a mere ideal of equality. He was demanding change in society in order that it might return to covenantal values. He was saying that, unless the nation returned to God's ways, enormous damage would result. He did not accept that the power structures had the last word, nor did his banishment suggest that his message lacked pragmatic challenge. Indeed, Jesus' teaching on 'turning the other cheek' does not appear to be presented in the Sermon on the Mount as an impossible ideal, but rather as a practical response to violence in an occupied country. One may question, therefore, whether the extreme contrast Niebuhr draws between the prophetic and the pragmatic is legitimate; just as it is no longer possible to treat the prophetic and wisdom traditions in Israel as if they belonged to different worlds.[38] In an open society, it must always be possible to confront the powers that be – and to do so with full awareness of contextual issues.[39] This incurs the charge of liberal illusion only if it assumed that the task is easy and painless.

Niebuhr's views have been influential but controversial, and among those who sought to controvert him, no one was more determined than G. H. C. Macgregor. While admitting the formidable rationale which Niebuhr presented, he claimed that in the light of the New Testament 'it is seen to be quite inconsistent with any but a badly maimed doctrine alike of the Incarnation, the Holy Spirit, the Cross, and the Kingdom of God'.[40] In Macgregor we find an attempt both to refute some of Niebuhr's basic presuppositions and to press divine command and covenantal ethics directly into the service of social ethics. Granted that Macgregor focussed his concern on the single issue of pacifism, how far does his attempt succeed?

On two fundamental theological points Macgregor particularly dissented: human depravity and the kingdom of God. He accepted the need for Barth's correction of facile, humanistic views of human perfectibility, but held that an extreme doctrine of human depravity was contradicted by the New Testament. 'Jesus saw the world always and everywhere as God's world'; and 'if a man will but "lose his life" in order to "find it"', then God's will can "be done *in earth* as it is in heaven – even though that will may prove to be a cross".'[41] Following C. E. Raven, he held that Christ is not a 'divine intruder' into an alien world but 'the first-born of all creation',[42] and contested the totally 'secular' reading of the world. In particular, the dualism of 'moral man and immoral society' was untrue and disastrous. Human collectivities *may* evince less moral characteristics than individuals, but they are open to moral criticism and may not be so morally obtuse as Niebuhr suggested. There are also moral communities, of which the churches are exemplars, which know the 'enabling grace' of the Spirit. The churches, the heirs of the covenant, must obey the teaching of Jesus – not least the command to love one's enemies – and confront society at large with such possibilities. The relation of church and society is therefore a dialectical one in which the church learns more of God's creation and challenges that creation to hear the call of its creator.

If some of the above criticisms seem over-optimistic, Macgregor pressed home his attack by contesting Niebuhr's remarkable claim that Jesus was not involved in the relativities of politics. 'Jesus' words... cannot be isolated from the actual social and political circumstances in which they were spoken.'[43] In so far as Macgregor is claiming that Jesus' teaching interacts with the socio-historical situation (for example, countering the violence of occupying forces, or dealing with the poor as victims of political and economic change in Palestine), his position has certainly been substantiated by later scholarship.[44] Following Otto and Dodd, he maintained the tension of the kingdom transcendent yet manifested on earth, future yet present in Christ. 'The obedient servant of His Kingdom must therefore be in the world, where alone the process of redemption may be carried on',[45] and where the dynamic of the kingdom operates. The wholly other-worldly view is to be rejected as an evasion of the intention of Jesus' teaching.

One of Macgregor's main criticisms of Niebuhr is that he fails to recognise what he calls the distinctively Christian method of overcoming evil: 'the redemptive power of active, self-sacrificial love, which has its symbol in the Cross'.[46] Interpreting the New Testament as emphasising 'non-retaliation' rather than 'non-resistance to evil', Macgregor goes on to reject the view that in social ethics we have to deal with the law as the expression of God's righteousness, while in interpersonal terms the gospel expresses his love. Jesus, like Paul in his own way, was concerned with love as the fulfilment of righteousness and law. He taught not retributive justice, but 'active, self-sacrificing love, which redeems and changes the evil will, so overcoming evil in the only way by which it can be truly overcome'.[47] The churches must convey the critical challenge, the prophetic witness, to a disordered world, and that is the essence of Christian social ethics. Even amid the chaos and disorder, the world will not be able finally to shake off the challenge, for there is a deep affinity between revealed teaching and the created order: a view which a world in ecological crisis may appreciate more than a mid-century world locked in mortal combat.

In spite of crucial differences, Macgregor acknowledged many points of agreement with Niebuhr. In truth, he was strong where Niebuhr was weak, and *vice versa*. He gave a sound and consistent exegesis to central features of Jesus' message, and insisted that the Christian's duty, like that of the churches, was to be faithful to the divine command. To compromise on such issues is to fail to use the saving power which God entrusted to his people: in short, the power to overcome evil with good. Here indeed is counter-force! The paradox is that, while one must accommodate to the context in order to communicate with it, by accommodating to the context one may lose the message. Although Macgregor argued that pacifists did indeed have a policy, he did not set his interpretation in the context of a structural account of the political and economic forces which largely determine national and international life. Although there is a deep affinity between the Christian message and the created order, Macgregor does not seem to take seriously enough how that order is constrained to operate: a charge that cannot be levelled at Jesus, with his evident interest in landowners and tenants, the hiring and rewarding of labour, money-lenders and creditors. What Macgregor achieved, per-haps more clearly than Niebuhr, was a critique of Christian obedience.

Niebuhr and Macgregor evince many shared insights, but also incompatible perceptions. They provide prime material for the study of biblical interpretation in relation to ethics, for they raise acutely questions of presuppositions, perspectives, faith-fulness to the text, dialogue with context, and the differentiation and merging of horizons. Both illustrate that, on the basis of the critical and theological scholarship which they share, there is acute difficulty in the area of social ethics. As a modern interpreter, Niebuhr is contextually strong but exegetically weak as he removes the imperative of the kingdom to the distant horizon. As a biblical scholar, Macgregor is exegetically strong and is prepared to overrule certain contextually based considerations in order to remain true to the divine command.[48] Niebuhr proposed to use Jesus' teaching as a principle of discriminate criticism when choosing between relative values. But will the world of systems hear Jesus' teaching? Macgregor is faithful to the motifs of Jesus' teaching, but is anyone listening other than the converted or the scandalised? If approaches can be so diverse, one may question whether traditional criticism is adequate to encompass all the elements involved in relating biblical interpretation and ethics.[49]

POWER STRUCTURES AS SYMBOLIC SYSTEMS

Power is so pervasive and so determines people's lives – is such an instrument for good or ill – that scholars have not been slow to evoke the imagery and reality of the 'principalities and powers', the deeper forces of the universe, to recapture something of the dimensions and dynamics of at least Paul's awareness of power. Although many had hitherto drawn attention to this ancient cosmic view, it was Barth's Christological interpretation of it, particularly in relation to the Nazi phenomenon, which caught the imagination of modern interpreters. Have not Christians always had to struggle with the demonic 'rulers of this age' who crucified Christ, but who have been 'disarmed' by God's action in Christ and whom Christ will bring into proper subjection?[50] In the heyday of biblical theology, O. Cullmann's interpretation of the state in these terms was highly influential,[51] and Amos N. Wilder, who made a special study of eschatology and ethics in the New Testament, applied this realm of discourse to social ethics.[52] Elaborated in many studies, this kind of thinking became widely accepted as 'the proper symbolic structure to enable Christians to understand the political realm, and relate to it in a Christian way'.[53]

In the perspective of biblical interpretation and its bearing on ethics, it is important to realise that such results were not obtained without some remarkably tendentious exegesis. As Bultmann indicated, this New Testament realm of discourse is rooted in a theological understanding of the 'cosmos' as the world of God's creation, the world of humankind, in its historical reality. An important feature of the cosmos (especially in Pauline understanding) is its alienation from God – 'this present evil age' (Gal. 1.4) – by virtue of which it both incurs divine judgment and establishes itself as the anti-divine power in the life of human beings. When God's work of redemption in Christ is brought into the equation, Christian social ethics has to reckon with the fact that Christians are still inescapably in the world ('cosmos' as the sphere of earthly life) and therefore 'in the flesh', but that Christ has overcome its alienating power. The cosmos in its alienation from God, can be conceived – and is conceived by Paul – as the domain of demonic forces (by whatever name), which continue to menace the lives of Christians even though they know them to have been dethroned and that ultimately the victory does not lie with them. What Bultmann sees as significant is that the spirit powers portray the human reality as full of conflicts and struggle, threat and temptation, in the face of which one must renew one's Christian discipleship.[54]

What are we to make of Bultmann's skilful interpretation of Paul's existential involvement with 'the powers'? In the face of the texts, we can hardly lay the charge of individualistic interpretation at Bultmann's door here, since his whole exposition shows human relatedness to the cosmic condition, although it is true that the socio-political dimension is absent in his interpretation. Bultmann's interpretation is certainly restrained by the existential analytic he received from Heidegger, and also by his assumptions about 'modern man' ('It is impossible to use electric light and the wireless... and at the same time to believe in the New Testament world of daemons and spirits").[55] What emerges is the elucidation of one aspect of Paul's symbolic world, set in the context of Bultmann's symbolic world! There is a fusion of horizons on the interpreter's terms. For all its perceptiveness, Bultmann's view contains a reductionist element. To compound the interpretive difficulty,

Paul did not have a systematised theology of power. He wrote of it as he encountered it: whether as the expression of cosmic forces or, empirically, as exercised by imperial agencies (as in Rom. 13.1–7). His cosmic reflections were not directly concerned with political forces, and there is no explicit reference to the 'angelic/demonic powers' theme in Romans 13. The *archontes* are (possibly minor) imperial officials and administrators, and the theological perspective of the passage is concerned simply to depict them as the servants (*diakonoi, leitourgoi*) of God.[56] Christians have a duty to co-operate with them, at least to the extent of discharging any indebtedness. This teasing out of different strands in the apostle's thinking is an important aspect of biblical interpretation, ensuring that the interpreter applies the principle of 'distantiation' – the differentiation of contexts and of strands of thinking within contexts.[57] Only if this distantiation is carried out efficiently can there be a proper correlation or fusion of horizons in the ongoing process of interpretation.

What then of the 'fusion' of horizons after the 'distantiation' of historical elements? This step is, of course, taken by interpreters in their own right and must not be ascribed retrospectively to Paul! The apostle recognised that human life was at the mercy of powers which posed a threat to its freedom and integrity: these powers being frequently conceived as angelic or demonic as well as human. The language games in which Paul engages compound the difficulty: he is presumably speaking metaphorically of the human opposition he encountered when he recalls how he 'fought with beasts at Ephesus' (1 Cor. 15.32). Life is rather more complex than sweeping statements about the 'three-decker universe' represent! At another level, people lived within the political and imperial authority structure and came to terms with it as they could.

Today, we recognise this sense of being at the mercy of forces other than our own. Our cultural conditioning inclines us to think of them in sociological, political and economic terms, but at times we reach out linguistically to other dimensions, especially when attempting to comprehend the power of evil in the world. It may therefore be possible to *reinterpret* Paul's cosmic picture of the human condition in such a way as to set issues of social ethics in a holistic context. This seems to be what W. Wink attempted when he approached the Pauline texts in the light of his experience of the structural poverty and injustice in the Latin American scene and found them to resonate to questions about the nature of power.[58]

Wink's approach, which reflects a well-articulated hermeneutics that is reaching out towards a new paradigm,[59] insists that Satan, for example, is not simply a piece of flotsam from the wreck of an ancient world view, but carries existential truth relating to alienation in human life.

If Satan has any reality at all, it is not as a sign or an idea or even an explanation, but as a profound *experience* of numinous, uncanny power in the psychic and historic lives of real people. *Satan is the real interiority of a society that idolatrously pursues its own enhancement as the highest good.* Satan is the spirituality of an epoch, the peculiar constellation of alienation, greed, inhumanity, oppression and entropy that characterizes a specific period of history as a consequence of human decisions to tolerate and even further such a state of affairs.[60]

Similarly, demons are not disembodied spiritual beings, but actual spirituality or interiority, whether of a person or a state. Interpreting 'the *stoicheia* of this world' (Col. 2.8) as basic principles (of philosophy, of the physical universe, of cosmology), Wink proceeds to show that, existentially, we are all subject to these invisible determinants: hence the tendency of the ancients to depict them as malevolent spiritual powers enslaving their victims. Over against this regime the faith of Israel and of the gospel asserts the sovereignty of God the Deliverer. Wink quotes a trenchant passage from Buber explaining why Israel, called to witness to the absolute, negates the overweening claims of the nations. 'That is why every nation is bound to desire to get rid of us at the time it is in the act of setting itself up as the absolute.'[61] In so far as the state dropped out of redemptive concern in Christendom, space was created for the emergence of the autonomous secular state 'which subverts religion to the role of legitimating its claims, and which makes its own power the sole arbiter of morality'.[62]

This observation is not limited to totalitarian states: it is true of most states, 'our own included'. The churches have largely abandoned the task of mediating the absoluteness of God to the nations, yet this was the commission they were given. In their refusal to offer worship to the emperor, the first generations of Christians were indeed touching the heart of the matter. The refusal of the Romans to accede to their scruples shows that they recognised the force of their refusal.

Wink has shown, in a Faustian way, that through biblical interpretation dimensions of the problem are uncovered which might well otherwise remain unexplored. Thus it is arguable that a holistic symbolic structure can be created which comprehends deep perspectives of alienation – even 'the demonic' – in the world, as well as underlining the interrelatedness of humankind in its manifold worldly and cosmic structures. At least, this is *one way* to express human bodily existence in its complexity, although to some it may remain a highly mythological – let us say, symbolic – way of achieving these ends. It is important, however, to have some way of conveying human entrapment in the power of evil, whether in global or personal terms; and also of expressing the liberating dynamic of the gospel.

The range of possible Christian responses to the use and abuse of power in society moves through a wide arc, from confrontation to collusion.[63] It is the task of biblical interpretation to illumine these choices through engagement with the gospel, with its indicatives as well as its imperatives. In the process, there is development in self-understanding, in community understanding, in spiritual understanding, and – in a positive sense – in worldly understanding. In Christian ethics there must always be a return to the heart of the tradition, precisely at the point where one is engaging with the most contextual of modern problems. It is thus that one begins to hear what the Spirit is saying to the churches.

PART THREE

Participation in meaning

The radical split between knowledge and commitment
that exists in our culture and in our universities is not
ultimately tenable. Differentiation has gone about as far as
it can go. It is time for a new integration.

(Robert N. Bellah)[1]

A DOUBLE ETHICAL RESPONSIBILITY

THE 'POST-MODERN' ERA IN INTERPRETATION

Biblical interpretation has long been moving away from the
older forms of positivism which affirmed historical fact as
objective truth, and from the empiricism which held that
traditions could be validated in terms of 'presuppositionless'
scientific rules. Such stances are often held to constitute
'modernism', which is nothing other than the expression of
Enlightenment dynamics, in which the subject comprehends
and dominates the object, and 'objective' knowledge is separated from 'subjective' attitudes like commitment and faith.
Such presuppositions prompted both an exaggeration of the
'objective' element at the hands of a 'neutral' interpreter, and
an over-emphasis on the 'subjective' element as in romanticism.
Claims to neutrality are now seen to be illusory, since the
reading transaction impinges upon the readers as a demand to
enlarge and change the perception of their world.[2] At the same
time, there has been a breakdown of the romantic view that
reading involved thinking the author's thoughts after him or
her. Now the weight is on engagement and encounter with the
text so that its 'word' may be heard, as dialectical and
kerygmatic theology insisted in their various ways. As Dodd's
'zero hour' and Bultmann's 'moment of truth' indicate, we not
only interrogate the text, we are interrogated by the text – and
may be transformed by it.

The newer 'post-modern' approach is part of a wider concern about how one identifies and understands meaning and value in tradition. It is essentially a participatory activity.[3] Every text, tradition or culture has its own horizon, as we have in our own life situation. Interpretation involves the fusion of horizons in the 'moment' of dialogue when worlds interpenetrate and translation becomes possible. Therefore, to understand a text, tradition or culture, one must try to get inside it, to read it from the inside out, and to discover it as meaningful social action.[4]

There are various implications of such a stance. As Gadamer emphasised, the term 'horizon' itself indicates a wider holistic view, an ability to see things rationally and in proportion. But horizons are shared by a great many people. Habermas therefore underlined the fact that interpretation is not a private viewing, but involves a consensus of critical meaning, which is then internalised and acted upon.

Again, if the interpreter is to discern the author's meaning, he/she must try to grasp the *reasons* that lend rationality to what the author wrote, spoke or did. This does *not* mean that the interpreter necessarily agrees with the author's meaning, but that there is engagement between them: 'a stream of agreements and disagreements that appeal to *reasons*'.[5] Such an emphasis is particularly important in relation to criticisms that this approach puts too much weight on tradition in itself, and it has obvious relevance to biblical hermeneutics which is much concerned with assessment of the moral issues raised by the text, as well as with the relation of values and tradition, and how values come to be invested with authority.

Language is the medium in which we live and move and have our being. It is the reservoir of tradition, on which all social institutions are dependent. Much work has been done to elucidate the reading process, especially through reader-response theory and communication studies.[6] But language can be used as the tool of ideology and power. Hence the logic of hermeneutics ('from the inside out') must be supplemented by a critical appraisal 'from the outside in'.[7] In other words, the manipulation of traditional values by those in power requires to be subject to the 'hermeneutics of suspicion',[8] which for present purposes may be taken to denote the discerning of the real objective behind the rationalisation.

A consequence of this new approach is that the ethical dimension in interpretation is enhanced. Ethics is bound up with language: not only because the latter is concerned with truth or authenticity (and therefore gives rise to the possibility of untruth or inauthenticity), but because language conveys moral advice, guidance, judgment, admonition, analysis of moral issues, and so on, and expresses personal conviction.[9] Ethics is reflective language directed to moral practice. In this sense it is endemic to the interpretation of the Hebrew scriptures and the New Testament, as well as to literature ancient and modern. Ethics therefore implies a hermeneutic, and hermeneutics presupposes ethics.

Church communities or at least their representatives are catalysts in this process, but recognition of value in society takes place in public. Christian ethics is thus a dialogue about values which draws from tradition, rests on rational premises and transcends traditional boundaries of the sacred and the secular. It has roots in the tradition and social reality of the Christian community.

SOCIETY, INTERPRETATION AND ETHICS

It is now virtually axiomatic that ideas and concepts, beliefs and ethics, are grounded in the context of the society from which they emerge. This is not, however, to reduce ethics or ideas to economics or sociology, nor to undermine the integrity of either ethics or theology (or philosophy) as a discipline. It *is* to insist that these stand in close relation to their socio-historical matrix.[10] To what extent is ethics predetermined by its roots in society?

The language of 'rootedness' suggests an organic link with systemic processes in society itself. The outcome of this line of thought is an organic or structural view of society in which, internally, the parts function through interaction with the whole, and people fulfil various roles and acquire status in relation to the structures of power or the dominant value system. According to this *structural–functional* view, associated with Talcott Parsons in particular, when society is in a state of equilibrium or balance, it evinces widely shared values and norms, which are expressed and fostered by its institutions and conserved through adaptive change.[11] Structural–functional views which emphasise equilibrium and stability tend to be static and to present 'typical' views of a society's norms and behaviour patterns. Non-adaptive social change is regarded as deviant behaviour. Moral and social codes, noted for their inflexibility, are likely to relate well to this model.

A model of this kind, however, fails to take adequate account of the factor of *conflict* within society as a means of effecting change. Not all change comes about through adaptation and co-operation. There may be tension, struggle and conflict between competing groups, each defending the interests of its members while relating to the demands of wider society. The *conflict* model presupposes a continuing process of change. Disequilibrium or dissonance characterises societies in development and transition, just as cognitive dissonance may be an essential step in finding more adequate understanding of a problem.[12] Where conflict occurs, there is less consensus and less agreement about values. Indeed, on this view, social systems and their subsystems are held together not by consensus, but by constraint.[13] Religion may still be used as a kind of social glue, but it may also serve as an agent of transformation and a sponsor of alternative values. The case of religious ethics is similar. If the *Haustafeln* reinforce the social status quo and Romans 13 political constraint, Paul tends elsewhere – for example, in *Philemon* and in his handling of issues such as meat offered to idols – to interpret the gospel as transformative.

There is a third possibility, which focusses on *perceived symbolic meaning*. When people respond to a situation, they do so by referring it to a shared social symbol system and by defining it in terms of a range of possible meanings. This *symbolic interactionist* model comprehends the processes which the structural–functional and conflict models describe, but takes the interpretation into the complex of symbolic patterns which governs human interactions. These patterns, however, are not timeless ideals, but develop in interaction with the historical process.[14] Biblical texts, not least those bearing directly on ethics, respond well to this approach – particularly as it does not exclude the value of other models, gives due weight to the symbolic core of a community's life, and insists on the interaction of symbolic core and historical praxis. It can come to terms with the factor of tradition in society and assist the recognition and appraisal of what Alasdair McIntyre has called the 'fiduciary foundations' on which a society's value system is built.[15] It can also shed light on minority groups in society, indicate their distinctive values and consider their relation to the organism as a whole; and it is applicable in comparative studies of ethics.

Two features may be underlined. One is the factor of power in society: where it is located, how it is administered and the extent to which it permeates the social structure. Power structures have their value system and promote certain values in society. Moral questions have therefore a public aspect, whether positive or negative, in relation to the values of power. Are values but an extension or projection of power? Or do they imply a critique of it? These questions must be pursued not simply in terms of the 'view from above' or the 'view from below', but also in terms of the variety of perspectives which manifest themselves in society. Here, indeed, is a need for debate and dialogue: consensus will probably take a little longer!

THE HERMENEUTICAL CIRCLE

All interpretation moves in a circle or spiral. The metaphor may not be completely valid. Theoretically, one may engage at any point in the circumference, although if one adopts the spiral model there is usually only one entry – at the foot of the stairs! However, as we have emphasised above, the entrance ticket is self-understanding (including social understanding): without it, one harbours dangerous illusions and is not fit for the course. In reading a 'classic' text, there is a double dimension to interpretation: a historical contextual approach is essential to understanding the ancient text itself, and the text in turn may open up new perspectives on one's own world. In fact, there is a many stranded dialectic. One may make a relatively direct approach to the world of the ancient text, as in a historical reading, and allow issues to emerge for contemporary engagement, or one may first explore issues in the modern world and, in the light of this contextual interest, proceed to engage with selected texts. In either case the circle is completed, although an even more important issue may be how correspondences are discerned between the world of the interpreter and that of the text.

The ethical dimension of biblical interpretation thus involves both horizons. E. Schüssler Fiorenza has spoken of a *double ethics*: the ethics of historical reading and the ethics of accountability.[16] These dimensions will be explored in the next chapters.

CHAPTER 7

Ethics and historical interpretation

> An *ethic of historical reading* changes the task of interpret-
> ation from finding out 'what the text meant' to the
> question of what kind of reading can do justice to the text
> in its historical contexts.
>
> (E. Schüssler-Fiorenza)[1]

In modern biblical scholarship, the historical critical method
has acquired the status of foundational discipline. It has
provided focus, method and apparent objectivity. It has served
as Occam's razor to cut away all pre-emptive moves to
undermine the critical probing of tradition at the instance of
dicta, or to prescribe the meaning of the text before a critical
examination of it has been executed. Its weakness has resided in
its imperialism, in its tendency to claim too much either in
determining 'what the text meant' or in discovering 'what
actually happened', and in becoming an end in itself. Like fire,
it supplies essential energy, but it needs to be controlled.

There are good reasons to be concerned with historical
context and the critical readings which do justice to the text in
this respect. All biblical material is contextual material, and
must be treated as such. If it is correct to say 'so-called biblical
ethics is situation ethics that often sets itself up as immutable
divine decree',[2] then the danger of distortion through dogmatism is great indeed. A contextual reading – that is, reading
primarily in ethical–political terms – can therefore serve as a
corrective to later dogmatic impositions and to modern accommodations.[3] Setting the text in context 'relativises' it in the
sense that the interpreter views it *in relation to* its context,
observes its interaction with it and focusses on vital issues.

Interpreters must bring their own understanding of societal processes to the text, in order to illumine the intratextual world and bring it to life while respecting the integrity of the contextual world. The ethics of historical reading no longer presupposes that there is a single, original meaning inherent in the text, but searches for the kind of readings which do justice to the text in the various perspectives in which it may be viewed.

In so far as Christian ethics has a fundamental relation to the biblical text, it has a hermeneutical involvement, and a historical contextual reading has a place in its interpretative processes. It must, therefore, be bound by the rules of hermeneutical engagement when it appeals to biblical material. On the basis of its own awareness of the relation of ethics and values to societal context and the operation of power within it, it can supply the interpreter with pertinent questions as he or she approaches the exploration of the moral world in which Jesus and his disciples, as well as Paul and the first Christians, lived and moved and had their being. Indeed, as Wayne Meeks put it, they not only lived in their world, but that world lived in them.[4] For this reason, we shall survey attempts to read the ethics of Israel, as well as the moral teaching of Jesus and the first Christians, in primarily socio-political terms.

A SOCIO-POLITICAL READING OF ISRAEL'S ETHICS

A hypothesis

In relation to socio-political approaches to Israel's history, Norman Gottwald castigated what he called non-methodical idealism in traditional scholarship. John Bright, for example, had treated the religion of Israel in isolation from the course of Israelite society: socio-historical, let alone socio-economic, factors were given slight attention.[5] George Mendenhall showed his dependence on an idealistic model by deriving Israelite society directly from Israelite religion. The latter was unconnected with the exercise of power on earth, and ethical norms were simply grounded in revelation or divine authority.[6] As Gottwald put it, 'Yahwism enters history from the transcendent realm of the Idea (the revealing God) and goes to work enfolding itself with no more than token debt to its environment.'[7] This is all the more remarkable since Mendenhall applied sociological methods to the understanding of other aspects of Israelite society, but finally ran for cover when the sociology of religion posed its acutest questions. By contrast, Gottwald pressed home the materialist hypothesis. Sovereignty is a political matter, whatever symbols are used to express it, and whether one is speaking of tribal society or nation state.

The ethical norms of Yahwism, far from being ahistorical and antipolitical generalities, speak directly and adamantly to the problem of how the community is to be organized internally so as to channel nonabusive power toward the necessary ends of communal viability.[8]

But Gottwald went even further, frequently using the language of 'function'. What he calls 'mono-Yahwism' was 'the function of sociopolitical egalitarianism in premonarchic Israel',[9] one of the features of which was a body of norms and rules enforced by social pressure – by judges, priests and mantics. As distinct from the totalitarian city states from which the Israelite farmers and herdsmen supposedly broke away, the ethos of Israelite society presupposed a high degree of social cohesiveness and decentralisation of power, both of which were symbolised at the cultic–ideological level by 'mono-Yahwism'. Instead of submitting to repressive human powers, the people entered into covenant with Yahweh who, in turn, gave them his blessing, the potential of productive life.

Gottwald's hypothesis is not without its difficulties and dangers. More traditional historians would have serious reservations about the evidence on which the hypothesis is based. How much do we really know about the ethos of these ancient city states? And what evidence is there for viewing them as the negative matrix for Israel's political self-understanding? It is as if the evidence can be deduced from an attractive hypothesis! Admittedly, this is one of the *cruces* in post-modern interpretation. Whereas a 'modern' reading dissects evidence and sources, 'post-modernism' reads the whole situation in the light of recognised power struggles in emergent societies. A degree of caution is appropriate. To illustrate further, Gottwald sometimes uses the language of 'cause' and 'projection': religion, including ethics, is a projection of power interests, and the latter stand in a causal relation to the former. If he had maintained this view consistently, his work would have been yet another instance of Enlightenment reductionism in the tradition of Feuerbach. But, he concedes, not only was Yahwism a product of socio-political egalitarianism, but the latter was in some ways a function of Yahwism.[10] The correlation between society and religion in Israel is apparently more complex than simple projection, and involves an element of interplay. Here Gottwald is more in line with symbolic interactionism, and with the 'humbler' sociology of which Robin Gill speaks. The materialist hypothesis in itself may be as unbalanced and prejudiced as the idealist. What is required is the recognition of a hermeneutical circle in which there is constant interpretive interplay between the socio-historical and the transcendental poles.

Substantiating the hypothesis

Even a cursory reading of the traditions of the settlement period suggests a time of transition, of power struggle, of adjustment in ethos, and of reappraisal of values. One might trace the new dynamic to the change from nomadic to agricultural and city life, with the consequent acceleration of stratification in society on economic lines.[11] Gottwald underlined the importance of state-dominated agriculture, with accompanying city-based trade and light industry, although his use of the term 'state' often seems loaded.[12] One could also note that the effect of replacing a barter system with a money economy was to stimulate trade at the cost of dividing the population into rich and poor. Radical changes of this kind were bound to have had consequences for religion and ethics. For traditional interpreters, the dearth of evidence always weighs heavily, and objections to Gottwald's procedures have been well aired.[13] But simply to stand by positive evidence may also be tendentious, an argument from silence.

Modern participative approaches attempt to advance a hypothesis, based on study of sufficiently analogous situations, which may afford some insight into the dynamics of the society in question. If the hypothesis begins to present a coherent picture, it is then necessary to look at other elements in the evidence which also claim a place in the pattern, but which may modify the original hypothesis. Thus, the interpreter has to give due weight to the peculiar logic of covenant language, describing the special relationship between the pastoral/ agricultural community and its God, Yahweh, who is sovereign over his people, and who therefore subordinates to himself all worldly power, whether of city or clan, fertility or arms, kings or peoples. Here is a key factor in controlling the abuse of power. Against all attempts to usurp power – political, economic or cultic – the God of the covenant is the ultimate counter-force, prompting diffusion of power, socio-economic goals, and social equality before him,[14] yet securing also the survival of his people in a menacing world. Gottwald puts it somewhat differently: 'one way of viewing the relationships of religion and society in old Israel is to recognize in Yahwism an experimental conceptual–institutional alternative to repressive human authorities'.[15] Moral instruction is set within this context and fuses with religious requirements, such as the prohibition of idols, for Yahweh can brook no rival. Yet many disparate elements, moral and theological, are received from a variety of sources and built into the basic covenantal understanding.[16]

An organic view of tradition regards it as a process which involves transmission, interpretation, retrojection and re-creation. It is thus possible for the interpreter to identify recurring interpretive motifs in the cumulative body of tradition as denoting ways in which tradition *came to be understood* and signifying values. There is a plurality of such motifs: value judgments about kings who did what was right in the eyes of the Lord; or divine wisdom; or obedience to the word of the Lord. Not the least remarkable fact is that narrative tradition is characteristically recounted and interpreted *from the angle of people who have been liberated.*[17] In other words, the counter-force had worked in their interest. Hence, in monarchical as in pre-monarchical times, Yahweh in his sovereignty is the counter-force arraigned against all the agents of oppression, external or internal: whether these are kings or gods, political enemies or economic tyrants, demons or other malign forces. And Israel – people and leaders – is pledged to obedience, to allowing the counter-force full play in her corporate being. Therefore, at every stage and level of its life, ethics for Israel is more than obedience to laws: it is obedience to God's *torah*, to his teaching of the people. Ethics is therefore inseparable from interpretation, for teacher and taught alike.

If social egalitarianism were the operative norm in Israel, then the kingship could only appear as a crisis of ethics, a contradiction of basic values. Yet the echoes of the debate which surrounded it indicate that, while there were indeed tensions – between priestly and kingly leadership, between charismatic leadership and the centralisation of power, between the demands of tradition and the need for effective action, between obedience to Yahweh and rebellion against him and usurpation of what belongs to him – the key factor was the preservation of the sovereignty of Yahweh in the midst of constitutional change.[18] Implicit in these tensions was the awareness that religious belief in Israel had a political function: namely, the limitation of power in human hands. Somehow, this had to be squared with the pragmatic concern for executive effectiveness. If 'the democratic intellect' may be seen as a prime Western value or aspiration in modern times, the ancient Israelite equivalent was equality before Yahweh.

Nevertheless, the dynamics of power dictated that the counter-force was harnessed as far as possible to the interests of dynastic power! One might look, for example, at the issue of Naboth's vineyard in 1 Kings 21, where foreign influence on royal practice was also a factor, or at the encounter of Nathan and David in 2 Samuel 12.[19] The 'prophet of Yahweh' emerges as the proclaimer of the divine counter-force. In any assessment of this dissonance, however, one must also reckon with the functional contrast of priest and prophet: the former stressing purity, regulation, cultic action; the latter gift, revelation or grace. The priest was the servant of the counter-force through cultic duties, but as an establishment figure he also related to the given power structure: Amaziah was a case in point. The prophets who were not attached to the cult or the crown had greater freedom to focus radically on the demand of Yahweh and to articulate his will.[20]

The outcome of this line of thinking is engagement with the paradox of power and powerlessness: in merely human perspective, the latter was experienced as disaster, negation, undeserved suffering. Partial responses were given through the notion of judgment, or in the pragmatism and agonising of Ecclesiastes and Job, or in the visions of coming retribution, vindication and renewal. But, in so far as Yahweh himself negated power in its totalitarian expressions and the misuse of power in analogous directions, there was a sense in which he himself endorsed the powerlessness of the victim. Thus, not only did the *Torah*, as the expression of his will, require justice and compassion for the poor and needy, but powerlessness began to emerge as an instrument of his peace: as the divine counter-force to the brutish forces which oppress and destroy. The notion received glorious expression in the so-called servant songs in the Isaiah of the exile,[21] but it is also found in the apocalyptic tradition (cf. Dan. 7) and as an element in renewed Davidic expectation (cf. Isa. 9). Truly, in the purpose of Yahweh, the meek shall inherit the earth.

A SOCIO-POLITICAL READING OF ETHICS IN THE NEW TESTAMENT

Introduction

Various attempts have been made to apply sociological theory to the elucidation of the social and moral dimensions of New Testament material. J. G. Gager, operating with a social conflict theory, adapted Festinger's theory of cognitive dissonance to the phenomenon of conversion, and drew also on millenarianism to elucidate early Christian mission.[22] An approach which combined sociological and psychological insights was used by G. Theissen to delineate the main features of the Jesus movement as a religious and social phenomenon in first-century Palestine.[23] His method required that he pay close attention to the roles, values, norms and symbols which the movement enshrined, to its impact on Palestinian culture and to the inner coherence of its beliefs and practices. In view of the scarcity of sociographic elements in the sources, he drew heavily on inferences from historical events, social norms and religious symbols. Wayne Meeks did a similar service for the study of Paul's social and moral world.[24] The early Christian communities were taught to regard themselves, corporately and individually, as separated from 'the world'. Terms such as conversion and transformation denote the gulf. Yet, because Christians could not but encapsulate much of the world of the Roman Empire in their thinking, language and relationships, the study of the moral practice of such groups must open out on to the canvas of wider society. Indeed, Meeks contended that the history of the early Christian movement could be written as the emergence of 'communities of moral discourse' (the terminology is Gustafson's) or 'communities of character' (so Hauerwas): a line of interpretation which involves the recognition of the extent to which the first Christians shared the symbolic and social world of their contemporaries, and the extent to which their worlds could, and did, change through the process of resocialisation or conversion.

This interrelationship of religious communities to the wider life of society entails an understanding of society as an organic whole. Thus, J. H. Elliott has called for 'a *systemic* analysis of Palestinian society' which 'reveals a configuration of conditions and forces that influenced the perceptions, attitudes, collective behaviour and alliances of various groups within this society'.[25] H. C. Kee found a systemic model of society adumbrated in the work of Piaget.[26] Those who have produced the most dramatic accounts of the contextual nature of Jesus' ministry have emphasised economic and social factors: among them, Machovec, Pixley, Belo, Stegemann and, at a popular level, Clévenot.[27]

Power structure and ethics in Jesus' world

To read the text of the New Testament in socio-economic terms is to allow oneself to scan the material with certain priorities in mind. Thus, while a systemic view of Jewish society is presupposed in what follows, two socio-political factors are emphasised: the agrarian nature of society (which, when dislocated, produces evident distress – unemployment, homelessness, beggary, thieving and brigandage – in the towns and on the roads), and political and economic subordination to Roman imperialism.[28] What follows is a highly selective account of a complex phenomenon, but it is sufficient for our purposes here.

While Roman rule, which commenced in 63 BC and inherited the social and political tensions of the Hellenistic age, allowed a degree of autonomy to subject nations, the social consequences of imperial rule were serious for the Jews. Among the factors noted by W. Stegemann, for example,[29] was social dislocation brought about by forced repatriation. The Jews, who had settled in Samaria and elsewhere in Hasmonean times, were expelled by the Romans in a politically motivated 'ethnic cleansing' or decolonisation, and repatriated to the ancient heartlands of Judaea. Some found their way into the Diaspora, as many had done before them; others became refugees in their own country. Another factor was the appropriation of land by the Herods. It was sold off to the highest bidder, causing dispossession and upheaval.

Our socio-political scanner is bound to pick up the iniquitous system of double taxation: that is, Roman and temple taxes. Whatever concessions the Romans made to Jewish scruples, relief from taxation was not among them. Direct taxes were levied on land and *per capita*; indirect taxes included tolls, duties, market dues and inheritance tax. Some groups benefited from the system; others were impoverished. Taxes were farmed out, to the mutual benefit of the authorities and their agents, but, since the landed classes could pass on the burden to tenants, the lower classes inevitably suffered. As for the temple, which was itself of economic importance, the institution was maintained by the temple taxes, which had a religious sanction (cf. Exod. 30.13–15) and were paid by all males of good standing in the community. Not to pay was to lose status and become one of the 'people of the land'.[30] Other factors which made for impoverishment included crop failure, which occurred frequently on marginal land, while indebtedness was the inevitable outcome of a system loaded against the interests of the peasant majority. Losses due to the demoralisation of the people and resentment against the system were incalculable. For such reasons, Clévenot – with antennae trained on the underdeveloped world of today – described the social formation of Palestine in Jesus' day as 'sub-Asian': 'village communities and a temple-state, which took the surplus from the villages, and was integrated into the Roman imperial system.'[31]

The degree of resistance was largely determined by one's relationship to the power structures. Those in positions of responsibility were virtually required by circumstances to co-operate with the imperial authorities, whether willingly or with reservations. By and large, the aristocracy and priests of the Sadducean tendency took this line. Others could choose a more independent course – and pay the penalty. Crucifixions, en-slavement and the destruction of towns were by no means uncommon; and those who protested non-violently against Pilate's seizure of temple funds were beaten up by undercover security agents. Those with least to lose resorted more readily to open violence: robbers or social bandits, the *sicarii* or terrorists, and eventually zealots or revolutionaries. Yet in unsettled times activists emerged from well-to-do families also, frequently providing leadership and channelling feelings of outrage in more effective ways.[32]

The religiously inspired minority movements of the time offered certain solutions to those caught in the crisis. Of course, the zealots and their precursors had a religious motivation in the cleansing of the land from idolatry, and the mantle of the Maccabees was readily assumed: religion can supply a powerful motive for direct action, not to speak of fanaticism. The Pharisaic movement was of very different mettle, being rooted in the settled village and town communities, where the synagogue had become the religious and social focus and one could combine one's daily avocation with total commitment to the study and observance of the *Torah* as the divine gift to Israel. It represented a small but articulate and critical artisan class, with a set of values potentially antagonistic to the national and imperial establishments. Its own expertise sponsored an alternative authority system. Another response was that of withdrawal. The Qumran community, whose location in the Judean wilderness was of the essence of its being, protested by its very existence against the profanation of temple, priesthood and land, and the political policies that brought it about. The tragedy of its demise came about with the triumph of its eschatology over its ethics.

The community around John the Baptist – like the covenanters of Qumran he constituted 'a voice crying in the wilderness' – focussed on a leader who compared Israel to a rotten tree which had to be felled. Here was counter-force which derived from the prophetic intensification of the *Torah*, embracing a recognition of the pervasiveness of sin and a new solidarity in baptism, cleansing and promise. Here was challenge to the ruling authorities which was judged intolerable when related to specific moral practice within the ruling house.[33]

The majority of the population, however, had no affiliations with any tendency, and were largely the victims of the system. These were the crowds on whom Jesus was said to have compassion, for they were leaderless and vulnerable, having been effectively abandoned or exploited by those who should have been the protectors of Israel. In such a context, any religious or moral initiative was inescapably political.

THE ETHICS OF JESUS IN SOCIO-HISTORICAL PERSPECTIVE

God and Caesar

An obvious starting-point for a discussion of Jesus' relation to the power structures is Mark 12.17, the question about paying taxes. This tradition was not unrelated to concerns in the

Christian communities, and probably derived its form (a 'pronouncement story'), if not a further element of ambivalence, from that context. The situation reflected in the text itself suggests that circumstances inhibited discussion in explicit terms: a hostile questioner, an easily alienated audience, a tense political ethos, and no lack of informers in a totalitarian regime. The language and rhetoric are thus important in this connection.

The rhetorical situation related to the exigency created by the taxation problem;[34] but the emotional and partizan features created a dangerous political situation in which it was impossible to speak freely, as Jesus' questioners well knew. Jesus therefore had to speak credibly without falling into the trap they set. If his word was to be memorable, he had to make an impact on the situation: hence the strategy of the coin and the 'riddle' statement, with its formal association with wisdom teaching, and perhaps barely concealed irony. His statement had to be indirect, but the encoded message cannot be treated as if Jesus was simply side-stepping the issue. There are, in fact, indications that this saying or pronouncement was taken seriously and variously interpreted. Romans 13.7 seems to reflect the emphasis on the sovereignty of God and the duty of paying taxes, without quoting a 'word of the Lord'. Luke, however, suggested that it was cited in evidence against Jesus as urging non-payment of taxes (Luke 23.2). In its political and economic context, the saying lacks conviction if it is taken as a 'two-kingdoms' view which gives unequivocal endorsement to taxation policy. That would assuredly have alienated one part of the audience – and needlessly so, for Jesus' concern was with the kingdom of God rather than with Caesar's problems with the poll tax. The saying therefore underlines giving what is due to God. As Belo observes, Jesus' strategy was to shift the question so that his response was inscribed in the logic of the Jewish symbolic field, which his audience accepted.[35] He thus required them to face the implications of God as counter-force. Is not this God's world? Do we not owe him everything? – except perhaps what is alien to him – money: especially when it bears Caesar's image, 'the mark of the uncleanness inflicted on the country by the occupying power'.[36] Does it involve a political point – the rejection of the imperial monetary system as the service of idols? Such options are for his hearers to decide. There may well be irony in Jesus' invitation to pay Caesar precisely what he is due!

As for the temple tax, the story of the widow's mite can be taken as an evaluation of its moral worth: sacrificial giving is relative to the giver (Mark 12.41–4). Western scholars tend to note its Jewish antecedents and its literary function. Belo, however, emphasises the class economy. The priests administer what the rich give (Mark 12.41c), but Mark understands Jesus to commend to the churches 'a radicalized economic practice in which people share the means of life they have as a condition for blessing'.[37]

It is unlikely that this story is unrelated to Jesus' attitude to the temple. Here we hit upon another problem. Jesus made some kind of challenge to the temple authorities on their home ground (an account is given in all four Gospels), but this crucial event was worked over in such detail by the evangelists (and possibly others) that it is difficult to be sure of its precise nature.[38] Belo points out that in Mark Jesus drives out sellers, buyers and moneychangers – as if they were evil spirits. 'The money from commerce is connected with the temple, and this is why the temple bears no fruit. Money, the money of the traders, is master there.'[39] In fact, John 2.14–16 provides stronger grounds for Belo's view. Typically, Western scholars have suggested that Jesus' anger was directed against the greed of the traders, but the buyers were expelled also and, as Nineham indicates, Mark makes no mention of anger. Nineham concludes, 'It would appear that what Jesus objected to was the "secularization" of a place which should have been kept holy for worship.'[40] But, if we accept the consequences suggested in the Synoptics, this explanation is rather weak, and it would be necessary to spell out precisely what was involved in such 'secularization'. Jesus can hardly be depicted as a High-Church liturgist! His action was clearly a radical challenge to the priestly establishment, however expressed. It doubtless countered their operation of the temple with a proclamation of the will of God – as the citations of scripture suggest. And his protest must have been seen as a threat, or at least an affront, to the institution: hence the drastic steps taken to silence him. After all has been said, it may be that the materialist interpretation has something in its favour; and the story of the widow's mite may give a clear enough indication of the direction of Jesus' protest.

God reigns!

Underlying Jesus' entire ministry is commitment to God as king. The first commandment is love to God and neighbour. The corollary is the rejection of 'mammon' (Matt. 6.24). Jesus had apparently no interest in economics, whether of the temple or the state (although his disciple group had its treasurer). His concern with the victims of the system was to bring them to a power of a different sort, which could transform their lives and bind them into the people of God. They might well experience it as healing or cleansing, as release from entrapment or as enablement of sight, hearing, speech or movement: indeed, as veritable life from the dead. Truly the Spirit of the Lord was upon him (Luke 4.18), bringing good news for the poor (cf. Matt. 11.2–6). The power in question was not of this world, yet exerted a transforming effect within it (cf. Matt. 12.28; Luke 11.20). Jesus thus laid hold of a symbol which went right to the heart of Israel's awareness of God as sovereign counter-force: a symbol which had been marginalised in Israel's power struggles, and somewhat distanced by its eschatology and apocalyptic. We can discern Jesus' ministry as presenting the kingdom in word and action so that it became an intimate and immediate reality for those who were brought to participate in it. This is not 'realised' as opposed to 'consistent' eschatology; the transcendence and 'futurity' of the kingdom are not in question. Nor is it an inaugurated process, to grow from strength to strength in the future, fostered by ecclesiastical or other agency. Jesus gave *performance* to the kingdom,[41] so that its coming was not longer to be sought in apocalyptic signs nor in any other kind of external event, but as a powerful presence in the midst – even of the resistant Pharisees (Luke 17.20–1). It is not an inner possession, for its power emerges in the heat of controversy and opposition. It is *counter*-force: the power which puts in question all earthly and demonic oppression and impoverishment. It is thus not a static condition nor a Platonic idea, but a leavening power, a disturbing force making for wholeness.[42]

Here it may be observed that the ambiguity of the kingdom is an essential part of its being. This arises from its transcendent nature, which – as in dialectical theology – never endorses any existing state of human society or any human creation as encapsulating the reign of God, but always points to the divine qualification, to the human order – however changed – as imperfect and unfulfilled, and to the future which is God's gift. We can certainly point to the intimations of the kingdom – the alternative order rooted in divine sovereignty – in the ministry of Jesus (and perhaps elsewhere); and to the call for action in line with the divine requirements; but in so far as the materialist hypothesis presupposes that, by changing material conditions, the kingdom of God is adumbrated, it harbours a dangerous illusion.[43]

The praxis of the kingdom

We can, therefore, see Jesus' disciple group as an 'alternative' community, devoted to a life style, an ethic, that gave complete priority to the reign of God (Matt. 6.33), a reign manifest in the poor rather than the rich (Luke 6.20, 24), and coming as a gift of the Father's love. The ethos of the community was defined over against worldly power structures: 'you know that those who are deemed masters over the nations subjugate them, and the great use their power against them: it shall not be so among you' (Mark 10.42). Powerlessness is a keynote: it is the meek who shall inherit the land – and this is asserted in a context of spiralling violence![44] Jesus demonstrated the paradoxical power of such a policy in the ethos of his times: turning the other cheek and going the second mile are strategies designed to create a new situation, arising even out of sheer surprise. Jesus taught a quality of response which might transform the relation of oppressor and victim (he gave no guarantees). No doctrine of pacifism is involved, although the strategy might be described as non-violent. It deploys moral force, and is designed to have an effect on the situation.

The disciple's calling is to be 'servant of Yahweh'. The ethos of the disciple community was at least compatible with the sharing of goods (Matt. 5.42; Luke 6.30) and extended little sympathy to the rich (Luke 6.24, 16.25). The prayer pattern for disciples contains the petition, 'forgive us our debts as we also have forgiven our debtors' (Matt. 6.12), where the seeking of forgiveness is pointedly related to one's treatment of debtors. In the social conditions of Jesus' times, this point would have had impact. Indeed, a whole series of parables draws on the world of debtors and creditors.[45] The aim is not to commend an enterprise culture, but to focus on the kind of response to oppression which reflects the divine counter-force. The community also opened its fellowship to those who had lost status (Mark 2.15–17 par.). The counter-force was thus exerted against the exclusions of ritual purity, although when occasion demanded it Jesus apparently commended ritual action.

Such emphasis on divine counter-force was bound to bring Jesus into collision with authority systems of all kinds, for it was subversive by nature. The most intractable system was that built around the *Torah* by the scribes. It was not that Jesus lacked common ground with the scribes in his respect for the *Torah*: rather, with charismatic insight he reoriented its interpretation in the light of the purpose of God, and thus proposed an alternative symbolic code. Mark gives several examples. In the cornfield episode (2.23–8), the Pharisees directly challenge the action – the social code – of the disciple group. 'Why are they doing what is not permitted on the sabbath?' Jesus' strategy is to present an alternative behaviour pattern from scripture, with David as the model for the disciples. He thus undermines the Pharisees' symbolic code – and therefore their authority – by suggesting that David correctly read the moral priorities. This alternative interpretation of the sabbath rests on the perception of the purpose for which it was made, viewing it as God's gift for the benefit of humankind: a reading which, Mark suggests, is underscored by eschatology. A similar strategy is discernible in the healing of the man with the withered hand (Mark 3.1–5). The alternative symbolic structure focusses not on the notion of what is permitted on the sabbath (the legalistic symbol), but on whether it is right to do good on the sabbath and thus realise its blessing (the religio-moral symbol). His opponents are once again outmanœuvred, but unrepentant, in that they resist the truth displayed before them: in the evangelist's view, a manifestation of 'hardness of heart' which angered and grieved Jesus.[46]

A final example is the question of divorce (Mark 10.2–12): his opponents 'bringing him to the test' as a teacher of divine wisdom. As the symbolic code of his opponents seems to be endorsed by scripture (Deut. 4.1–4), the case is not easy. Jesus first relates the Mosaic provision to human 'hardness of heart' (realistic provision, we might say) and then develops his alternative code by adverting to the question of purpose, human and divine. In biblical interpretation it is important to take direction from the fundamental texts and to set other texts in relation to them. To identify a text as fundamental requires the insight of a charismatic teacher or the guidance of a community of faith which has embodied such insight. It could be argued that what Jesus is subverting here is not merely legalistic interpretation, but sexism and class privilege: since the woman in Jewish society belongs to her husband's house and submits to his authority, she is at his disposal (but not vice versa); and the poor cannot afford divorce in any case.[47] These points, however, are not explicit in the text.

In short, Jesus' alternative ethic made such an impact on the religio-political establishment that the latter speedily encompassed his downfall. As Luise Schottroff put it:

The Jesus movement was not a political movement, in the sense of having a political goal, such as the expulsion of the Romans. But since its aim was to transform the whole nation into the children of God, serving God only, and no other master, it presented a massive threat to the *de facto* power[48]

A radically contextual reading of Jesus' ministry entails its own paradox. It sets him in his own times, yet, while he is utterly contemporary with his period, he somehow also transcends it. This question of transcendence is a key issue for the interpreter. Does one locate it in the 'secret' of his being, as Mark did and as Christian doctrine later taught? Should one set it in the sweep of Jewish religious history, as arguably the fulfilment (a loaded traditional term) or the encapsulation (a pretentious modern term) or at least a version of the essence of Israel's moral and religious tradition? Does one speak simply of the power of his integrity and the constancy of his concern for others – especially the poor and victimised – which he maintained against all institutional pressures? Should one emphasise the shared praxis of the community of disciples (either in the narrower or wider frame of reference) in which the divine purpose of the covenanted people was celebrated and at least in part realised? Or does one speak in terms of 'reversal', with particular reference to the resurrection faith?[49]

Whichever readings commend themselves in the interaction of interpreter and text, all must be set in the religio-ethical context of encounter with evil: an encounter attested in the passion story as in the gospels as a whole. In making the supreme demand of one who refused to compromise the nature of his ministry, the Cross proclaims a powerlessness which is paradoxically more powerful than the powers which perpetrated it, and which picks up a similar motif in the Hebrew scriptures. It is the final expression of counter-force, in context with all the manifestations and demonstrations of counter-force enshrined in his ministry and teaching. Thus his praxis passes into story: and his story is one of divine vindication in the face of evil (only too easily translated into triumphalist language), of life through death, of hope transforming life. As such, that story will always stand at the heart of Christian ethics.

THE ETHICS OF THE FIRST CHRISTIANS IN
SOCIO-HISTORICAL PERSPECTIVE

Changing social patterns in early Christian communities

The early Christian communities embodied socio-religious change. They had to deal with divisions within families, the breakdown of marriages, social ostracism and official displeasure. In religio-social perspective, Jewish Christians were in a particularly invidious position, and this could have economic consequences. The church as a whole had to come to terms with geographical expansion, with the change from predominantly rural to Hellenistic urban settings, with recruitment from a wider range of social classes and religio-cultural groups, with emergent leadership roles within the communities, with changing patterns of mission and with strained relationships with the imperial authorities, at worst in spasmodic outbreaks of persecution. All of these raised sharp ethical issues, some of which are singled out for comment below.

Economic tensions
Economic considerations forced themselves on the Jewish Christian community addressed in James. Serious attention is given to social and economic distinctions (2.2), which rendered it open to worldly temptations (1.12–15). The prosperous and the gifted were in danger of dominating the community and setting false standards. The writer not only corrected partiality towards the rich – it is the humble who are truly exalted (1.9), the rich who have no future (1.10–11) – but felt obliged to remind members of political and economic reality. 'Is it not the rich who oppress you? Is it not they who drag you into court?' (2.6). These questions reveal awareness of structures of economic oppression and domination which victimise members of the community and constitute a blasphemy against Christ who called them. The political and social situation which faced some Jewish Christians meant that they were at the sharp end of economic sanctions and urgently needed support. Hence faith must be put into practice; love to neighbour must become the

praxis of the community (2.20). Orphans and widows – those deprived of the maintenance that others take for granted – are a God-given charge on the community (1.27). The brother and sister in need require more than a 'God bless!' (2.15–16); and leaders – teachers (3.1) and those who have some learning (3.13) – must validate their words by their actions, avoiding the rivalries of the power game. This brings the writer back to the entrepreneurial business people, so vulnerable to false values (4.13–17), and to a final blast against the rich (5.1–6). Thus the ministry which this letter reflects serves to awaken the oppressed to the reality of their situation. As for the rich, their ill-gotten gains, the rake-off from the system, is their condemnation on the day of judgment. Their fraudulent appropriation of the wages of the farm-labourers – were there farm-labourers in the congregation? – cries out against them (5.4), like the cries of the oppressed in Egypt. The rich who spirit away the livelihood of the labourer condemn him to death; they murder the righteous! They themselves are fattening for slaughter (5.5). This is no threadbare moralism![50]

Community ethics
It has been seriously questioned whether the Johannine writings have anything to contribute to the study of ethics.[51] The peculiar ethos of the Johannine communities probably owes much to their socio-political situation. Their relatively defensive and inward-looking perspective, allied to their fear of outside forces and the strengthening of eschatological hope, bear witness to experiences of disturbance occasioned by external events. This accords with the disruption of Jewish life post AD 70 and of the possibility of the migration of the community, under duress, to Asia Minor. The members had much cause to distrust 'the world'. The establishment of brotherly love within the community in response to divine love and in imitation of Christ was the priority in ethics.

The deep distress of the Johannine community in the face of active persecution is reflected in the Apocalypse of the seer of Patmos, where ethics is virtually overtaken by the intensity of eschatological hope, with its strident notes of divine retribution and the vindication of the saints. Conflict with the empire is the underlying theme, so that steadfastness and endurance are moral priorities and cowardice the leading sin (Rev. 21.8). In the judgment against Babylon, merchants who have grown rich on her wealth and luxury (18.3) lament her passing: no one buys their cargoes any more (18.11). As W. Schrage has commented, 'In the tradition of prophetic social criticism, we hear the ironic voice of a prophet's wrath in the face of social injustice and wickedness.'[52]

Similar stress in Hebrews results in a call for perseverance in the faith, and courage to be a pilgrim in an alien world. Otherwise, the moral stance is unremarkably conventional in community terms: stimulating one another to love and goodness (cf. 10.22–5), peace with all (12.14), hospitality (13.2), honouring the marriage bond (13.4) and not living for money (13.5).

Social and political factors in the Pauline mission

Unexpectedly, the Gentile mission takes us into areas of relative prosperity, where the Christian communities enjoyed a wider social mix that included some, if not many, of the 'wise, powerful and noble' (1 Cor. 1.26) and that brought its own difficulties and opportunities.

Mission strategy Social factors had a part to play in changes in mission strategy. Gert Theissen has described the first Christian missionaries as 'homeless, roving propagandists without roots or a means of livelihood', who 'embodied a form of socially divergent behaviour' not unlike that of the itinerant Cynic.[53] They encapsulated the 'missionary disciple' ideal set out particularly in Luke, and deeply grounded in the social crisis of the Jewish and Hellenistic worlds. They resembled the Cynics in other ways also: in their penchant for moral 'topics' like wealth or freedom, and their self-sufficiency (*autarkeia*: cf. Phil. 4.11). Thus, when Paul and Barnabas went forth as missionaries, they were doubtless typecast as itinerant preachers in the Cynic mould, whose life style was the critical criterion of their authenticity. Put crudely, this amounted to the question as to whether they were serious 'philosophers' or mountebanks; and the answer was found in assessing whether they were in the game for profit or whether they were genuinely concerned for truth. The sharp division goes back at least to Socrates' discrediting of the sophists, and is reflected by Paul when he disparages the 'peddlars of God's word' (2 Cor. 2.17), although the fact that he declined to receive payment from the Corinthians must be balanced by the fact that he was maintained from elsewhere. Paul's argument is somewhat convoluted: he actually *defends* his right to maintenance, even though he gave up this right at Corinth and was criticised for doing so![54]

What then are the moral issues? A general issue is that of avarice or self-seeking; to outstay your welcome (three days!) was a sufficient indicator for the (Jewish) Christians of the *Didache*. A more particular issue is that of conformity to a charismatic model held to derive from Jesus and his disciple community. This combined total trust in God for sustenance with a complete disregard of human foresight – in effect, the combination of an ideal of poverty with a claim on the generosity of the faithful communities. Paul insisted on a moral and logical appraisal, maintaining that the claim made on the faithful was not a right, but a privilege. He in turn was accused of not observing the apostolic pattern – since he worked to maintain himself and his dependents, and accepted the support of communities other than those he was immediately serving. Was he being 'worldly'? Paul, of course, denied such a charge, although by the standard of charismatic poverty he was vulnerable, just as the charismatics by their practices – letters of commendation, indeed! – were also open to criticism. Ethically, Paul had replaced a traditional observance of charismatic poverty with an emphasis on not being a burden on those one was immediately serving. More importantly, Paul was engaged in a new kind of ministry – or an extension of the previous stage in mission. As Theissen put it, he was now 'the goal-oriented community organiser, breaking new ground and establishing groups apart from Judaism rather than "grazing" among existing groups of sympathizers'.[55] Paul therefore has a distinctive mission strategy (2 Cor. 10.13–18); his praxis is, to that extent, functional. He will not allow an older authoritarian pattern to stand in the way of the latter-day needs of mission, especially as these can be justified on moral and social, as well as theological, grounds. His missionary endeavour – self-consciously ascribed to the grace of God – is in practice legitimated by its success!

Urban setting   Almost all the letters of Paul are addressed to Christian communities in an urban setting. The social consequences of such urbanisation are considerable. There was a greater interaction of social classes, especially on the fringes of the synagogues. Christian converts now included some from the business community, who could provide meeting-places for the house churches and offer leadership as well. These people were more sophisticated both in intellectual outlook and in social interaction: hence the problem of 'meat offered to idols' (1 Cor. 8–10), where this group appealed to a criterion of 'knowledge' or 'enlightenment' to justify class-based social mores in the face of objections from 'weaker' members. Behind the religious objection there might well be a degree of social resentment, which also made itself felt within the fellowship of the churches themselves where the different socio-economic groups had different ideas about what constituted a community meal (1 Cor. 11). The financial competence of such groups enabled them to support Paul in his missionary strategy, and doubtless to underwrite the collection for the Jerusalem poor. This group was inevitably concerned with conditions for trade within the Roman Empire, placing weight on law and order, and being much exercised over taxation policy (cf. Rom. 13.1–7). They were also accustomed to having recourse to law, which caused particular difficulty if they found themselves suing a church member (1 Cor. 6.1–8). In short, the churches now included a potent middle-class constituency; and catechetics accordingly adopted the family image of the well-established Hellenistic household (the *Haustafeln*), patriarchal in tone as it prescribed the duties and desiderated attitudes for all household dependents, including slaves.

Cultural pluralism   A variety of moral issues at Corinth related directly to cultural pluralism: to the fact that, in Meeks' phrase, they not only lived in the Hellenistic world, but it lived in them. Such issues included immorality within the Christian community (1 Cor. 5.1–5), questions of retaliation for wrongs suffered (Rom. 12.17–21); marriage and celibacy (1 Cor. 7.1–11, 25–40); mixed marriages (1 Cor. 7.12–16), and the problem of religious and social status (1 Cor. 7.17–24).

Paul's responses are a curious mixture of eschatological concern, pastoral care, dominical and apostolic tradition and concession to the human situation. The situational element is strong. While Jesus' discussion of marriage has now hardened into a prohibition of divorce (1 Cor. 7.10–11), Paul ends up by declaring that, if the non-Christian partner insists on separation, the Christian partner is not bound by the marriage (1 Cor. 7.12–16). When people are agitated about their present status or that of others, Paul has a 'rule' that each should continue as he was when God called him – whether circumcised or slave – but the 'rule' is subject to some give and take! (1 Cor. 7.17–24). For example, slavery is undesirable: the Christian who is a slave should take the chance of freedom if opportunity offers (1 Cor. 7.21),[56] and those whom Christ has redeemed should not become slaves (1 Cor. 7.23). The eschatological factor is powerful, qualifying moral stances and transforming the human outlook (cf. 1 Cor. 7.29–31). Hence the state of marriage does not receive unequivocal endorsement, but is a concession to human frailty. In eschatological perspective, married life is full of distracting anxieties, so that the single state is preferable, but 'in a time of stress like the present' the hassle of changing marital status should be avoided (1 Cor. 7.26–7). Eschatological images can be invoked for moral ends: not simply in terms of facing the last judgment, but also to demonstrate why God's people should not resort to pagan law-courts (1 Cor. 6.1–8).

This last feature points to the deployment of powerful traditional symbols – whether eschatological, dominical or apostolic – within the social situation. Paul had a strong community ethic, which emphasised corporate interdependence and the absorbing of violence in love. The policy of non-retaliation, so strongly emphasised by Jesus, was incorporated into the community ethic, often in traditional gnomic form, rather than as explicit dominical teaching (cf. Rom. 12.14–21). It is directed towards 'loving one another with brotherly affection' and 'living peaceably with all' – as far as possible! Finally, the element of pastoral care is apparent in Paul's sympathetic approach to human crises, evident in his handling of the exclusion of the person guilty of an immoral sexual liaison (1 Cor. 5.1–5), as well as in his firm but reasoned correction of errors in community policy (1 Cor. 6.1–11).

Christians and the state   The socio-political context is best illustrated from 1 Peter 2.11–17. The writer emphasises the distinctive nature of the Christian community as God's people: its election, vocation and enjoyment of God's mercy, Christ being the corner-stone. (1 Pet. 2.1–10). But, being in the world, it is also involved in socio-political and economic structures which entail the recognition of the pyramid of authority, recognised almost universally throughout the Graeco-Roman world.[57] At its apex is the emperor, and below him the officers of government and administration who are the instruments of law and order (1 Pet. 2.13–4). The writer emphasises the importance of getting these relationships right – not least because it will correct wrong impressions formed by outsiders and influence them for their own good! (1 Pet. 2.12). In any case, the service of God entails silencing ignorance and stupidity (1 Pet. 2.15). Christian freedom should not be made a cloak for wrongdoing – which, in this context, would mean refusal to submit to authority. Christians honour all in appropriate ways: fellow Christians, God and emperor! (1 Pet. 2.16–7). It is worth adding that the pyramid of authority embraces the household relationship of master-slave and husband-wife (1 Pet. 2.18–25; 3.1–7). For the Christians addressed in this letter, the system left no room for anything other than compliance: a fact which they should 'freely' accept. To be sure, Roman imperialism left space for individual liberties, and abuse of the system, as far as 1 Peter is concerned, was more likely to occur in the relatively domestic scene. The Christian response, under grace, is to follow the example of Christ in enduring undeserved suffering without retaliation or sin, and putting oneself in the hands of 'him who judges justly' (1 Pet. 2.21–3). Here is the one possibility of transcending circumstances. Indeed, Christ has shown that such powerlessness is creative, for 'by his wounds you have been healed' (1 Pet. 2.24).

Romans 13.1–7 uses recognisably the same paraenetic tradition, but its orientation is significantly different. Here, since God is recognised as the apex of the power pyramid (this is only implicit in 1 Peter), the status of the authorities is almost divinised (Rom. 13.1–2) and, as in 1 Peter, they are God's agents (Rom. 13.4). Here is a theological version of the Hellenistic political world view, adapted for Christian theological use, but compatible with Stoic ethics, which might indeed have been its source.[58] But the writer is using this material for rhetorical purposes. Having identified submission to the authorities in broad terms as the basic issue (Rom. 13.1, 5), he has to develop a strategy which enables him to carry his audience with him (the 'ethos' of the passage), and then to focus on the particular issue which is his concern. The crunch is reached in verse 6: 'That is why you pay taxes.' This note is absent from 1 Peter 2.

The explanation may well be found in terms of social context. The Roman Christians were in a different position from those addressed in 1 Peter: a mobile community of craftsmen like Aquila, perhaps, striving to maintain business in the face of political and fiscal disincentives.[59] According to both Tacitus and Suetonius, taxation was a *cause célèbre* in the reign of Nero, who ran a constant balance of payments and public expenditure deficit; while the *immodestia publicanorum* was notorious. When Christians like Prisca and Aquila were expelled from Rome, along with their fellow Jews, in the reign of Claudius (Acts 18.2–4), they had to shoulder the full burden of 'tribute' (direct taxation on imperial subjects, not paid in Italy), as well as indirect taxation such as customs duties, so iniquitously administered. Both types of taxation are named in Rom. 13.6. As they tried to regain their market position, Christian business people might well be tempted to join in the popular agitation over taxes, and even to attempt non-payment or tax avoidance.

For this reason they are commanded to 'discharge your obligations to everybody' (Rom. 13.7), remembering to act in love towards the community as a whole (that is, not out of personal advantage alone) and not to be ensnared in the pagan life style, since 'this is the hour of crisis' (Rom. 13.11-14). The question of validity arises in relation to the praxis advocated in 1 Peter 2 and Romans 13, both of which are liable to be misunderstood if taken out of context. It is true that 1 Peter considers difficulties in the master–slave relationship, rather than the problems of submission to the state, but a similar praxis would apply. Indeed, reflections of 1 Peter occur in the *Martyrdom* of Polycarp. To follow the pattern of Christ, who suffered for all – 'the faultless for the sinners'[60] – is to absorb violence, even to the point of death, trusting in God for vindication. Neither 1 Peter nor Romans 13 considers all the circumstances of the relation of Christians to the state. Polycarp added an important qualification: 'we have been taught to render honour, as is befitting, to rulers and authorities appointed by God *so far as it does us no harm*'.[61] This may well have been a hidden premise in the two passages under consideration: there were limits to submission. An explicit qualification of this kind is found in Acts 5.29, where the apostles tell the Sanhedrin: 'we ought to obey God rather than men'. Paul's problem in Romans 13 was quite different. If our socio-historical interpretation is correct, he sought to detach the Roman Christians from political involvements which put at risk their single-minded concentration on faith priorities. The Christian's relation to the state is always one of checks and balances. The most remarkable feature is that, while the state is recognised as God's instrument in restraining evil and commending those who do right, there is nothing of the prophetic passion for social justice as the expression in society of the righteousness of God.

Multi-cultural community   In the Graeco-Roman world, there was a crisis of personal identity which was not met by official religion. Whatever its origins, the latter was primarily oriented to public and political concerns, now largely divorced from the intimate life of family or clan. Private religion, groups and cults therefore began to exercise a strong attraction. Some found satisfaction in voluntary communities such as the Cynics, Stoics and Epicureans.[62] A multiplicity of cults, many of foreign origin, were also attracting devotees throughout Italy and elsewhere, speaking of salvation, providing assurance and administering healing, all attested by compelling private testimonies in inscriptions and other documents. As H. C. Kee observed, 'it is precisely the appeal across barriers of family, ethnic origin, and social status that aroused the hopes of the alienated as well as the anxieties of the privileged'.[63]

Some looked to Judaism, with its uncompromising mono-theism and its high-minded ethics, to meet these deeper needs. But the multi-cultural scene brought its own problems for ancient Judaism, in spite of a universalistic strain which ran through its ancient scriptures. The Judaism of the times remained focussed on Israel as the covenanted people: the main stock into which others might be grafted by a carefully controlled process which included instruction, immersion and circumcision. Nevertheless, the more usual status of Gentiles was as God-fearers on the fringe of synagogue communities. The position of women converts is less clear, although the feminine *proselyta* is found in some inscriptions. It was also relatively easy for ordinary people in Judaea, particularly under economic pressure, to lose status and become mere 'people of the land', as alienated from their roots as their Hellenistic counterparts. Who had the vision to match the hour?

Visionaries do not necessarily have an easy ride! For Paul, the apostle to the Gentiles, the people of God 'in Christ' trans-cended the boundaries of race, gender and status. Giving practical expression to this – for example, in table fellowship when the community comprised Jewish Christians and un-circumcised Gentile believers – led to clashes with more con-servative elements in the churches, who found a focus in Jerusalem (cf. Gal. 2.12). Undeterred, Paul 'did not yield submission even for a moment' (Gal. 2.5) to the 'circumcision party' and 'opposed Cephas to his face' (Gal. 2.11) when he failed to stand by Paul's multi-cultural concept of the gospel. With their Jewish roots, the churches had inherited something of the Jewish problem, and it was Paul who shifted the centre of gravity. As Jesus had recovered certain emphases so as to constitute a radically different symbolic system, so Paul brought the concept of the faith community, characteristic of covenantal discourse since Abraham, to unqualified expression. His mission and message thus required that through baptism in Christ 'you are all sons of God' (Gal. 3.26).

There is no such thing as 'Jew or Greek', there is no such thing as 'slave or free', there is no such thing as 'male and female', for you are all one in Christ Jesus. (Gal. 3.28)

A brief comment is offered on each of the three dimensions. *Race* In spite of ambivalences in their tradition, the Jews had strong religious, social and political reasons for maintaining their identity, even while recognising the importance of the interface with the outside world. One unintended result of Paul's mission was the separation of Jews and Christians, to his own evident anguish (cf. Rom. 9–11). His hope was for a genuinely multi-cultural church, embracing both circumcised Jews and uncircumcised Gentiles. The unity of the whole community rested on faith in God. The particularities of race and its differentia, such as language, were overcome in the spiritual community whose focus was a common meal, and who offered the service of worship and discipleship in Christ.[64]
Gender Equality of the sexes in the sight of God is reflected throughout the gospels, whether in the celebration of the birth of Christ, membership of Jesus' family of faith, or witnessing to the resurrection. The allocation of roles within the faith communities is more problematic: whether the all-male twelve (corresponding to a traditional symbol?) or Paul's silencing of women in church (1 Cor. 14.34–5). The latter case relates to Paul's disciplining of disorderly worship, and women are not the only ones placed under constraint. Nevertheless, his presentation is conditioned by cultural and traditional assumptions (1 Cor. 14.34), including Jewish patriarchy and Hellenistic notions of proper order. One feature that requires to be related to its socio-historical setting is the interpretation of scripture applied to the justification of positions taken up on

socio-historical grounds. A case in point is 1 Tim. 2.11–15, where selective use of Genesis supports a particular form of female submissiveness. A more obscure Pauline passage occurs in 1 Cor. 11.3–16, in which Paul actually makes no objection to women prophesying (11.5)![65]

Slavery A similar tension applies to the status of slaves in the Christian community. By baptism they are received into full membership. Paul is clear that slavery is undesirable and that Christians should not become 'slaves of men' (1 Cor. 7.23). But it is not clear that he recommended that slaves seek manumission,[66] not even in the case of Onesimus. Socio-historical conditions serve as partial commentary. Manumission was a complex legal process. The transition to free status raised economic and other problems of adjustment for the person concerned. Slavery was as essential to ancient households as the motor-car is to their modern counterparts; and Christian masters, on whose support the churches depended, could hardly contemplate the ruin of their economic establishment. Then there was the eschatological crisis to consider...There is no evidence that Paul ever contemplated the emancipation of slaves as a priority of gospel mission. He did not like the system: that much is clear. In the remarkably wide social mix of the Christian communities (whatever difficulties arose in practice!), slaves enjoyed full membership: freedmen of the Lord! (1 Cor. 9.22). They were 'beloved brothers' (cf. Philem. 16), and performed notable service. What fine tuning was needed to enable the community to work with such tensions we can only surmise.[67]

POSTSCRIPT

This chapter has attempted to demonstrate the ethics of historical reading by considering leading aspects of Israel's story and that of Jesus and the first Christians in relation to their socio-historical contexts. The attempt, while basically exegetical, prompts hypotheses, demands theological awareness and involves sensitivity; yet the entire process is regulated by the texts themselves, singly and together. The reader brings to the task insights relating to society and the structures of power within it, but applies them in such a way as to identify the tensions of living in obedience to the transcendent Lord within a context or contexts in which power, authority and social pressures constrained possible responses. The highlighting of this divine counterpoint and its contextual problematic is perhaps the main contribution of historical reading to biblical interpretation and biblically related ethics. In its execution it requires integrity on the part of the interpreter to ensure that its Otherness, its strangeness, is fully recognised, even as the operation of forces immanent within its world is explicated through structural analogy. This process may be described as the ethics of historical reading.

CHAPTER 8

Ethics and contemporary reading

So we listen to the text. But with whose voice does it speak?
It is a text still, not a person. It has no voice of its
own... The text is *mute*. So apart from the *prior* assumption,
from the very outset, that something speaks through the
text which called the text *and myself* into being, the text is
cast into a swamp of total relativism, and interpretation is
reduced to ventriloquy. So I repeat: in the text I hope to
encounter an alien speech which is finally the self-
disclosure of God.

(Walter Wink)[1]

We listen to the text: to the Other. With this observation we are
brought back to Schweitzer, with his living Stranger; to Barth,
with his insistence on the One who is qualitatively different
from ourselves; and to Bultmann, with his emphasis on
encountering the Word. As Ricoeur has emphasised, the text
comes to us as the witness of the faith community to the object
of its faith, so that as we engage with the text we hear the
summons that it brings to us. In the text, interpreted with
integrity, we find, not our mirror image, but a wholly different
reality which relativises us, yet comes as a gift of grace.

But there is a difficulty. In order to listen to the text, we must
overcome the fact that, at least for many, western scholarship
has expropriated the Bible, so that many are no longer confident
that they have access to its interpretation. Such a situation
underlines the need to recover the art of reading the Bible, so
that insights may be shared through group interaction with the
text. In this way it may be possible, once more, to speak of
encountering the Word.

Indeed, if we are truly to listen to the text, and if that listening is to the Other and not simply to ourselves, we must think both of the quality of our approach to the text and of the ethics of reading. More than that, we must take responsibility for the consequences of our reading. As E. Schüssler Fiorenza has put it:

The rhetorical character of biblical interpretations and historical reconstructions... requires an *ethics of accountability* that stands responsible not only for the choice of theoretical interpretive models but also for the ethical consequences of the biblical text and its meanings.[2]

There is, therefore, a correlation between being alive to the Other in the text and being aware of the others around us. Indeed, reading in community may be particularly creative, since human interrelatedness prevents us from adopting the model of the solitary reader as normative.[3] But when interpretation takes place in community, the possibility arises of a multiplicity of readings. Is the text genuinely pluriform? Are we ready to accept that there may be a legitimate plurality in interpretation, and that others' interpretations may bring out the inadequacies and distortions in our own? Approaching the text in community also underlines the fact that interpretation is a public event, at least in so far as meaning is shared and disseminated. We must therefore be ready to take responsibility for the varied consequences of our interpretation.

It is conceivable that some people, because of their conditioning, may find satisfaction in a reading which affirms their presuppositions about biblical authority and Christian values, but which at the same time is racist or sexist or shows class prejudice. It is a sobering thought that the Bible has been used to legitimate tyranny and oppression, to incite to war and destruction, to excite guilt, to advocate slavery, to fan the flames of prejudice, to depersonalise women and so on. Biblical interpretation should carry a health warning! But *rightly divined*, it conveys the word of joy, peace and salvation as it responds to the address of the Other.

To explore these dimensions, this chapter is divided into four parts, dealing in turn with the question of approach to ancient texts; with understanding the process of interpretation; with relating interpretation and ethics; and, finally, with a consideration of our hermeneutical responsibility, illustrated in relation to selected texts or themes.

APPROACHING THE TEXT

Pre-understanding – Western style

As David Tracy has indicated, the status of the Bible as a 'classic' of Western culture ensures that it is a book which most people possess but seldom read; and when they do attempt to read it, they encounter an extremely strange world.[4] Biblical criticism has not lessened the gap. Bultmann, supreme exegete and interpreter, attempted to bridge it. He recognised that the horizons of the ancient and modern world do not fuse without considerable effort on the part of the interpreter (hence the 'demythologising' programme), the hermeneutical key being found in the existential analytic of Heidegger and the pre-understanding of the interpreter.[5]

Pre-understanding, for Bultmann, relates to our knowledge of human existence which, when structurally analysed and clarified, enables the crucial issues to emerge in the ancient context (the *kerygma*) and presents the interpreter with live options for decision today. Thus interpretation, like education, begins where we are – at least, theoretically! But, for Bultmann, as we have seen, 'where we are' (or 'modern man') is defined in broadly cultural, philosophic and academic terms. The social sciences are kept at bay, not to mention the particularities of daily life such as work, leisure, making ends meet, unemployment, sickness, health…: in short, the corporate involvement of humankind! Today it is clear that pre-understanding must include awareness of how our existence is bound up with socio-economic and political structures, and so prompt questions to put to the text. We come to the text alive to *our* vital questions. The result is a direct link between interpretation and ethics, which Bultmann ascribed to a separate discipline, in traditional post-Enlightenment style.

Paul Ricoeur differed from Bultmann in important respects: not least in his rejection of Bultmann's attempt to make the secularity of 'modern man' axiomatic for interpretation. He also faulted Bultmann's failure to take seriously enough the language of scripture, with its rich imagery, and its power to create a new awareness in the reader – even to prompt the recovery of what has been lost in modernism.[6] 'Modern man' is himself the victim of his enculturation. Like him we need to be inducted into a situation in which the text can activate questions and generate response. We need to be inducted into an interpretive process which is nothing less than the deciphering of life through the medium of the text.[7] This is also to encounter the witness of the apostolic community to the object of its faith, so that we can respond, through that witness, to the summons to faith.[8]

But if we are to read and re-read the Bible, and thus to read and re-read ourselves, we need to change key from philosophical abstraction to human community. To decipher life in the mirror of the text involves the sharpening of sensitivity towards the faith question (that is, love to God) and towards praxis (that is, love to neighbour). If the former engages with the illusory self-sufficiency of secularism, the latter focusses on its selfishness and injustice: on the cry of the victims of the system which neither Bultmann nor his putative interlocutor effectively challenges. It might well be said that racism, sexism and class divisions are much more potent and destructive powers in human life than the so-called vital questions of faith which ignore such realities.[9]

People need to be helped to question the stultifying shallowness of 'secular man' and, in fellowship with others, set out on a mission of rediscovery. T. H. Groome calls this stage 'naming present action', as the groundwork for further critical explorations of the participants' stories and visions: an exercise in self-understanding and social awareness in which much is discovered through a new capacity for sharing and dialogue.[10]

Pre-understanding – feminist style

A particular critique of Western values from within Western culture arose out of the modern feminist consciousness, which embodied an acute sense of patriarchal oppressiveness and thus made common cause with liberationism.[11] Feminist interpretation dramatically recovers perspectives neglected and distorted by the insidious influence of patriarchal authority and assumptions down the centuries.

A prime example is provided by the reading of the Magnificat in Luke, with its extraordinary overturning of the accepted order of things. Confessing that she had long failed to appreciate its revolutionary content, Dorothe Söllee describes her discovery that it was more than a collection of verses from the Hebrew Bible:

> ... when I studied theology I simply dissected the text in literary-critical terms: this bit comes from here, that bit comes from there ... I now think that this is a foolish procedure which only distracts attention from the content. The content, the redistribution of hunger and luxury, helplessness and power, was not perceived by those who studied it, either in the socio-historical context of the New Testament or in the context of their own lives. And the figure of the girl who sings this song of jubilation suffered precisely the cultural fate that women have to expect elsewhere: they are made invisible.[12]

Here is the rediscovery of a lost perspective, the highlighting of an element of suppression in critical interpretation and, in consequence, the disowning of the 'Ave Maria' tradition, with its desensualised figure of humble devotion that so gravely distorted the biblical picture.[13] Here too is a claim to 'biblical realism' which stands in sharp contrast to theological syntheses which have used this appellation, and to charges that feminist hermeneutics is subjective. The only point to be made in response to Sölle is that some importance must be given to the fact that, in Luke, the text itself did survive – doubtless because of the tradition of 'the poor' in Israel which persisted in, and even characterised, a strand within the early Christian communities. In consequence, one may see Mary as a model of discipleship for all – a theme developed effectively by Rosemary Reuther.[14]

Feminist consciousness operates as a powerful pre-understanding, ready to subject texts to searching scrutiny for sexist bias, but also to develop biblical perspectives neglected in male-dominated exegesis. Here is a veritable 'hermeneutics of suspicion', a radical perspective on biblical scholarship, which shrivels, at least in part, under the intensity of the scrutiny. It also offers a revolutionary challenge to long cherished assumptions – for example, in political and ecclesiastical life – which, although hallowed by 'tradition', may prove to be no more than the accumulated expressions of the masculine will to power. It is sensitive to oppressive structures of all kinds, and thus joins with liberation movements in the cause of social justice and the right exercise of power. Finally, it is conducive to the development of an ethos in which feminine values (if the phrase is legitimate) contribute fully to a new and distinctive ethics.

Pre-understanding – liberationist style

In liberation terms, pre-understanding is an integral part of the hermeneutical process in which, as Carlos Mesters put it, the Bible provides the text and the community the context, while 'reality' – the real-life situation of the people – supplies the 'pre-text': the reality which lies in front of the text when read in context.[15] Located in the South rather than the North, liberation perspectives reflect the people's hard won experience of life and their vision of the future. They know they have a history of their own; they reject all patterns of world domination; they accept ideological and religious diversity; and they long for equality and fraternity. Their reflections, perceptions and aspirations are articulated through small interactive groups, in which the essence of the church is found. At their centre is the Bible which, when rightly used, is a liberating instrument. Such usage is beautifully illustrated by the study sessions of the base communities in Ernesto Cardinale's *The Gospel in Solentiname*.[16]

In a thought-provoking contribution to the international

ecumenical congress on theology at Sao Paulo in 1980, Carlos Mesters threw light on this dynamic by offering a sketch of three groups using the Bible.[17] The first engages in a very narrow type of Bible study: the letter of the text is what matters, not wider meaning about life in the world today. The Bible, he observes, may be applied as a force for liberation or oppression. When literalism treats the text as a monolithic edifice, it is often an oppressive force, ready to ally with other oppressive forces. It can be corrected through the life of the church when it is committed to the oppressed. The second is the more traditional Bible-study group, where people come together as a community to 'learn about the Bible'. This is often led by the 'expert' who wishes to educate the group in more enlightened ways of understanding the Bible. One result may be alienation, since the line of approach is alien to the people. Mesters gives graphic examples:

One time a nun went to give a course on the Old Testament. Halfway through she had to close down the course because no one was showing up. The people said: 'Sister is destroying the Bible!' A certain priest offered an explanation of the Exodus. Many people never came back. 'He is putting an end to miracles,' they complained.[18]

This kind of situation is not unknown in the West! Often the 'expert' may put it down to resistance to 'scientific methods'. More often, the fault lies in the failure of the leader to relate to the group, and in the difficulty of moving from the academic perspective to contemporary moral issues. As Mesters puts it, 'when the community takes shape only around the Bible, then it faces a crisis as soon as it must move on to social and political issues'.[19] The third situation is a thoroughly contemporary one: 'a community of people meeting around the Bible who inject concrete reality and their own situation into the discussion'.[20] The future, Mesters believes, lies with such groups.

Such a rich pre-understanding of the interpretive process is accompanied by an element of impatience with traditional ways which no longer meet the requirements of the situation. As J. L. Segundo puts it, in an age of rapid change, traditional formulations of the Christian faith, like traditional modes of interpretation, resemble quaint museum pieces which provide a doubtful refuge for people sheltering from the radical challenge of life today. But this kind of pre-understanding entails a critical consciousness, a willingness to probe the situation. Segundo raised four major points. The first – shared alike by Marx and the sociological approach indicated earlier – is that current ideas (political, ideological or whatever) are bound up with existing social reality. The second involves our willingness to see that theology – including *our* theology – is related to the whole ideological superstructure and finds expression within the ideological struggles of our time and place. The third is directed to biblical exegesis and the tendency in much of it to ignore or minimise the effect of the social context of the interpreter. Hence one must work for change in theology and church as well as in the world – and particularly in Latin America to which these reflections are directly related. The fourth and final stage is to recognise the emergence of a new hermeneutic, characterised by the kind of commitment evoked by the Bible itself. Segundo prefers to use the term 'partiality', over against the dubious 'impartiality' claimed by much Western scholarship. This is where the texts from the past link with the present, and make their own demands in relation to the context in which they are heard.[21]

The demand which all this makes on Western interpreters is not that they speak as if they lived in Latin America, but that their self-understanding and their social understanding be equally radical. The question of identity is pressed upon the interpreter, for a defensive interpreter will produce a defensive interpretation. In the global perspective of today's world, it may be easier in some ways to pick up the signals of culture-bound prejudice, but the reality thus signified is as intransigent as ever.

HERMENEUTICAL PROCESS

Western hermeneutics in transition

Paul Ricoeur can probably be cited as representative of the Western hermeneutical tradition. Ricoeur underlined the importance of the critical moment: not in any historical positive sense (although distantiation is important to an awareness of belonging to a world, a culture or a tradition) but as a questioning of what the text means by its testimony.[22] Our first *naïveté*, as L. S. Mudge suggests, contains a dim awareness of that to which the text is calling us.[23] Ricoeur speaks of critical explanation not in a destructive sense, but as an opening of the way towards a second *naïveté*: a conducting of us, as readers, through the rich diversity of genres and modes of expression that constitute the language of faith, until we appreciate the poetic or creative function of the text as revelatory *poesis* and thus arrive at the 'post-critical moment'.[24]

And so we come full circle: from our initial naïve fascination with texts in which testimony is preserved in *poesis*, through the critical disciplines which help us overcome idolatry and dogmatism, to the post-critical moment when we ourselves begin to testify in a divestiture of consciousness, which implicates our lives in the world 'in front of' the text.[25]

The world 'in front of the text' opens up the future to a theology of hope, and is of prime importance for ethics and praxis, but Ricoeur resists converting religious discourse without remainder into political or even moral discourse. There is always a 'something more' in the *kerygma*, an impossible possibility in faith ethics, which does not debar us from commitment to social and political action, and indeed positively encourages the questioning of institutionalised power; but it has even wider horizons, for it is a resurrection faith, deciphering the signals of new life amid the contradictory appearances of death.[26]

Ricoeur's work is a very positive contribution to biblical interpretation, but it is limited by its abstract philosophical mode of expression and may not, in the end, completely avoid the debilitating separation of personal and social ethics which has plagued Western interpretation. Walter Wink presents an alternative imaginative attempt to break through to a characteristically dynamic view of the interpretation process. Faustian and Freudian in his approach, he views the process in terms of three moments: fusion, distance and communion.

Fusion Approaching the task of interpretation from within our culture and tradition, which provides horizon and orientation, we initially exhibit the *naïveté* of uncritical fusion with the world which shaped and nurtured us. Then comes its negation – through suspicion, doubt, questioning. It is an eye-opening experience, an unveiling of reality, a 'distancing of oneself from prevailing culture and intrapsychic images and preunderstandings, and consequently a dialectical moment of necessary alienation on the way to freedom and truth'.[27] It serves to give us space to question received ideas and hear new truth. It is a process of distantiation, a distancing of ourselves so that we can have a better look at the world. It involves apparent loss, in order that there may be much gain – a paradoxical movement towards liberation.

Distance Wink has a highly symbolic way of depicting distance. Objectification is part of Satan's business, an alienated consciousness which is nevertheless an essential part of the growing-up process.[28] Biblical criticism is part of the '"diabolical" rebellion against the superego of dogmatic Christendom'[29] – a recurring theme (without the Freudian overtones!) in much critical scholarship. But biblical criticism '"got stuck" in the Faustian moment of alienated distance':[30] it failed to realise its liberating potential (Satan's doing again!). Today the guild of biblical scholars, rather than Christian dogma, 'functions as the harsh superego in the self of many exegetes'.[31] We need, therefore, a second negation, to shake us out of this complacency. One route is the sociology of knowledge approach, which Wink uses not only to show how far biblical criticism became the tool of secularisation – embodying as it did methodological or functional atheism – but how far it alienated the reader from his or her true objective of finding faith or God or truth.[32] A second route is that of psychoanalysis: shedding the ill-founded arrogance of critical modernism; recovering from the repression of the radical questions enshrined in the language and concepts of another time; and renewing an awareness of the power of symbolism in what Ricoeur called a second *naïveté*.[33] Thus this second negation points the way to transformation, and enables a reading of the text in its own right.

Communion   The goal is the communion of horizons. If at the outset I was the object of a subject (my cultural heritage) and, in revolt, I became a subject with an object (the text), now in the communion of horizons I am 'both the subject and object of the text *and* the subject and object of my own self-reflection'.[34] Now in the reading of the text the horizons of one's own life are illumined, affording new self-understanding, and the horizons of the text are illumined as we bring to it interpretive understanding from our own world. There is interaction, interpenetration, communion. Wink, however, makes it clear that this is not an individualistic exercise, although like Kierkegaard he emphasises inner transformation. Interpretation is best done in community, where horizons can be explored and shared.[35] And the fact that the text does not release meaning unless our world is clarified at the same time means that there is no gulf between understanding and application. Indeed, reading arises out of praxis – or, as Wink would put it, out of our interest in applying what we read to our world.[36]

Wink comes nearer, and actually presupposes, group or community study. His intriguing use of symbolism enriches his interpretation, although terms such as 'fusion' and 'communion' may contain an element of overstatement. Moreover, the emphasis he places on psychoanalysis in his description of the interpretive process, probably highlights the inward struggle and personal transformation at the expense of engagement with the power structures, which as we have seen receives dramatic attention elsewhere in his writing.[37]

To describe and analyse the hermeneutical process is therefore no easy task. It probably requires a consciously multidisciplinary approach, combining academic reflection and practical engagement. T. H. Groome, for example, presents the hermeneutical operation in terms of five movements. The first two, already noted, embrace naming present action and exploring the participants' stories and visions. The starting point is thus with present experience, shared and critiqued. The third movement is the presentation of the Christian community's story and vision, the hub of which is biblical material, particularly in narrative form. Here is potentially a great extension and enrichment of the horizons of the interpretive group, provided that the dynamics of the interaction between the community's story and vision are fully recognised: the church is under the judgment of the Word! Hence, in the fourth movement there is what he calls a dialectical hermeneutic between the story and the participants' stories: in short, 'What does the Community's Story mean for ... our stories, and how do our stories respond to ... the community Story?'[38] The final movement is the dialectical hermeneutic between the vision of God's kingdom and the visions embodied in our present action. There is thus in Groome's proposal a progression in community from praxis through gospel interpretation to renewed praxis; and the presupposition of it is a critical correlation between the data of the Christian faith and the data of human experience and empirical reality.

It is remarkable that in Western scholarship, for the most part, one has to go beyond the usual range of critical studies before a complete hermeneutical model emerges. Even so there is need for caution, for Wink's emphasis on personal transformation requires to be related to, and qualified by, his understanding of the determining influence of structural factors in the social situation, which he brings out very clearly in other writings. Groome's third and subsequent movements turn on the quality of the correlation between the interpretive group and the dynamics of the text. There is a danger that the group might find comfortable correlations – a 'comfortable' reading of the story, a 'comfortable' vision – which simply confirm its presuppositions without undue disturbance. The essential factor is that it is prepared to see the strangeness of the Other, to confront radically different possibilities, and to let itself be reshaped in understanding, vision and action by the Spirit of the divine Other.

Feminist hermeneutics

Feminist hermeneutics embarks on nothing short of a rereading of the gospel. It identifies with liberation perspectives, for example, by showing the material affinity between the Magnificat and the manifesto for Jesus' ministry in Luke 4. It illustrates the thesis of suppression, for example, from the fact that, in the resurrection narratives, the women's primary witness is brushed aside – 'idle tales' – in favour of the eventual authoritative testimony of Peter and the (male) disciples; apostolic power was an issue here. It appeals to the practice of Jesus. As E. Schüssler Fiorenza has shown, the episode in Mark 14.3–9 in which an unnamed woman anoints Jesus with seeming extravagance is particularly revealing.[39] She it is – not the twelve – who performs the act of true devotion. She it is who will be remembered for her deed of discipleship. Besides, Jesus' teaching can show a remarkable inclusiveness: 'whoever does the will of God is my brother, and sister, and mother'. (Mark 3.35) Without de-contextualising Jesus, it is possible to see that his liberating ministry included women, and that he placed value on their faith and discipleship.

An important plank in the feminist position is distantiation. This is obviously true of the approach to the Hebrew scriptures,[40] but is equally important in relation to the New Testament. In Paul's letters, for example, we find a remarkable expression of baptismal egalitarianism in Gal. 3.27–8, in which there is a clear reflection of the 'male and female' motif of Gen. 1.27. This was the moral high point of Paul's argument. If baptism was the one action that united all Christians, then it could be interpreted Christologically and ecclesially as affirming oneness in Christ, and its social implication was an equality which transcended the differentiae of race, economic status and gender. Acceptable both for catechetical and missionary or apologetic purposes, it was the kind of formula Paul required to validate his Gentile mission.

Distantiation is important when we come to the particularities of the Pauline context. For example, feminist hermeneutics has to come to terms with Paul's specific directions on female participation in worship (1 Cor. 11.3–16; 14.33–36), which have earned him in modern times the imperceptive soubriquet of male chauvinist. A sensible strategy is to relate them to the wider context of Paul's churches, where women like Chloe were prominent in leadership (1 Cor. 1.11) and where marriage was understood as a full partnership (1 Cor. 7.3–4). Thus Paul is seen to have maintained a relatively liberal attitude – he went out of his way to stress that the temple of the living God comprises God's sons and daughters (2 Cor. 6.16–18) – but his rhetoric expressed a reaction to what he regarded as an abuse of this freedom.[41] There is a temptation for affronted modern writers to assume a regression on Paul's part from the Christian egalitarianism of Gal. 3.28. There is undoubtedly a tension between Paul's acceptance of the interdependence of the sexes (1 Cor. 11.11–12) and his underscoring of the subordinate role of women, which is a challenge to Christian feminist hermeneutics.

A possible line of approach is to understand Paul as constrained to use the synagogues of the Diaspora as his model of religious community and to relate practice within his churches – certainly in regard to behavioural convention – to Jewish tradition. His rhetoric therefore reflected the subordination of women so strongly expressed in Josephus and Philo (in Gentile culture too), as well as current androcentric exegesis of the stories of creation and fall in Genesis. The point of all this was to reinforce a certain kind of practice. While, as in synagogues, there was no problem about the participation of male and female together in worship nor, indeed, the joint holding of responsible positions in the community, women lacked the authority of the *Torah* to read and lead prayers in public. Paul reaffirmed this tradition (1 Cor. 14.34). Charismatic excesses elicited his sympathetic but firm constraint, which applied in double measure to women's utterances: in no way was it acceptable to follow the practice of Gentile cults here. In his insistence that women should consult their husbands rather then enquire in public, Paul was even leaning to the conservative side. He was fairly conservative also in relation to dress and head-covering, thus distancing Christian practice from certain Graeco-Roman customs. And to all this he lent the weight of apostolic and even dominical authority. Paul had very definite ideas about decent and orderly behaviour. His position, complete with appeal to the *Torah*, was indistinguishable from the standpoint of a Jewish Christian who had broken with the synagogues but was determined that the 'congregations of the saints' (1 Cor. 14.32) should not offend against the customary norms of behaviour. In a curious way, he was affirming the unity of praxis which bound Jew and Greek together in Christ.

All this is cold comfort for the feminist interpreter. 'Of course, I feel humiliated when I read what 1 Timothy says about women', wrote Dorothee Sölle, and took refuge in the thought that Paul did not write 1 Tim. 2.11–15. This, however, is not a complete solution. The problem is that the Bible is androcentric, patriarchal: a fact which has persuaded some to abandon it in favour of a post-Christian feminist ideology. Those who resist this failure of nerve tend to affirm the liberation strand – the call for justice for the oppressed and the victims of discrimination – as central to the positive message of the Bible and affirmed by Christ. There is no way forward in terms of a literalistic interpretation which takes all biblical statements, whether of Paul or others, as of equal validity, without reference to socio-historical conditioning or other relativising factors. To do so would be to act irresponsibly. The biblical writers – like Paul – are not always true to their highest insights, and exercise power in patriarchal fashion. This becomes a negative marker, a red signal as it were. It denotes a point at which cultural presuppositions have not yet been challenged – or challenged adequately – by the gospel. Doubtless this happens in all situations, ancient and modern, for here we see through a glass darkly. Moreover, unless we are disembodied voices crying in the wilderness, we all have to accommodate to some extent to the culture which shaped us and supports us. The challenge is to engage with it as part of a dynamic for change which truly 'urges Christ', as Sölle puts it. The hermeneutical path is, once more, from praxis through reflection to renewed praxis.

Liberation hermeneutics

Introduction

The merging of horizons, which has been a most notable feature of liberation theology, is anticipated and well illustrated by Martin Luther King's celebrated 'dream' speech, which in turn reflected the rhetoric of his people's spirituality. Such linguistic and interpretive virtuosity produces not distortion, but persuasive force, as the power of the ancient imagery of renewal and restoration courses through the utterance, sharpening the rhetorical purpose and homiletic appeal. In liberationism there is much rhetoric, much persuasive argumentation. There is multi-media communication: poetry and hymns, cartoons and sermons, group discussion and public demonstrations, pastoral concern and academic writing. There is commitment – to the expression of the gospel in the contemporary social and political context, and therefore to the poor, the oppressed and the disadvantaged, and to economic, political and social change. The central interpretative concern is the relation of Bible and gospel to the oppressive structures identifiable in the context of the interpreters.

Viewed in this perspective, any approach which is merely idealist or literary or other-worldly is seen as a betrayal or domestication of the Bible, which is thus, in the words of Gutiérrez, 'rendered as innocuous as a lap dog'.[42] So far from presenting the power which 'put down the mighty from their thrones, and exalted those of low degree' (Luke 1.52), it gives the mighty remarkable consolation! Moreover, as we have seen, liberation theology is ambivalent towards biblical criticism. There is a perception that the exclusive guild of biblical critics who build up expertise in history, philology, theology and so on, and seek to induct others into the club, has little to offer the unlettered masses.[43] It is cast as a Western phenomenon of strictly limited value to genuinely contextual interpretation. The latter finds its roots in the base communities: in groups of believers sharing the scriptures in the light of their human experience, finding their voice and learning to 'name their world'.[44] It is in historical (that is, contemporary) experience that God is found and human transformation effected. Such spirituality, being itself grounded in historical experience, does not disintegrate into individualism, but involves action, a 'liberating commitment' to the poor and oppressed, and a solidarity with the marginalised and the victims of the system.[45]

Gradually, the inherent interpretive process was better articulated. Leonardo and Clodovis Boff summarise leading features of liberation hermeneutics: people are more important than theological explanation, and the latter should serve the former; human transformation is central to the process; and the Bible is read or reread in the context of moral and political concern.[46] As liberation theology and praxis developed, more systematic accounts of the underlying hermeneutical process began to appear.

Clodovis Boff analysed the hermeneutical process in some detail, understanding interpretation as a dynamic process in which biblical meaning emerges in community. It is no longer a question simply of the meaning created for the original audience, long since removed from the scene. The concern is now with a new reading in a new setting, with new life concerns pressing in, and with the generation of new meaning. This freedom, as Mesters also noted, can be abused: for example, when the Bible is manipulated to underwrite norms acceptable in particular circles for other reasons (Boff has certain kinds of fundamentalism in view here, though the point has a wider application), or when an oversimplified correspondence is established between biblical motifs and modern cases (as in some forms of liberation theology, where identification may be enthusiastic, but uncritical). This latter point is particularly significant for interpretation. It inhibits the drawing of facile parallels between, say, Jesus and ourselves: such as – if Jesus was a pacifist, we should be pacifists; if Jesus was a zealot, we should be zealots! This kind of interpretation does not pay due regard either to the particularities of the ancient or the modern context.

A genuinely contextual model, as Boff is at pains to demonstrate, will indeed attempt to see Jesus in dynamic relation to the context of his own times, as we tried to do in the last chapter, and will insist that the community's theological understanding of the text takes due account of that dynamic. It will also relate its theological reflection on the text to the sociological comprehension of its own context. Thus there is a distancing of ourselves from the text in order to see the dialectic within it, and also an identification with the dynamics of the text (not in isolation, but with awareness of it as a biblical theme) as we bring it to bear on our modern situation, of which we need the fullest possible understanding. It is thus that we acquire 'hermeneutic competence', discernment 'according to the mind of Christ' or 'the Spirit' for the new situations which no rule of thumb can settle. Here is a model, an orientation towards praxis in the name of Christ. It rests on a 'correspondence of relationships' which expresses and channels the element of analogy implicit in all hermeneutics and it relates the correlation to the dynamics within the text.[47] There is a consequent praxis element in which our transformed understanding is expressed.

J. S. Croatto has pursued the matter even further, drawing on linguistics and semiotics, and making much of the distinction between diachronic and synchronic exegesis.[48] He is thus at home with notions of polysemy and multiple meanings, which can be illustrated in diachronic perspective by the changes of meaning which occur in the course of history. Synchronic exegesis engages with the text as a whole in order to find meaning and to discover new interpretations. He works with the notion of event, of word interpreting the event, and of the creation of a reservoir of meaning around it – three stages of a 'circular dialectic'. A new question put to the text unfolds a surplus of meaning to readers far removed from the original readers in time and situation.

There are undoubtedly insights here which could be used to illumine the relation of ethics and interpretation. As Fuchs and Ebeling showed, the word which itself interprets event creates a new 'word event' through the encounter of text and interpreter.

It is this 'word event' which taps into the surplus of meaning so that each reading of the text is a reinterpretation, a voyage of discovery, a generation of new meaning. Yet the original text is never thrown away. It remains active as testimony to the power of the original event which is realised afresh through community involvement with it.

INTERPRETATION AND ETHICS

Convergence on community

Liberation ethics has always been based in communities, and J. L. Segundo has supplied it with a convincing ecclesiological understanding.[49] Feminism has produced women's groups, and in its Christian form has evinced hermeneutical concern. One of the more notable initiatives in recent Western Christian ethics has been its emergence from captivity to academic moral philosophy, and its attempt to recover an interactive community base.[50] Christian community has an inherent concern for ethics in that it enshrines and witnesses to the Christian *way of life* as the bedrock of its existence. It is therefore, by definition, a moral community, or a community of moral concern for its own members and the world in which it is set; and it is also a hermeneutical community, gathered round word and sacrament. This grounding of hermeneutics and ethics in community can be extended further in three directions.

(i) Christian community is capable of further definition in terms of its eucharist and worship. The eucharist relates to memory and story, but intrinsically it celebrates the sharing of life: God with us and for us. It affirms acceptance, forgiveness and reconciliation, and establishes community. It is for the world, in intercession and loving service. Hence the eucharistic orientation, like worship itself, is deeply moral, reaching down into motivational roots and sustaining service.

(ii) Christian community enshrines the ministry of word and sacrament. Worship is divine–human communication in varied dimensions. If the sacrament is the climax of worship, the ministry of the word is its centre-piece. The latter is more than the reading of scripture; it is encountering realms of meaning which do not proceed from ourselves and which, by setting our actions and aspirations in the perspective of the Other, redirect our way and chasten our spirit. Indeed, one can speak of the hermeneutics of worship, in which encountering otherness is the central feature. Christian worship in its fullness (admittedly not always achieved) combines prophetic word and priestly action in community. Hence, while it may be true in practice that the church's prophetic message is largely proclaimed by individuals, it is a misrepresentation and impoverishment of Christian worship to exclude the prophetic element from the understanding of liturgical practice or to marginalise it. The consequences are important for ethics. In place, the ministry of the word supplies a prophetic challenge. Its exclusion or marginality opens the way to collusion with cultural values.

(iii) Christian identity is expressed in Christian story. Christian memory is integral to word and sacrament, through which it emerges into the present. Christian ethics not only relates to community story and personal narrative, it stands precisely at the intersection of the two. Here is another way of conceiving of the correlation of horizons, the faithful community being itself the catalyst. Narrative theology has had its champions and its detractors in recent years. It has seemed to make sweeping claims which ignored the need to clarify concepts. The strongest claim for narrative (if not narrative theology) is that it expresses a fundamental aspect of Christian identity and community memory, and has thus a clear role to play in Christian ethics.[51]

Increasingly, Western, feminist and liberation ethics are seen to have much in common: a sense of community, a concern for justice and power sharing (each according to its vision), a willingness to welcome the social sciences into the process of reflection, and a distinctive view of the future in terms of hope and transformation. But there are also severe tensions.

Worlds in collision

Liberation ethics, it should be remembered, stems from the socio-historical context of Latin America, and has achieved expression world-wide, wherever the cry of the marginalised, the victims, or the poor is heard. Feminist ethics can be regarded as part of the liberation scene, although its base-line is distinctive and it emerged from Western experience. Both movements are well situated to pose the most radical questions about the system which has so evidently depersonalised and marginalised many people. To this extent they contrast with the prevailing character of Western ethics, which has traditionally analysed norms, virtues and values, treasured its 'autonomy', considered the 'social determinants' of ethics and even endorsed the importance of community, but has not consistently questioned – sometimes it has even expressly affirmed – 'the system'.[52]

To promote dialogue, the contrast has been set out vigorously by M. Vidal in a series of antitheses:

(i) Western autonomous ethics is bourgeois: the moral projection of the aspirations of the dominant economic group. Liberation ethics is ethics 'from below'.

(ii) Western autonomous ethics fosters an individualistic ethics, which evinces a kind of rational arrogance and endorses self-sufficiency and progress through competitiveness, while discounting the human cost. Liberation ethics is an ethics of grace and expresses human solidarity.

(iii) Western autonomous ethics gives priority to rational reflection at the expense of the narrative aspect, which comprises the 'moral memory' of the people. Liberation ethics recalls the people to their own story and enables them to find their voice again.

(iv) Perhaps most seriously of all, western autonomous ethics has produced an excessive conformity to the modern world. Liberation ethics gives back to Christian ethics its prophetic, even messianic, role.[53]

Feminist ethics may be associated with liberation values here, with some qualifications. If feminist perspectives are 'from below', they are so in a slightly different way (for example, in relation to cultural origins and often in social class), but they champion the underclass who, by reason of their gender, suffer oppression and discrimination in a male dominated world. Feminist ethics tends to regard the Western competitive ethic as expressing male aggression, and emphasises personal values such as compassion, gentleness and community in an aggressive and violent world. It articulates women's story, and seeks fundamental change in the power structures. F. M. Réjon has pointed the contrast in a slightly different way. For him, the autonomous ethics of the modern West is:

progressivist rather than new; *elitist* in the type of questions it tackles; *idealist*, in that it points to goals but ignores the means of reaching them; *privatising*: not so much individualist now, but personalist, arguing about concepts such as dialogue-encounter, but not those like domination-dependence; *functionalist*: its interlocutor is the modern-bourgeois world, which it legitimises, not the world of the poor and the people...[54]

There is powerful advocacy here, and reply could be made at least to some points, although it is important not to be side-tracked. Vidal himself, while admitting the moral character of liberation theology, complained that liberation ethics has never been systematically formulated. The result, he suggests, is confusion: faith is reduced to moral demand, and religious sanction may be given to worldly decisions (significantly, the example given is the 'sacralisation' of left-wing politics). There may be at times a political naïvety: a refusal to see both sides of the equation. The same criticism could, at times, be made of Barth and Niebuhr! But liberation ethics refuses to be domesticated by Western assumptions. The insistence on the sharp division between moral and theological reason may well be as invalid as the old divide between dogmatic and moral theology; while to speak of liberation ethics as resting on the 'clichés of Christian orthopraxis' is notably imperceptive. There is an holistic integrity about liberation ethics (at its best) which deserves to be recognised. One could also take issue with the sharp distinction Réjon draws between the personalist and the public, between dialogue and the acceptance of domination. At least some Western ethicists have attempted to relate personalism, interactionism and political concern, without sensing a contradiction in their procedures,[55] while modern paradigms reinforce the link between public dialogue and the possibility of change. Besides, the process of alienation has to be very advanced before one can reject outright one's obligation to the society in which one lives. Such a stance, however, is perfectly capable of being sharply critical and calling for change. Our central concern here, however, is with interpretation and ethics, a theme only indirectly represented in the strictures advanced above. One might observe that, while liberation ethics is rooted in biblical concern, there is sometimes evident a lack of distantiation which tends to narrow and absolutise the vision. Besides, without minimising the force of the criticisms (which are often all too justified), Western ethics is not monolithic: it is in fact extremely varied, and some sections of it have learned from the stronger points of liberation ethics.

E. Dussel, in his careful formulation of liberation ethics, distinguishes 'morality' – the prevailing moral order within the existing order of things – from 'ethics', which he relates to 'the future order of liberation'. He uses the term 'society' to denote the existing 'worldly' order of domination, as distinct from 'community' – 'the face-to-face relationship of persons standing in a relationship of justice'.[56] Echoing Revelation, he calls the prevailing social morality 'the "Babylon" principle'; it has been moulded within the structures of oppression and made to serve their interests. Hence, since the eighteenth century, 'natural law' has been assumed to safeguard private property, while 'the habit of amassing wealth fails to remind anyone of the usury or avarice of feudalism'.[57] By contrast, the 'Jerusalem principle' (cf. Rev. 21.1–4) represents the future, fulfilment, the praxis of love, true community, and its 'pull' is felt here and now. The Sermon on the Mount represents the ethics of the new age, contradicting the prevailing morality and setting forth the 'ethical' requirement which is 'absolute – valid in every situation and age'.[58] To some extent, old *cruces* of interpretation are re-emerging here, but the force of the ethical vision cannot easily be swept aside.

Sharing renewed vision

A disturbing feature of the present situation is the tendency to withdraw behind defensive walls, and thus to make dialogue impossible. It is seen – understandably – in the impatience of liberation ethics with Western paradigms. It is found – less excusably – in the dismissiveness often evinced in the West towards the liberation scene. Both camps require an element of negation, to challenge the limitations of their perspectives. Increased self-understanding and social awareness provide one corrective, while socio-historical perspectives on the text effect proper distantiation.[59] Through the negation there comes renewal of vision, not as a projection of one's own self-interest, but as given by the Other through the text. Thus biblical interpretation, following the process discussed above, is integral to the renewal of vision; and, in this multi-cultural world which we inhabit, the recovery of vision may be assisted by insights shared in community across the globe.

However, in the examples briefly worked out below, the aim is not so much to highlight this global interchange as to illustrate the interaction of biblical interpretation and Christian ethics in a selected cultural setting. For our purposes, that setting is mainly Europe in the second half of the momentous twentieth century, but global concerns have not been ignored, even if constraints of space prevent a fuller treatment.

HERMENEUTICAL RESPONSIBILITY

In this final section we bring the hermeneutical approach adumbrated above to the discussion of selected themes in Christian ethics: both those explicitly treated in the Bible and some not directly discussed there. The aim is not to sharpen our approach into an automatic tool. The subject matter is too varied, and biblical interpretation too much of an art, to allow such a procedure, even if we wanted it. Nor do we treat it as a case-study from a biblical interpretation group, although the importance of community in interpretation is underlined throughout. We take for granted that the basic movement in interpretation is from present praxis through interpretation to renewed praxis. The hub of the enterprise is the correlation with the biblical material – distantiation and its consequences – on which interpretation and reflection depend. The following six cameos (they can be no more) may serve to illustrate the range of possibilities and difficulties.

1 *Responsibility to the state*

Romans 13.1–7 is probably the most notorious *crux interpretum* in the New Testament. As John O'Neill has observed,

> These seven verses have caused more unhappiness and misery in the Christian East and West than any other seven verses in the New Testament by the licence they have given to tyrants, and the support for tyrants the Church has felt called on to offer as the result of Romans 13 in the canon.[60]

Any reading of the text today must take into account the fact that it has played a notorious part in twentieth-century politics. There is much scope for exploring the structures by which we are governed, the way in which they seek to shape our values, and the sense in which they serve a God-given purpose. There is scope also for having our ideas challenged by the story of the twentieth century and the ways in which religious attitudes were exploited by demonic regimes. These reflections represent the first two stages of the hermeneutical process.

The next step is to view the text in its context and to establish the dynamics which operate within it. E. Käsemann found Paul's dynamic in God's grace, rather than in any over-arching system of ethics or law. Paul's view of Christian behaviour is charismatic.[61] The grace and compassion of God (cf. Rom. 12.1) empower us to serve, even as Christ did. Political authority is a symbol of the transitory world, to which one discharges one's obligation. Even this, for Paul, has the character of charismatic service, 'a fragment of the Christian's worship of God in the secularity of the world'.[62] Käsemann's theological hermeneutic relies heavily on an interpretation of the wider context of this passage, rather than on its immediate context or inherent features. One wonders how far Käsemann is reading a theology of grace into Paul's position here.

This brings us to the question of correlation, as in the 'hermeneutics of correspondence'. Käsemann presented a critique of four common types of interpretation which got it wrong. Briefly, type one was the traditional Catholic metaphysic of the state, which deeply influenced Protestantism also.

Paul, however, was dealing not with the state in the abstract, but specifically with government officials – from tax collectors to magistrates. Type two was conservative Lutheranism, with its theology of 'orders' rooted in cosmic design. But Paul was not on this wavelength. He simply envisaged the 'ordinances' of the divine will and the functions of those in office. Social ethics has, therefore, to do with the service to be rendered to God in the contingencies of everyday life. It is important, Käsemann argued, to remain true to Paul's 'demythologising' of the contingent, for type three invested political authorities with the cosmic significance of 'principalities and powers', whether angelic or demonic.[63] There is no evidence for this in this text, and Käsemann reminds us of the part played by such interpretations in the *Kirchenkampf*.[64] Finally, type four was the Barthian affirmation of the lordship of Christ over the world (as in early Christian hymns): hence state and authorities are in a sense 'for' the faithful, and political responsibility is a Christian avenue of service. Yet seldom could this have been a reality for Christians of New Testament times, and the conditions are lacking which would allow Romans 13 to be transposed into the modern situation without distortion (such as the 'passive obedience' common in some forms of Protestantism). Interpretation must take full account of the differentiation of contexts. 'Earthly institutions and authorities cannot be grounded in Christology – only the community of believers and Christian activity.'[65] But are we not in fact talking about Christian activity in Romans 13? And would not Logos Christology – which, admittedly, is not Pauline – relate Christological understanding to the whole of creation?

Correlation is thus seen to be a critical factor. Perhaps it is better focussed when we turn to the question of submission in a hierarchically organised world where superiors and subordinates are facts of life. Paul had, in effect, accepted the conservative standpoint of the Diaspora synagogues, and his unrevised social attitudes are all too evident in relation to slavery and the equality of the sexes. He was concerned here only with the worldly order as an arena of Christian service. But interpretation cannot rest content simply with historical clarification, as if the question of content was irrelevant to us. There can be no question of simply reprocessing the social ethics of the apostle when some aspects of his stance have collapsed (slavery) and other parts are defective in argument (his defensiveness in relation to women in church). There is greater mileage in Paul's application of the concept of freedom to serve, and in his use of the term *syneidesis* ('conscience'), denoting critical awareness and self-awareness in relation to the moral issue. It is perhaps in Paul's recognition of the importance of the power structures, along with their possibilities for good (although power can always be misused), and his assertion both of freedom to serve and of conscience, that we find the creative correlation we need to pursue the issue today.

This takes us to the level of transformed praxis. Is there a limit to obedience? Käsemann's answer is that it ends only at the point where we cease to acknowledge Christ as Lord of the world (Christology returns!). Indeed, one needs discernment to judge between courses such as reactionary defensiveness, martyrdom, retreat into private religion – and the opportunity of the hour. Can the Christian participate in revolution? The option was not open to Paul: Käsemann ascribes it to modern democracy, although Calvin wrestled with the deposing of the tyrant. For Käsemann, the question is one of individual conscience and decision. It turns on whether the political authorities are creating a situation in which service is robbed of all meaning in the context of a nation's life. In Käsemann's judgment, these conditions obtained in the Third Reich, at least after Stalingrad. But do freedom and conscience constitute the dynamics of the Christian story and vision?

Käsemann's interpretation reflects an informed awareness of the hermeneutical process. He takes account (more fully than this brief review permits) of the horizon of paraenesis in an eschatological context, registers lessons from the history of interpretation, identifies important issues in Paul's moral discourse and discusses the implications of reading this passage today in the context of Christian social ethics. But when all is said and done, Käsemann's discourse retains the characteristics and limitations both of liberalism and existentialism. Central to it are ideas of freedom, critical awareness, the transitory nature of the world, and charismatic service. The issue of revolution is discussed with the detachment of the academic seminar. Although the discussion appears to take seriously both ancient and modern contexts, in fact it does not penetrate in any depth into the context of Paul's paraenesis,[66] nor does it go beyond general policy in relation to the modern. Indeed, it illustrates how difficult it is for modern Western scholars, shaped by the Western intellectual tradition (and therefore liberal, academic, bourgeois, existentialist, Protestant or Catholic), to transcend the limitations of individualistic ideology, even through community faith ethics, and to take on board a structural understanding of society and the forces which determine and define the horizons of human experience.

At the very least, this passage needs to be discussed within an interactive community which proceeds to consider not only how its members may discharge their responsibilities day by day, but also how far the existing structures could be said to fulfil a purpose within the divine economy, how far they serve the interests of the dominant class (in social, economic, gender or racial terms), and how they could become more democratic, more accountable and better channels of God's righteousness, so that they might indeed be 'God's agents working for your good': and what action the community and its members might take towards this end. Thus we would reach more convincingly to Christian praxis dynamically related to Christian story and vision.

2 *Social ethics: the family*

The family has had a prominent place in Christian ethics and church teaching, particularly since the Reformation. Many still see it as the linchpin of society and, in a spirit of bravado or helplessness, blame the troubles of society on its breakdown. A modern Christian ethicist such as Hauerwas would make it a pivot of Christian social teaching today, and most church leaders agree. Sociologists have described families as primary groups in society, mainly because of their fundamental role in socialisation. Sprott called the family the 'natural' group.[67] The interpreter's pre-understanding may thus be naïvely positive towards family life, although many experience its breakdown, and challenges can be made to it in the name of ethics. It is therefore important to note that pre-understanding may be affected by the stereotype of the family to which the interpreter inclines. Families have, in fact, varied from clan proportions to the 'nuclear' family of modern industrial society, and each has its strengths and weaknesses which should be explored in discussion and by analysis. The element of prejudice as pre-judgment has to be recognised and controlled, as in Groome's first two movements.

As far as correlation goes, the fact that the New Testament may have a decentring effect in this case at least helps to focus the issue. Jesus inherited the tradition of strong family life, which had its roots in the Hebrew clan system and was built into the social fabric of Israel and Judaism; but he stood apart from it in important respects, applying the metaphor of the family to the community of the faithful and committing himself to the disciple group as the significant unit. A series of questions confronts the interpreting community. Is this factor to be ascribed to eschatological distortion? Is Jesus a 'special case'? Does his action sanction alternatives to family life, such as a religious community? Does it not, at least, put a question-mark against the unqualified endorsement of family life, especially in its 'bourgeois' form, which emerges so often from Christian circles? Or should we make more of the fact that Jesus did not apparently break all contacts with his family? (Some members may be prompted to reflect here on the activities of some sects in removing young people from their families.) Such correlations, even when negative, open the way for a re-evaluation of our story and vision.

The process can be taken further. In Pauline and post-Pauline circles, the family structure is affirmed, but in such culture-specific terms that once again the interpreter is faced with a problematic scenario. The so-called house tables (or *Haustafeln*) express the Diaspora patterns of two thousand years ago, minimally adapted for use in Christian communities. The family unit is the household, which includes slaves and endorses patriarchy. Wives are to be subject to their husbands, who should treat them with love rather than exert violent authority. Only in Ephesians, with its Christology of the family, is mutuality in relationship recognised (Eph. 5.28, 33), although this is perhaps close to Paul's own view (cf. 1 Cor. 7.3–4). Children have to be similarly submissive; fathers restrained in their discipline. Slaves should perform their servitude to the glory of God; masters should treat them fairly; any imbalance will be redressed on judgment day! (The group might consider why the young churches adopted this model, and how far it compromised their moral stance.)

The next step is to read the Bible in a more theologically creative way. One can not only develop the Christological understanding in Eph. 5.21–33, where an analogy is drawn between the love of man and woman and the love of Christ for his church, but one can take Gen. 1.26–7 and Mark 10.6 to proclaim 'in the beginning is the couple!' and to argue, with E. Fuchs, that the image of God in humankind is the desire for the other.[68] Conversely, when the integrity of the other is not respected, violence and oppression result (even the *Haustafeln* indicate the need to counter this ambivalence). Hence, the family can become the locus of strife, for freedom has its obverse in entrapment, fidelity in prevarication, conjugality in alienation, authority in violence and so on. A reading on these lines avoids the danger of absolutising culturally determined norms, and provides a context for further reflection.[69]

Christian tradition beyond the Bible is also an important factor. Arguments based on natural law, for example, have attempted to base the hierarchical and patriarchal structure of the family on the order of creation and the natural characteristics of man and woman. The 'sacramental' view of marriage is problematic on several scores. One set of interpretive problems was enunciated by Erasmus,[70] while another rests on an apparent discounting of relational features: 'The presence or absence of love is of no significance for the canonical continuance of a marriage entered into in this sacramental sense.'[71] However, modern Catholic writers such as B. Häring and K.

Rahner emphasise the role of conscience and the quality of relationships. The Lutheran counterpart of the natural-law view rested on the 'orders of creation', which took family, like state and occupation, to be part of God's design. Marriage functioned, according to Luther, to restrain sexual appetite, to procreate children and for Christian nurture. Bonhoeffer opted for the term 'mandates': one is obliged to express Christian obedience through these forms. This left room for a 'relational' or 'personalist' understanding.

So intimate is the theme for the interpreter that biblical correlation spills over readily into the renewing of our story and vision. Other material is relevant. The family is of socio-political importance: hence any view of it today must submit to sociological scrutiny. The traditional, affirmative view sees the family as a bulwark of freedom (for example, against the state); as the seat of paternal authority; as endorsing community values such as cohesion, kinship and positive healthy relationships; and as the procreator of future generations and thus fundamental to nation and race. The *Haustafeln* relate fairly convincingly to this scenario. The weaknesses of this view revolve around questions of social context (suggesting an oversimplified and stereotypical understanding), of individual needs (individuals vary and are disadvantaged if their needs and interests do not coincide with the stereotypes), and of ethical critique. Loyalty to the family concept may induce uncritical views which do not recognise that the family is a unit of self-interest which can be manipulated for political or other ends.

Feminism provides a powerful critique of all this. Feminist perspectives have tended to see the family as a bastion of oppressive socialisation and persistent gender stereotypes. Some feminists view it as an adjunct of capitalism, while more generally the family is seen as the setting in which radical changes in roles, expectations and personal consciousness must be effected to express mutuality in relationships. Some of these criticisms are themselves culture specific, and only some cultures allow space to challenge stereotypes. Nevertheless, feminist critiques are far reaching, and are perhaps best seen in the context of the search for liberation – for a new humanness –

which does not relate to one gender only, but underlines the feminine contribution.[72]

As far as the family is concerned, biblical interpretation can play a manifold ethical role in renewing vision. In critically assessing family values in the Bible (not least, in the New Testament), it can draw attention to the fact that *all* versions of family life and structure are relative to socio-historical context. It can thus not only point to the positive aspects of the family in the New Testament and elsewhere, but can also compare and assess goals for family development. Jesus' practice at least raises the possibility of alternative forms of familial community. Sometimes these are essential: for shelter, for service, for therapy, for devotion, for witness. Generally, however, the family is affirmed, with its strengths and weaknesses, but with an eschatological horizon. It can be much more than it is.

3 Sexual ethics: homosexuality

Homosexuality is selected here not only because it is a substantial issue in itself, but also because it illustrates in dramatic fashion the problem of the 'two worlds' for biblical interpretation. So acute is the problem that the complete hermeneutical process outlined above is difficult to effect in full. In group discussion, the initial aim is to dispel ignorance, to open up a wider understanding and to foster sympathy with those existentially concerned with the issue. Thereafter, the hermeneutical priority is to establish a proper correlation with the biblical texts.

Texts are sometimes cited in condemnation of homosexuality. Such attempts encounter the problem of definition. In the biblical world(s), whatever the term denotes is condemned without question. In the modern world(s), a totally different understanding is put forward by social scientists. Homosexuality is not a disease or disability, but a minority sexual orientation (2–10 per cent). The ambiguity of the term is noted. 'Few people pass through life without experiencing homosexual feelings, even if only slight and fleeting.'[73] A homosexual phase is often regarded by social scientists as a normal part of adolescent development, and problems in this area are ascribed to cultural intolerance. Why should a substantial minority of the population be described as 'psychologically, criminally or medically abnormal'?[74] In the same vein, R. Scroggs concludes:

> The *fact* remains... that the basic model in today's homosexual community is so different from the model attacked by the New Testament that the criterion of reasonable similarity of context is not met. The conclusion I have to draw seems inevitable: *Biblical judgments against homosexuality are not relevant to today's debate.*[75]

Before jumping to conclusions, we need to enquire what the various texts say in their own context, and whether the process of biblical interpretation has anything to offer in this connection.

Concern about homosexual behaviour took different forms in various epochs of biblical history. In the Holiness Code, the Hebrew tradition censured homosexual acts (Lev. 18.22) and even invoked the death penalty (Lev. 20.13). Like bestiality, sorcery and the sacrifice of seed to Molech, homosexual acts appear to be connected with idolatry. Certainly, when it encountered Greek culture, the Hebrew tradition maintained its strong opposition to such acts, especially in so far as they involved pederasty,[76] describing such practices as 'contrary to nature' – the terminology owes a debt to Stoicism. Thus, as Countryman argues, 'from being a largely theoretical dimension of the purity code, disapproval of homosexual acts... became a day-to-day defining characteristic of Jewish culture'.[77]

Paul's sweeping characterisation of Gentile culture as idolatrous (Rom. 1.22–32) was in line with this whole tradition, and homosexual acts (male and female) were simply an expression of typical Gentile error and uncleanness. The same is true of the sweeping list of vices in 1 Corinthians 6.9f., which includes the problematic phrase *oute malakoi oute arsenokoitai*. Scroggs took this to denote the passive and active partners in the homosexual act, and Boswell as 'male sexual agents' and their clients (not necessarily male!). Scroggs argued that the juxtaposition of *pornois* and *arsenokoitais* in 1 Timothy 1.10 was parallel to the phrase in 1 Corinthians 6.9, but the context is, in fact, yet another long list of vices. Perhaps interpretation should remain true to the derivation of the word *arsenokoitēs* as indicating the perpetrator of homosexual acts, and simply note that it perpetuates the Hebraic attitude stemming from Leviticus, whether reflected in rabbinic usage or not, and depicting typical Gentile impurity. The most significant statement Paul makes is that even *malakoi* and *arsenokoitai* have been received into the Christian community, washed, sanctified and justified: 'and such were some of you'. (1 Cor. 6.11) Modern interpreters will note that conversion does not change one's physical being. What it does transform is one's motivation and self-understanding, and not least one's actions in relation to others.[78]

What all this amounts to is that it is difficult to find a precise correlation of ancient and modern horizons on this issue. How then can we suggest a new vision for today? It is one thing to observe a Judaeo-Christian clash with Hellenistic mores, although not all Hellenistic writers were on the devil's side! It is quite another to relate our reading of these texts to homosexuality as an issue in Christian ethics today. Our exegesis has not adopted the liberal strategem of arguing that the texts were actually dealing with pederasty, which could then be interpreted with relative ease for today. Equally, we shall not adopt the conservative strategem of assuming that, because the texts deal with homosexual actions, the attitude of Christians today must accord with that reflected, but not fully explained, two thousand years ago in a few scattered passages of the New Testament. That line is completely blocked by two factors. The first is that the practices differ sharply:

Ancient Greeks and Romans seem to have assumed that human beings are attracted sexually both to their own and the opposite sex. They could even debate the relative merits of the two types of love. The idea of the homosexual person as one who is exclusively or predominantly attracted to members of the same sex appears to have been unknown to them.[79]

The second is the related point that the modern understanding of the phenomenon is so radically different from that of the ancient world as to rule out direct appropriation of their attitudes. This is as true of understanding the basic biological processes as it is of psychological factors. In this sense, Scroggs is at least partly justified in ruling out the relevance of Biblical judgments for modern debates about homosexuality. In terms of the 'correspondence of relationships' hermeneutical model, there is no real correspondence!

Has Christian ethics, therefore, no biblical basis on which to build? Some moral and pastoral discussions seem to proceed as if this were so.[80] A contextual point which can be drawn from Paul's passages is that homosexuals (however defined) are included with all others, Jew and Greek alike, in their need of the transforming grace of God (and it is a blatant assumption that they must, or can, become heterosexual in the process!). This factor is the only genuine *tertium quid* in the hermeneutic engagement. In such extremes, the interpreter is obliged to place the hermeneutical transaction in a fiduciary context and affirm the common ground solely in terms of gospel understanding. Paul acted in good faith in affirming conventional wisdom in relation to the problematics of his context. We must act in good faith by expressing the gospel of God's grace in relation to the radically different situation of today. This does *not* mean that we affirm the whole range of contemporary attitudes to homosexuality, but that we appraise each aspect of the problem in the light of the gospel.

It would appear, therefore, that we require a reserve strategy, to be followed when the full model of biblical interpretation cannot be implemented – drawn from central biblical themes and related to praxis today.[81]

4   *The parable of the talents: ethics and economics*

There is a double purpose in looking at the parable of the talents in this context. The first is that it *is* a parable and it does exemplify the use of parable – even a controversial one such as this – to open issues and promote discussion. The second is that it relates to economics: a subject of great significance to North and South, as well as being highly controversial in the public mind. The first two interpretive movements in Groome's scheme are therefore invaluable as an approach.

Distantiation is the necessary prelude to correlation. The attitude of Jesus to wealth and wealth creation appears fairly consistent in its indifference and detachment, but he stood in a tradition of wealth creation through the harvesting of land and sea, crafts and marketing, and his ministry took place within parameters which forbade usury. His engagement with economics was therefore not through the medium of abstract theory, but through human involvement. Debt was a major factor in his society,[82] and his concern for people in their economic straits is above question. He asserted their worth in the sight of God in and through their poverty: 'the poor' qualified as a positive religious symbol in a way that the rich did not.[83] And he enacted the year of release, of the jubilee which God was declaring: for nothing less could break their captivity and suffering.[84]

No parable is more at the mercy of the interpreter's preunderstanding than the parable of the talents. R. M. Grant assumed that, as Jesus evinced detachment from the amassing of wealth, he was concerned with religion rather than economics. One could therefore drive a wedge between the gospel and the material realm, as if the latter was of little consequence. As a modern interpreter in a capitalistic society, Grant placed the parable in a similar context, taking the first two characters as fulfilling a proper role in wealth creation (and gaining the approbation of the landowner) and castigating the third and vocally rebellious slave for failing in his duty (to invest at a proper rate of interest). This is basic to Grant's attempt to develop an ethic of wealth creation based on scripture, reason and tradition.[85]

Several criticisms fall to be made. (i) *The separation of the religious and material* in Jesus' ministry will not stand. He is sensitive to the poor as victims of the system, who will receive massive compensation from God when Israel is restored! This system, therefore, cannot be built up uncritically into a Christian economic ethics. (ii) *The tradition is complex.* Political factors are of overriding importance in Luke. The landowner is a nobleman in quest of vassal power (Luke 19.12) – like Archelaus in 4 BC; the people are alienated from him and send a counter-petition (Luke 19.14) – as happened in Archelaus' case;[86] the two 'successful' servants obtain preferment (19.17, 19), while the third slave is a non-collaborator who, when confronted by the ruler with his newly confirmed political powers, attempts to express the fear which his regime engenders and to protest against the severity of his requirements (Luke 19.21): his fellow citizens even make a plea against the ruler's sentence (19.25). The wrath of authority comes down against the vocal slave and the rebellious subjects (19.26–7). However, running through this story are motifs from a rather different story based on a commission given by a departing trader to his employees. This motif is given clearer expression in Matthew 25.14–30, which turns on the contrast between the faithful servants and the third unfaithful one. The judgment falls on the unfaithful servant alone. It is difficult – and perhaps unnecessary – to find the 'original' form of the story. Luke's version may be an elaboration of the 'trader' form. Matthew's version may have simplified the narrative by omitting the political dimension and exaggerating the moralistic or 'spiritual' dimension. Both evangelists link the parable to the theme of the coming kingdom and Jesus' ministry in Jerusalem. In short, whichever narrative we read, we are faced with complexity. (iii) *The power structures reflected in the parable are not endorsed in it.* If this is clear in the political version, it also applies to the merchant version. The employer is still a hard man! In his parables, Jesus can conjure up pictures of the hard realities which ordinary people have to face. This is not to commend the systems which so distort human life.

   If the interpreter is reading this passage in the context of moral concern today, there is a fundamental option to be exercised. Does one read it 'from above', from a dominant position within the power structure; or does one read it 'from below', with concern for its effects on the people involved? To use it to present a theological justification of capitalism is to exercise the first option. Two considerations then arise. One is the question of the *consequences* of such an option, and whether they evince justice or injustice or are compatible with the gospel. One should take account not only of the benefits of wealth creation for some, but also the consequences of debt for others. The second is whether such a stance is compatible with the ethics of historical reading. Is the orientation of Jesus' ministry compatible with such a reading? Did not Jesus identify with those whose perspective was 'from below'? Did he not set all human activity in the context of the sovereign Lord who alone had the right to look 'from above?'

With a view to the rethinking of our own stories and the renewal of our vision, we refer here to the work of Bob Goudzwaard, a Dutch economist who clearly believes not only that freedom and justice are relevant to the economic and political realm, but also that the gospel is relevant to notions of freedom and justice.[87] Citing 'the deliberate effort to exclude the awareness of sin and injustice from the world of economics and politics' as 'in itself one of the root-causes of our present problems and miseries', he set forth the thesis that

the social, economic and political renewal of Europe stands or falls with our willingness to re-orient our social and economic life to other principles than a maximum rise in our standard of living, and to re-structure social-economic life to become a platform for the fulfilment of still vacant responsibilities.[88]

To mull over such claims is an important contribution to the correction and renewal of our vision.

5 *Ecological ethics: creation*

Ecological ethics has caught public imagination and aroused popular concern. Who does not know of the 'greenhouse effect', global warming, the breach in the ozone layer, the poisoning of rivers and oceans, acid rain, the felling of the rain-forests, radioactive waste, threats to species, population explosion, 'Greenpeace' and CFCs?[89] The ecological crisis is expressed in the terminology of Western technological society, and is largely its creation. It is the riposte of the natural order, one might say, to the technocratic imperialism of a culture which assumed that *homo faber* had the world at his disposal, to exploit and exhaust at will to fit his materialistic and expansionist goals. Paradoxes abound. Wealth creation has its cost; and we are all implicated, for our lives are sustained by the destructive culture we deplore!

Complicity is extended to Christianity. After showing the relation of modern science to natural theology, and modern technology to 'the Christian dogma of man's transcendence of, and rightful mastery over, nature',[90] Lynn White concluded that, if the powers thus afforded humankind are now out of control, 'Christianity bears a huge burden of guilt'.[91]

What 'correspondence of relationships' or 'correlation' can we find with biblical material? The key text (though not the only one) is Genesis 1.26–8, in which the central, but problematic, concepts are the creation of human beings in the 'image' and 'likeness' of God, their 'dominion' over the created order and its 'subjection' to them and perhaps even the command to be fruitful and multiply. Etymological forays are not reassuring. 'Image' and 'likeness' are extraordinary words for a Hebrew writer to use in this connection, for the terms are normally used to indicate the unacceptability of idols as images and the impossibility of finding an adequate likeness to God.[92] The text is literally a shocker, making its point in daring language. The term 'to have dominion' is no less perplexing ecologically: the word means 'dominate' or 'lord it over', while 'subdue' literally means 'trample on'! And the command to 'be fruitful and multiply' is not qualified by a specific limitation. A non-contextual, literalistic misreading of this text could itself spell ecological disaster!

How then does one find the context and overcome the literalism? Socio-historical context is not particularly helpful here: it could only refer to the context of the author, about whom we know nothing. The most meaningful context is found through intertextuality: relating the text to other relevant texts in the Hebrew Bible. Here we find the paradox of humankind. On the one hand, there is spiritual status: 'a little lower than the angels' – a phrase rightly interpreted only when related to the graciousness of God: 'O Lord, our Lord, how majestic is thy name in all the earth!' (Ps. 8). On the other hand, we are dust, clay, breath or vanity; as transient as grass or flowers; suffering from the weakness of the flesh and beset by troubles. Here, then, is the paradox of humankind: exalted above all creation, made for communion with God, yet inexorably part of the created order, destined to return to the dust whence we came. If humankind is exalted in the Bible, it is also cut down to size.

Genre is another important consideration which helps to correct literalism. The Genesis passage uses word pictures, elements of story and folk literature which have their own rhetorical strategy and purpose. As the pictures pass before us in succession, almost like a children's frieze, we are carried through the wondrous unity of creation which embraces humankind (in the latter part of the sixth day!) and culminates in the sabbath on the seventh day when God rested and all creation was in perfect harmony.[93]

In the New Testament, the Prologue of John's Gospel not only echoes creation as it introduces the Logos, but strikingly proclaims the Logos as active in creation (John 1.1–5). It was the Logos, the life and light of humankind, who became incarnate in Jesus Christ (John 1.14–18). Hence, at the heart of the gospel there resides the profoundest respect for creation, so that its 'sabbath' – its perfect harmony, its *shalom* – is restored through the Logos, incarnate in Jesus. (Heb. 4.4, 9) Conventional interpretation therefore summons to faith and obedience (Heb. 3; 12–4.11); but obedience to the Creator involves respect for all creation.

Returning to the creation story, we recall that 'dominion' in the Hebrew tradition was exercised by kings as the vassals of God. It was not an absolute power (only Yahweh is truly sovereign), still less a permit to destroy at will; it was a responsibility, a stewardship of that which was entrusted to them by Yahweh, God of Israel. This is a useful concept, as long as it is remembered that we who are given this trust are also part of the creation: just as the Logos who became flesh for us and for our salvation is the Logos active in, and sustaining, the creation of the world. There is, therefore, an affinity with the created order which requires to be underlined. We are part of the creation that is entrusted to us. If we diminish it we diminish ourselves. If we poison it, we ourselves drink of the poisoned chalice.

Correlation of horizons has already passed into the question of our story and vision. If, with White, we take Francis as the patron saint of ecologists,[94] we do not go the whole way with him in laying the ecological disaster at the door of Christianity. The latter is implicated particularly insofar as it encouraged Christians to believe that the world was a gift of God's providence to be used for human benefit and profit. But there is more to it than this. The classical strain, with its indifference to matter, also informed the Age of Enlightenment, which, in its turn, affirmed the dominance of rational mind over matter. The result was the alienation of our personal and physical worlds.

The personal and physical universes we inhabit have been so divorced that the morality we should adopt to our world is a matter of scandal and confusion. Understanding is so divorced from questions of our being and that of the world that we are seeing a mindless rape of nature in the interests of short-term human gain. This divorce of the natural and moral universes is perhaps the worst legacy of the Enlightenment, and the most urgent challenge facing modern humankind.[95]

Never was there a greater need for renewed vision and for a new way of understanding our own story. It is unlikely that technology alone can solve our problems for us. A transformation of lifestyle, involving a much greater awareness of our interdependence with nature, is a priority. With renewed confidence, we can point to the spiritual malaise of humankind as the root of the problem.

6   *Racism: anti-Semitism*

In our final cameo, we focus on the moral evil of racism in its anti-Semitic (that is, anti-Jewish) form. Preliminary reflection should recall the horrors of the holocaust, the most striking single manifestation of the evil of racism – indeed, of evil itself – in modern times. One might look at the sociological and psychological factors involved, particularly in view of the persistence of racism in its many different forms. Then, in preparation for the biblical correspondences, we have to face the unpalatable fact of Christian collusion in anti-Semitism. As B. E. Olsen has put it, 'Hitler's pogrom was but the crown and pinnacle of a long history of hatred toward the Jew, participated in (if not initiated) by those whose duty it was to teach their children the truths of Christianity!'[96] Even more disconcerting is the suggestion that the evil can be traced to the New Testament itself, although all reasonable critics agree that it is foreign to the gospel of Jesus. Hence it is particularly important in this case to identify the dynamics at work in the biblical material. But first let us ask how Christianity could ever have fuelled the flames of anti-Semitism.

Anti-Semitism has deep roots which antedate Christianity but were nurtured on its soil.[97] Jules Isaac, a Jew deeply affected by the holocaust yet an advocate of reconciliation, pointed to three main themes in the propagandistic 'teaching of contempt', which suggested that the dispersion of the Jews was a providential punishment, or alleged degeneracy in Judaism at the time of Jesus, or spoke of the death of Jesus in terms of deicide.[98] Socio-historical criticism goes some way towards undermining propaganda, which appeals to unthinking prejudice. The Diaspora, which existed before the crucial dates (CE 70 and 132), represented (according to Isaacs) a progressive impoverishment of Palestinian Judaism rather than a definitive dispersion;[99] critical scholarship has served to show the vitality of the Judaism of the first century;[100] and the allegation of deicide is a pernicious spin-off from later doctrine. The tragic course of the twentieth century has shown that 'the scapegoat is with us still; the flow of blood – Jewish blood – is still unstaunched'.[101]

In such a context, the story of the death of Jesus must be told today with sensitivity. Socio-historical criticism goes some way to illumining Jesus in his times. He was a Jew, living and teaching in a Jewish environment. His message – concerning the nearness, the reality of the kingdom of God – was controversial and divisive as existing institutions and conventional understanding came under ultimate review. He marks the point of division between those who accepted his message and those who did not; and this factor colours the subsequent accounts of controversies which have led to a manifestly unfair popular assessment of the Pharisees in particular, which requires critical redress.[102] Apologetic has tended to hold the Jewish authorities mainly to blame for Jesus' death, and to minimise Roman involvement: again, a balance must be struck. But the real problem centres on how the Passion narrative is told. The telling of it in the gospels is probably influenced by later controversy, leading Mark in particular to emphasise the charge of blasphemy brought against Jesus (Mark 2.7; 14.64). By the time Mark wrote, to confess Jesus as Christ might well bring Christians before a Roman law court; and in this situation they correlated their situation with that of the story of Jesus' trial, at which Jesus himself makes 'the good confession' (Mark 14.61-2). This fact influenced the tenor of the gospel accounts. The hub of the matter for today is to see the death of Jesus not merely as the particular sin of those directly involved (although the historical contours of the event are not in dispute) but, much more importantly, as the sin of humankind; just as the sublime forgiveness, which may also be found in it, may be seen as an expression and fulfilment of that ministry of vicarious suffering so memorably articulated in the servant image in Deutero-Isaiah and realised, at least to some extent, in the historical experiences of Israel itself.

In reading the New Testament one has to identify the dynamics of particular passages in their context, and to note their embeddedness in that context. It was part of the rhetoric of anti-Judaism in early Christianity to speak sweepingly and deprecatingly of 'the Jews'. Even Paul, a thoroughgoing Jew, is apparently affected by it in an apocalyptic passage in 1 Thessalonians (2.13–16);[103] yet he would wrestle throughout his ministry with the problem of the *Torah* now that God has sent his Son (Ga. 4.4–5) and with the bitter fact that so many Jews did not accept Jesus as Christ (cf. Rom. 9–11). His hope and belief remained strong that in the end 'the whole of Israel will be saved' (Rom. 11.26), just as 'in Christ there is neither Jew nor Greek...' (Gal. 3.28). In interpreting this issue, we must carefully distinguish the socio-historical features which belong to the ancient horizon from the thrust of the gospel, to which we can correlate our horizon. Thus we may be able, in Rosemary Reuther's words, 'to drop this "left hand" of anti-Judaism '[104] and hear the authentic claim of the gospel of God's reconciling love. And it is not Christians alone who speak this language. As we reconsider our story and vision, we do well to heed the words of a Jewish writer:

Confronted with a world which for two centuries now has set itself against the word of God, *per se*, to a degree which increases terrifyingly, the church and Israel – each in its proper way and in its place – have a common witness to bear; at *all* times, even contrary to appearances, God remains king over the whole earth.[105]

V   CONCLUDING COMMENTS: SOCIO-HERMENEUTICS

Throughout this study we have presupposed a biblically informed spirituality characterised by moral and religious concern. Interpretation involves reading the biblical text in its socio-historical context and discerning the dynamics at work within the text itself. It involves focussing on the religious and moral issue, and relating dynamic and issue to the gospel of Christ.

Interpreters are, of course, part of a chain of Christian interpretation extending throughout the centuries into modern times. There can, indeed, be meaningful dialogue between ourselves and interpreters who have gone before us, with whose judgments we may agree or disagree in terms of the faithfulness to the dynamics of text and gospel. Our biblically informed spirituality has, therefore, theological, as well as hermeneutical, dimensions, which are themselves indebted to interpretive experiences: both our own and others', positive and negative, in our contemporary setting and down the ages.

Correlation, or 'correspondence in relationships', between the horizons of our world and those of the text, is a key factor in interpretation. Imperfect correlation is almost bound to be tendentious: as in the 'modernising' of Jesus and the 'domestication' of the Bible. A proper correlation is dependent on 'distantiation', the differentiation of worlds so that each of them is treated with integrity; but it also involves the participation of the interpreter in the dynamics of the text, and theological reflection on issues arising from it. Without presumption, the interpreter may join in a dialogue about the adequacy or otherwise of the treatment of an issue in given texts and contexts: the primary criterion being the gospel of Jesus Christ. The text may be 'culture bound', to a greater or lesser extent. It may be situationally constricted and thus express the gospel less than fully when related to other contexts. It may even be theologically objectionable – as in the case of the slaughtering of the Amalekites or vengeance on the children of Israel's enemies. If carelessly correlated to the modern situation, a text might be morally objectionable: for example, if it were used to stir up prejudice, racism or sexism, to justify violence or war, or to further human greed and power.

If the gospel is the main criterion, the Christian ethicist dare not lose sight of the 'story' of Jesus; yet this 'story' is itself the product of the interpretation of texts, and therefore part of the process under discussion here. The intersection of Jesus' 'story' and our stories is, of course, dependent on the 'correspondence of relationships'. Throughout this book, we have surveyed various responses to these problems: from the liberals' eternal principles (one attempt at correlation), through the various encounters with the eschatological, and especially the 'word' or 'kerygma', to the more recent literary and socio-historical approaches. The view we have advocated may be tentatively termed the socio-hermeneutical.

Socio-hermeneutics presupposes the conjunction of the social and the hermeneutical, in ancient and modern contexts. It draws on the resources of academic scholarship and the insights of devotion and worshipping communities, as does theology at its best. It involves people, not simply ideas and logic: hence it may not be reduced, without remainder, to philosophical principles, whether of hermeneutics or morality. It also underlines the intrinsic relationship between biblical interpretation and Christian ethics. Interpretation involves ethics; texts raise moral issues; ethics considers the treatment of such issues, in ancient and modern settings; interpreters consider the moral consequences of their interpretations.

Socio-hermeneutics involves growth in religious and moral understanding, on the part of interpreters themselves and those instructed by them. At times, the process may be painful. An element of cognitive dissonance is part of the learning process: a disequilibrium, occasioned by critical studies or the widening of horizons, may characterise growth beyond 'first naïvety'. Immature instances have to be set aside: such as literalistic or uncritically authoritarian misunderstandings of tradition, whether biblical or moral. The support of a sympathetic interpretive community, whether academic or religious, is helpful in ensuring that people grow through this stage, with all the disturbances that may be involved, to a more mature faith and renewed vision.

Biblical interpretation and Christian ethics are both concerned with the transcendent in human life. The Other – the transcendent reality whom we encounter in the Bible – is beyond our imagining or control, and meets us in Christ as grace and judgment, as *kerygma* and completion. The human temptation is to make an attempt at control and thus reduce the threat or fear of the unconditioned, of genuine Otherness. Even when appeal is made to story, that story must be open to the Other: a witness to the moving of the transcendent God in love, mercy and judgment upon his creation. The Bible has, in fact, a rich variety of forms and genres, embracing narratives and poetry, confessions and creeds, concepts and principles, lifestyles and relationships, all reflecting the dimension of the transcendent, the Word enfleshed in Christ, and all of them potential contributors to interpretation and ethics.

Since all human endeavour, individual and corporate, takes place under God, interpretation and ethics are vitally concerned with the exercise of power on earth, and its bounds and consequences for people and for all creation. In this way the gulf which often separates personal and social ethics is overcome: they are separable but interrelated disciplines, both in theological and human terms. Moreover, since all human life is lived in social context, sociologically based disciplines are of obvious relevance to the understanding of ethics, and the ethicist can make use of them without capitulating to an imperious secularism which has so often accompanied them in the past. Christian ethics may thus generate an internal dialogue between disciplines as diverse as social sciences, language studies, history and hermeneutical/theological disciplines. In addition, it may create possibilities of dialogue, which may in part be ecumenical, as Christian ethicists in different continents deal with pressing moral issues, but should also be with the world in all its diversity. If nation is to speak peace unto nation, people must be encouraged to grow in trust and understanding, and to learn to be open with regard to their traditions and commitments. Dialogue does not presuppose a dissolution of commitment into a spurious neutrality, according to the dictates of a dogmatic secularism. Dialogue presupposes diversity and rejoices in mutual discovery of truth. Thus interpreter and ethicist are alike concerned to unveil a vision of reality, yet to do so in all humility, for others, too, have their insights. No human being or institution has a monopoly of truth, which is essentially a transcendent category. It may be appropriate, therefore, to sign off this exploration of interpretation and ethics in the words of the sage who hailed from the land of Uz:

> These are but the fringes of his power,
> and how faint the whisper that we hear of him!
> Who could comprehend the thunder of his might?
> (Job 26.14 *REB*)

Notes

INTRODUCTION

1 *Sermons, or Homilies, Appointed to be Read in Churches* (1562: rp. 1986), p. 1.
2 R. Detweiler and V. K. Robbins, 'From New Criticism to Post-structuralism: Twentieth-Century Hermeneutics', in S. Prickett (ed.), *Reading the Text: Biblical Criticism and Literary Theory* (1991), p. 274.
3 cf. E. Schüssler Fiorenza, 'The Ethics of Biblical Interpretation: Decentering Biblical Scholarship', *JBL*, 101/7 (1988), pp. 3–17.
4 For example, J. L. Houlden, *Ethics and the New Testament* (1973); J. T. Sanders, *Ethics in the New Testament*, (1975); W. Schrage, *The Ethics of the New Testament* (Eng. tr. 1988: German edn 1982); W. C. Kaiser, Jr., *Toward Old Testament Ethics* (1983); C. J. H. Wright, *Living as the People of God* (1983); B. C. Birch, *Let Justice Roll Down: The Old Testament, Ethics, and Christian Life* (1991).
5 cf. J. L. Houlden, *Ethics and the New Testament*, pp. 4–5. Houlden is countering the procedure adopted by R. Schnackenburg, *The Moral Teaching of Jesus* (1965): German rev. edn 1962.
6 cf. W. Schrage, *The Ethics of the New Testament, passim*.
7 E. Schüssler Fiorenza, *Bread Not Stone: The Challenge of Feminist Biblical Interpretation* (1984), p. 24.
8 cf. George Steiner, *Real Presences* (1989).
9 J. T. Sanders, *Ethics in the New Testament*, p. 130.
10 B. C. Birch, *Let Justice Roll Down*, p. 34. J. P. Wogaman, *Christian Ethics* (Westminster, 1993), pp. 2–15, 270–76, interprets the biblical legacy to ethics in terms of points of tension or conflicting tendencies.
11 The Hebrew scriptures can be studied in their own right as part of the history of religion, but they are also inseparable from Christian usage. It is in this latter connection that they claim the attention of this study.
12 cf. J. Reumann, *Variety and Unity in New Testament Thought* (1991), pp. 3–13 and *passim*, who takes 'faith in Jesus the Christ' as the key towards unity in reading the New Testament. Others have seen the

247

New Testament, collectively and in its separate parts, as a 'Jesus book': cf. C. F. D. Moule, *The Birth of the New Testament* (rev. 1981); J. D. G. Dunn, *Unity and Diversity of the New Testament* (1977).

13 S. Prickett, *Reading the Text* (1991) p. 1.

14 cf. J. Fletcher, *Situation Ethics* (1966); *Moral Responsibility*, (1967).

15 cf. R. Gill, *The Social Context of Theology* (1975); *Theology and Social Structure* (1977).

16 Iris Murdoch, *The Sovereignty of the Good* (1970).

17 cf. chapter seven below.

18 cf. C. Gunton, *Enlightenment and Alienation* (1985), who is much influenced by M. Polanyi, *Personal Knowledge: Towards a Post-Critical Philosophy* (1962).

19 In moral theology, B. Häring exemplifies the new biblical orientation, to which Vatican II gave notable impetus. Documents such as the US Catholic Bishops' pastoral letters have a sophisticated apparatus of biblical scholarship. Catholic tradition has always emphasised that biblical truth must be mediated through reason, and the social sciences are now given some prominence. See, for example, B. Häring, *The Law of Christ*, Ramsey, N.J. (1961–6); H. Schürmann and others, *Principles of Catholic Morality*, Dublin (1975), esp. pp. 18–30. J. Fuchs, *Christian Morality: the Word becomes Flesh*, Notre Dame, Ind. (1981); and C. E. Curran, *Towards an American Catholic Moral Theology*, Notre Dame, Ind. (1987).

PART ONE   PHILOSOPHICAL AND CRITICAL GROUNDWORK

1 C. Gunton, *Enlightenment and Alienation* (1985), p. 50.

2 cf. G. Davie, *The Scottish Enlightenment and Other Essays* (1991), *passim*.

3 W. Wordsworth, *The Prelude*, XI 108.

4 cf. Kant, 'Groundwork of the Metaphysic of Morals', in H. J. Paton (ed.), *The Moral Law, or Kant's Groundwork of the Metaphysics of Morals*, London (1969) p. 67; Immanuel Kant (1724–1804) hailed from East Prussia and was from 1770 to 97 Professor of Logic at Königsberg University. His principal work was *Der Kritik der reinen Vernunft* ('The Critique of Pure Reason'), 1781/87.

5 On historiography, see below. On the development of critical studies of the New Testament, cf. W. G. Kümmel, *The New Testament: the History of the Investigation of its Problems* (Eng. tr. 1973).

6 F. D. E. Schleiermacher (1768–1834), who moved in literary circles, was a skilled philologist and translated Plato, became

professor of theology at Berlin. In his addresses *On Religion: Speeches to its Cultured Despisers* (1799), he tended to emphasise the inward disposition of piety or pious self-consciousness. He published his greatest work, the *Christian Faith*, in 1821. His hermeneutical work was subsequently elaborated by Dilthey (see n. 19), who wrote a *Life of Schleiermacher*: but Dilthey is not a good guide to understanding Schleiermacher himself: cf. T. H. Curran, 'Schleiermacher: True Interpreter', and W. G. Jeanrond, 'The Impact of Schleiermacher's Hermeneutics on Contemporary Interpretation Theory', in D. Jasper (ed.), *The Interpretation of Belief: Coleridge, Schleiermacher and Romanticism* (1986).

7 S. Prickett, 'Romantics and Victorians', in *Reading the Text* (1991), p. 206.

8 cf. W. G. Kümmel, *The New Testament*, pp. 116–17.

9 See below, n. 19.

10 A. Ritschl (1822–89) held theology chairs at Bonn and Göttingen. His work, *Die christliche Lehre von der Rechtfertigung und Versöhnung* (1870–4) – Eng. tr. *The Christian Doctrine of Justification and Reconciliation* – effectively launched a new theological movement which counted Harnack and Herrmann among its adherents. Other books include *Christian Perfection* (1874) and *Instruction in the Christian Religion* (1875).

11 P. Hefner, *Faith and the Vitalities of History* (1966), p. 56.

12 Ritschl, *Instruction*, para., 48. Ritschl has been accused of distorting and diluting the biblical notion of the kingdom of God, virtually identifying it with the group of disciples. Yet Ritschl sharply differentiated between church and kingdom. Christians had a teleological orientation, a purpose beyond their community. He refused to adopt an organisational or institutional view of the kingdom, but spoke of it symbolically, as mustard seed or leaven; cf. B. M. G. Reardon, *Liberal Protestantism* (1968), pp. 26–8.

13 Richmond, *Ritschl: A Reappraisal*, London (1978), p. 241.

14 Auguste Comte (1798–1857) was the founder of historical positivism and 'the church of humanity': for a brief discussion, cf. S. Brown, *Secular Alternatives to Religion* ('Man's Religious Quest' Unit 22) (1978), pp. 20–5.

15 B. G. Niebuhr (1776–1831) was professor of history at the new University of Berlin, where Schleiermacher was a colleague, was active in Prussian politics and served as minister to the Holy See: for an assessment, cf. G. P. Gooch, *The Cambridge Modern History XII*, (1910), pp. 819–21.

16 L. von Ranke (1795–1886), the proponent of objectivity, was described by Gooch as 'beyond comparison the greatest historical writer of modern times': as n. 15, p. 825. But time moves on!

17 cf. chapter seven below.

18 All of these elements are recognised in the work of Collingwood and are reflected in the historical procedures adopted by Bultmann.

19 W. Dilthey (1833–1911) combined in himself empirical philosophy and the transcendentalism of the Kantian tradition. He recognised three classes of statements in human studies: one relating to perceived reality, including the historical component; another showing the uniform relations between the parts of this perceived reality; and the third being the practical component, dealing with value judgments and rules.

I   ETERNAL VALUES

1 cf. Kümmel *The New Testament: The History of the Investigation of its Problems* (1973), p. 114.

2 Sir John R. Seeley (1834–95) was a historian and essayist who became professor of modern history at Cambridge University in 1869. He published *Ecce Homo* in 1865. Among his other publications was a study of *Natural Religion* (1882). Gladstone's views are contained in *On Ecce Homo* (1868), originally published as a series of articles in the monthly *Good Words*. Writing over forty years later (1907), Oliver Lodge declared that opinion had shifted to such an extent that 'it is difficult to realise the shock experienced when an historian set to work to deal with the life of Christ as he would deal with any other history...' (in the preface to the Everyman edition of *Ecce Homo*, p. viii.)

3 Ibid., p. 135.

4 Ibid., p. 202.

5 *Natural Religion*, p. 174.

6 Ibid., p. 178.

7 Ibid., p. 179.

8 cf. *Dictionary of National Biography* (ed. S. Lee), LI.

9 Dr Chr. Ernst Luthardt was professor of theology at Leipzig and in the latter part of the nineteenth century was, along with Wüttke, the foremost proponent of the history of Christian ethics. His 'Lectures on the Moral Truths of Christianity' were translated into English and gained wide acceptance. His *History of Christian Ethics* (hereafter denoted by *HCE*), published in German in 1881, was translated into English and published in 1889.

10 Luthardt, *HCE*, p. 23.

11 Ibid., p. 26; Seeley, *Ecce Homo*, p. 151.

12 Ibid., p. 48.

13 Ibid., p. 74.

14 Ibid., p. 77.
15 Ibid., p. 82.
16 Ibid., p. 82.
17 See above.
18 *HCE*, pp. 87–8.
19 e.g., D. F. Strauss faulted Jesus' withdrawal from family life, property matters and aesthetic concerns. Ziegler suggested that Jesus was indifferent to politics.
20 Luthardt took Jesus' maxim 'render to Caesar what is Caesar's, and to God what is God's', with its separation of the two spheres, as an outstanding political principle: 'all the political wisdom of antiquity did not attain to its "political" wisdom': *HCE*, p. 94.
21 *HCE*, p. 95. With this interpretation should be contrasted the socio-historical reading of James in chapter seven.
22 *HCE*, p. 99.
23 *HCE*, p. 101 (his italics).
24 *HCE*, p. 102.
25 cf. discussions of Johannine ethics in chapters four and seven.
26 *HCE*, p. 32.
27 cf. Ricoeur's hermeneutical programme: see, for example, Mudge (ed.) *Essays on Biblical Interpretation* (1980).
28 See also the discussion of Alexander below.
29 Adolf Harnack (1851–1930) is probably the outstanding exemplar of liberal scholarship. His skill in the handling of sources and his sound historical method ensured that he had much to give to the historical criticism of the New Testament. He saw Luther and the Protestant tradition as championing the spiritual liberty of humankind, and he believed this heritage to be under threat in his time. He took a prominent part in public life, was concerned for the relation of gospel and culture, and – like Schleiermacher – placed a premium on communication with a wider audience than his own academic world. The publication of sixteen public lectures which he gave on *Das Wesen des Christentums* (*The Essence of Christianity*: Eng. tr., 1901) in the University of Berlin during the winter semester of 1899–1900, was a notable event, not least for the study of New Testament ethics: cf. M. Rumscheidt (ed.), *Adolf von Harnack: Liberal Theology at its Height* (1989), pp. 9–41.
30 *Essence*, p. 51.
31 Ibid., p. 52.
32 Ibid., p. 56.
33 e.g., Matt. 6.9; Mark 14.36; Luke 10.21; 11.2; Luke 10.20; Matt. 10.3; Luke 12.7; Matt. 16.26; Mark 8.36.
34 *Essence*, p. 70.
35 Ibid., pp. 73f.

36 Ibid., p. 78.
37 Ibid., p. 81.
38 Ibid., p. 84.
39 Ibid., p. 101.
40 Ibid., p. 100.
41 Ibid., pp. 100f.
42 Ibid., p. 119.
43 Ibid., p. 120.
44 Ibid., p. 123.
45 D. Sölle, *Thinking about God* (1990), p. 38.
46 cf. his *History of Dogma, passim*; and see W. Pauck, *Harnack and Troeltsch* (1968), pp. 22–6; see also the discussion of Troeltsch in chapter two.
47 cf. Pauck, *Harnack and Troeltsch*, pp. 37–8.
48 cf. Luke 10.18; Matt. 5.18,26; 6.2,5,16 etc.; Mark 11.17 par.
49 D. Sölle, *Thinking about God*, p. 34.
50 In the Introduction to the 1950 reprint of Harnack's work (Eng. tr., 1957, p. viii.)
51 Archibald B. D. Alexander (1855–1931) was the epitome of the Scottish clergyman who combined scholarship and writing with his pastoral duties. Apart from devotional writings, he introduced English readers to the historical approach to the study of philosophy which had become predominant in Germany, and wrote several works of theology. His most notable book was probably *The Ethics of St Paul* (1910), which was a pioneering work, having few precursors in English or German. He also wrote *Christianity and Ethics* (1914), *The Shaping Forces of Religious Thought* (1920) and *The Thinkers of the Church* (1924).
52 W. Heitmüller's *Jesus* (1913) is a prime example of a tendency to 'psychologise' eschatology which was prevalent at this time, from conservatives such as Theodor Zahn to the liberals in Germany and Britain and the 'social gospel' movement in the USA (see chapter two); cf. Lundström, *Kingdom of God in the Teaching of Jesus* (Eng. tr. 1963), pp. 15–16. Much of the earlier work from Baur onwards was concerned with the relationship between Paul and Jesus, and with Paul's 'religious experience': cf. A. Schweitzer, *Paul and his Interpreters* (1912) and V. P. Furnish, 'The Jesus–Paul Debate: From Baur to Bultmann', *BJRL* 47 (1964–5), pp. 342–81.
53 *Ethics of Saint Paul* (*ESP*), p. 7.
54 Ibid., p. 8.
55 Ibid., p. 13.
56 Ibid., p. 13.
57 Ibid., p. 27.
58 Ibid., p. 58.

59 The seven terms are flesh, body, spirit, soul, heart, mind and conscience.
60 *ESP*, pp. 68–73.
61 Ibid., p. 84.
62 Ibid., p. 157.
63 Ibid., pp. 164–7.
64 Ibid., p. 167.
65 Ibid., p. 175.
66 The 'classical' virtues which Paul accepts include wisdom, fortitude, temperance or self-control, and justice. The 'amiable' virtues include humility and long-suffering, and forgiveness. The Christian graces or 'theological' virtues are faith, hope and love.
67 *ESP*, p. 201.
68 Ibid., pp. 208–11.
69 Ibid., p. 229.
70 Ibid., p. 235.
71 Ibid., p. 233.
72 Ibid., p. 256.
73 For a judgment on Alexander's verdict, one would require to consider the factor of eschatology (e.g., 1 Cor. 7.29), the implications of radical equality in Christian baptism (Gal. 3.27–8), the effect of gospel counselling in specific contexts (Philem. 15–6), the 'peace' tradition received by Paul (Rom. 12.17–21), etc.
74 *ESP*, p. 291.
75 Ibid., p, 319.
76 He can name only Ernesti's *Die Ethik des Apostels Paulus* (1868) as a predecessor, and even that was a small volume.
77 In the preface to his book, p.v.; cf. J. Weiss, *Paul and Jesus* (Eng. tr. 1909).
78 *ESP*, p. 323.
79 cf. T. W. Ogletree, *The Use of the Bible in Christian Ethics* (1983), p. 29.
80 E. F. Scott observed that the time was still far distant when thinkers could try to determine and analyse what we now call personality. Paul had the deepest insights into human nature, usually expressed in the triple formula of 'flesh', 'soul' and 'mind'. But, Scott insists, it is the soul which is the eternal jewel for which all the rest is merely wrapping! Cf. E. F. Scott, *Man and Society in the New Testament* (1947); see in general, pp. 140–66.
81 The impact of psychology was mainly felt in the twentieth century, with the work of James, Freud, Jung, Allport and others; liberal response to it tended to be elementary, while dialectic theology treated 'psychologising' interpretation as distortion. More recent works have taken it much more seriously: cf. G. Theissen,

Psychologische Aspecte Paulinischer Theologie (1983); and, in a wider scientific context, *Biblical Faith: An Evolutionary Approach* (Eng. tr., 1984); D. O. Via, *Self-Deception and Wholeness in Paul and Matthew* (1990), esp. pp. 10–18.
82 cf. A. Jülicher, *Die Gleichnisreden Jesu II* (1910), pp. 585–98.
83 cf. B. M. G. Reardon, *Liberal Protestantism* (1968); and *Roman Catholic Modernism* (1970), in which the most significant figure is A. Loisy (1857–1940).
84 *Thinking about God*, p. 30.
85 cf. S. Hauerwas, *A Community of Character* (1981).
86 Hauerwas, *Community*, p. 12.

2 THE PRINCIPLES OF SOCIAL ETHICS

1 G. Winter, *Social Ethics* (1968), p. 8.
2 Winter, *Social Ethics*, p. 6.
3 cf. E. F. Scott, *Man and Society in the New Testament* (1947), pp. 255–81.
4 For a brief discussion, cf. Fairweather and McDonald, *The Quest for Christian Ethics* (1984), pp. 170–6.
5 cf. Calvin, *Institutes*, IV, xx, 32.
6 In this separation of personal ethics and public duties, Hegel is of course indebted to Luther.
7 Herrmann provides an example: see below.
8 cf. M. Weber, *The Protestant Ethic and the 'Spirit' of Capitalism* (1958), and *The Sociology of Religion* (1965).
9 cf. R. Gill, *Prophecy and Praxis* (1981), pp. 21–30.
10 The Christian socialism of Maurice and Kingsley was the logical outcome; later, the Christian Social Union (CSU) brought together an impressive group of churchmen, including B. F. Westcott (its chairman), Hastings Rashdall and *Lux Mundi* contributors such as Scott Holland, Gore and Moberly. Another group, the Guild of St Matthew, included Headlam and Shuttleworth.
11 B. F. Westcott (1825–1901) was, with Lightfoot and Hort, one of the most distinguished English New Testament scholars of the nineteenth century, being particularly noted for his work on the Greek NT and a series of commentaries: cf. C. K. Barrett, *Westcott as Commentator* (1959), pp. 17–19. But he was also a leading churchman with a keen interest in social ethics, standing in the tradition of Maurice, Kingsley, and the *Lux Mundi* group: cf. D. Nicholls, *Deity and Domination*, (1989) pp. 52–60. Westcott published a popular work on the subject in 1888, *Social Aspects of Christianity*. He continued to express social concern in practice

when he became Bishop of Durham in 1890, and acted as mediator in the coal strike of 1892; cf. G. F. A. Best, *Bishop Westcott and the Miners* (1967).

12 In this respect he anticipated the work of Kittel and others.
13 *Social Aspects of Christianity*, p. 8.
14 Ibid., p. 12.
15 Ibid., p. 14.
16 Westcott took the family rather than the individual as the primary social unit. Family, he suggested, is essentially a fellowship and fatherhood, deriving its nature from one Father (Eph. 3.15). A context is thus prepared for a high view of marriage, as both gospel (Matt. 19.5) and apostle (Eph. 5.32) suggest, and for a lofty view of obedience.
17 In his view of nation and state, Westcott is noticeably bourgeois. Authority is expressed in nationhood and is to be recognised, as in 1 Peter 2 and Romans 13. Nationhood calls for the manifestation of brotherhood; 'each in his proper sphere – workman, capitalist, teacher – is equally a servant of the state, feeding in his measure that common life by which he lives' (p. 38). Thus he capitulates in the end of the notion of static hierarchy. Nevertheless, in relation to patriotism he is much more restrained than many exponents of Enlightenment thinking: Schleiermacher, for example, could be ardently Prussian.
18 Among Westcott's surprising omissions is his seeming failure to anticipate the destructive potential of racism and the mythology of race, which was to play such a heinous role in Europe in the following half-century, although there is no doubt about the direction of his thinking. For him, race was a positive universal.
19 A sharp distinction exists between the divine society and the many human societies. The divine society, however, is called in Christ to be 'a light for revelation to the nations' (Luke 2.32). The church reflects the three axioms in its social mission: to be a prophet of the eternal in the light of creation; to interpret the world in the light of the incarnation; and to be the quickener and sustainer of life in the light of redemption. As a bishop of the established church, Westcott was less radical than Harnack or Alexander in affirming the autonomy of the church, and much less radical than many of the social gospellers in America.
20 cf. W. A. Visser't Hooft and J. H. Oldham, *The Church and its Function in Society* (1937), p. 210; cf. J. Bennett, *Christian Ethics and Social Policy* (1946).
21 W. Temple, *Christianity and the Secular Order* (1942), pp. 61–74; A. M. Suggate, *William Temple and Christian Social Ethics Today* (1987), pp. 126–51.

22 cf. S. Spencer, 'History and Society in William Temple's Thought', in *Studies in Christian Ethics*, 5/2 (1992), pp. 72. The puzzle of Temple's thinking seems to lie not in any alleged insularity, but in his too great reliance, until a late stage in his career, on idealist philosophers such as Hegel, Bosanquet and Bradley: cf. *Mens Creatrix* (1917), *Christus Veritas* (1924) and *Nature, Man and God* (1934).

23 See below, Part Two.

24 D. B. Forrester, *Christianity and the Future of Welfare* (1985), p. 90.

25 R. H. Preston, *Church and Society in the Late Twentieth Century: The Economic and Political Task* (1983), p. 153; cf. Suggate, *William Temple*, pp. 148–50, 207–25.

26 C. Villa-Vicencio, *A Theology of Reconstruction* (1992), pp. 280–4.

27 Ibid., p. 5.

28 On Otto, see below.

29 cf. J. Bentley, *Between Marx and Christ* (1982), pp. 23–8.

30 C. Blumhardt, *Ihr Menschen seid Gottes* (1936), p. 328. L. Ragaz should also be quoted in this connection: cf. G. Lundström, *Kingdom of God in the Teaching of Jesus* (1963), pp. 20–3.

31 cf. Bentley *Between Marx and Christ* (1982), pp. x, 79–97.

32 cf. R. Ferguson, *George Macleod* (1990), pp. 369–86, 404.

33 cf. W. Herrmann and A. Harnack (eds.), 'The Social Mission of the Church'. H. Windisch commented that Herrmann always spoke as a philosopher who thought of ethics only in terms of a fundamental, consistent and universal principle.

34 *Social Mission*, p. 153.

35 H. Windisch, *The Meaning of the Sermon on the Mount* (Eng. tr. 1951), p. 45.

36 Herrmann, *Social Mission*, p. 77.

37 *Social Mission*, p. 88.

38 Windisch, *Meaning of the Sermon*, p. 46.

39 Herrmann, *Social Mission*, p. 19.

40 Herrmann, *Social Mission*, p. 20.

41 cf. Barth's disenchantment with his liberal teachers' 'Manifesto of the Intellectuals' in 1914: J. Bowden, *Karl Barth* (1971), p. 34.

42 cf. W. A. Visser't Hooft, *The Background of the Social Gospel in America* (1929).

43 cf. W. Rauschenbusch, *Christianity and the Social Crisis* (1907).

44 S. Mathews, *The Social Teaching of Jesus* (1910), p. 58.

45 W. Rauschenbusch, *A Theology for the Social Gospel* (1918), p. 139.

46 W. Rauschenbusch, *Christianizing the Social Order* (1916), p. 67.

47 Visser't Hooft, *Background of Social Gospel*, p. 50.

48 Mathews, *Social Teaching*, p. 3.

49 *Social Teaching*, p. 54.

50 *Social Teaching*, p. 104.
51 H. J. Cadbury, *The Peril of Modernising Jesus* (1937).
52 Visser't Hooft, *Background of the Social Gospel*, p. 50.
53 Visser't Hooft, p. 63.
54 Ernst Troeltsch (1865–1923), friend of Harnack and Weber, was professor at Heidelberg and Berlin. For his use of Weber's ideal types, cf. 'Stoic–Christian Natural Law and Modern Secular Natural Law', in *Religion and History* (Eng. tr. 1991), pp. 324–8.
55 Troeltsch, *The Social Teaching of the Christian Churches* (Eng. tr. 1931), I, p. 52 (cited below as STCC).
56 STCC, p. 56.
57 Ibid., p. 62.
58 Ibid., p. 63.
59 Ibid., p. 70.
60 Ibid., p. 78.
61 cf. Troeltsch's preface to the English translation of *Protestantism and Progress* where he clearly takes 'Anglo-Saxon Protestantism' as closely related to the modern spirit, and as having accomplished much in solving what he terms the practical problems of the Christian life.

PART TWO   ESCHATOLOGY AND THE CRITICAL METHOD

1 H. Zahrnt, *The Question of God* (Eng. tr. 1969), p. 33.
2 cf. A. N. Wilder, *Eschatology and Ethics* (rev. 1950), pp. 73–85, 86–115. His chapters on 'the fundamental sanctions' (pp. 116–32) and 'the significance of the eschatological sanction' (pp. 133–41) are also apposite.
3 cf. E. Käsemann, 'The Beginnings of Christian Theology', *New Testament Questions of Today* (1969), pp. 82–107.
4 cf. Käsemann, 'Primitive Christian Apocalyptic', as above (n. 3) pp. 108–37.
5 W. Wrede, *Das Messiasgeheimnis in den Evangelien*, (1901).
6 Interest in eschatology was rapidly increasing in Weiss' time: see below. He was not uninfluenced by the fact that E. Issel and O. Schmöller had published essays which focussed on the New Testament teaching about the Kingdom of God.
7 'New Testament and Mythology', in *Kerygma and Myth* (ed. Bartsch), Eng. tr., 1954, p. 5.
8 'Demythologising' is part of his hermeneutical strategy designed to ensure that the ancient world view is not an obstacle to the central message of Christ crucified, which is to be interpreted in existential terms.
9 See below.

10 cf. H. Clark, *The Ethical Mysticism of Albert Schweitzer* (1962), pp. 26-7.
11 *Von Reimarus zu Wrede. Eine Geschichte der Leben-Jesu-Forschung* (1906).
12 S. Kierkegaard (1813-55) was fighting on many fronts: against speculative idealism, nominal Christianity and the liberal cultural establishment. His critique of modern culture and conventional religion was brilliantly expressed and deeply perceptive. There was something of the gadfly in his approach, and it is not surprising to find him invoking Socrates as his only true predecessor.
13 Kierkegaard saw in this story 'the crowning proof that faith is wholly opaque and irrational – something given, something done to us, by which our whole being is convulsed': H. R. Mackintosh, *Types of Modern Theology* (1937), p. 224.
14 G. J. Stack, *Kierkegaard's Existential Ethics* (1977), p. 177. In glorifying 'the individual man', he was not alone: Mortensen, for example, took the category of 'the individual' to uphold 'the principle of personality'.
15 Husserl's method of interpretation has been influential in the study of religion, where attention is given to eliminating distorting preconceptions (particularly if the latter derived from a theological source) in order that the subject's relation to the phenomena may be as open as possible (phenomenology denotes 'that which is observable', as distinct from metaphysical substance). Methodological procedures which occur frequently are *epoché* (the 'holding back' or 'bracketing' of value judgments) and *eidetic vision* (discerning the given 'form' or essence of the subject under investigation). In practice, such an approach entails the application of a wide range of other disciplines (e.g., historical, sociological). Thus the ethics of the New Testament would be viewed in its textual setting, in its religio-cultural matrix, and in relation to the consciousness of the interpreter.
16 J. Macquarrie, *An Existentialist Theology* (1955), *passim*; cf. *The Scope of Demythologizing* (1960), pp. 25, 48-9, 143-4.
17 The consequences of Heidegger's work for ethics – and Christian ethics in particular – are considerable. Being-in-the-world involves moral action, which is the stuff of ethical reflection. Ethics is indeed concerned with 'authentic' and 'inauthentic' ways of living and acting. One finds a corresponding pattern in Paul's writings; cf. Romans 2.15, which can be taken as an acknowledgement of 'the law of nature'. Romans 1.25 describes the Gentiles' folly: the call to authentic being was available to them (Rom. 1.20), but they did not respond.

18 cf. L. S. Mudge (ed.), *Paul Ricoeur, Essays on Biblical Interpretation* (1981).
19 See chapters seven and eight in particular.
20 cf. Zahrnt, *The Question of God*, p. 207.
21 cf. ibid., p. 208.
22 cf. R. G. Collingwood, *The Idea of History* (1946), *passim*.
23 M. Kähler, *Historische Jesus* (1892), p. 66; for a discussion of Kähler, cf. P. Althaus, *The So-called Kerygma and the Historical Jesus* (Eng. tr., 1959), pp. 19–37.

3 INTERIM ETHICS

1 cf. J. T. Sanders, *Ethics in the New Testament* (1975), *passim*.
2 cf. G. Lundström, *The Kingdom of God in the Teaching of Jesus* (1963), p. 27.
3 The Blumhardts are a case in point: see above, chapter two.
4 cf. the introduction by Hiers and Holland to the Eng. tr. of *Die Predigt: Jesus' Proclamation of the Kingdom of God* (1975), esp. pp. 5–6. As the son of Bernhard Weiss and the son-in-law and pupil of Albrecht Ritschl, Johannes Weiss was in a position to appreciate the positive features of their respective contributions. Indeed, it appears that he withheld publication of his essay on *Die Predigt: Jesu vom Reiche Gottes* for several years, possibly out of respect for his father-in-law who died in 1889.
5 The parables, on the whole, do not score well in Weiss's tests. In Matthew, not only are the introductory formulae suspect, but also '*the whole point of view*' (his italics) which takes the parables to describe conditions within the kingdom of God. Parables have been reinterpreted as 'the secrets of the kingdom' on the basis of Mark 4.11, itself a secondary tradition.
6 This can be identified clearly enough in the logion underlying Mark 1.15, and it is explicit in Matthew 10.7 and Luke 10.9,11.
7 J. Weiss, *Jesus' Proclamation of the Kingdom of God*, p. 73.
8 Ibid., p. 93.
9 Ibid., p. 105.
10 Ibid., p. 106.
11 Ibid., p. 107.
12 Ibid., p. 108.
13 Ibid., p. 111.
14 Ibid., p. 135.
15 Ibid., p. 135.
16 cf. Hiers and Holland (eds.), *Jesus' Proclamation*, pp. 49–53.
17 cf. E. Ehrhardt, *Der Grundcharakter der Ethik Jesu* (1895). The title

is given as 'The Fundamental Character of the Preaching (*sic*) of Jesus' in the Eng. tr. of Schweitzer's *Quest*, p. 249, and this error persists even in later editions. Ehrhardt supplied much of the contextual material which Weiss could not include in his brief sketch.

18 cf. E. P. Sanders, *Jesus and Judaism* (1985), pp. 106–13. For criticism of Sanders, cf. Chilton and McDonald, *Jesus and the Ethics of the Kingdom* (1987), pp. 40–2, where it is concluded that 'repentance, a turning back to what alone has value, is a necessary and inescapable aspect of entering the Kingdom' (p. 41).

19 Alexander spoke of 'reducing the Son of Man to the level of a Jewish rhapsodist, whose whole function was to incite his countrymen to look away from the present scene of duty towards some mystic state of felicity which had no connection with the actual world in which men lived, and no real bearing upon their present character and moral discipline': cf. 'The Kingdom of God and the Ethics of Jesus', *Exp. T.* (1928–9), pp. 73–7.

20 C. Rowland and M. Corner, *Liberating Exegesis* (1990), p. 92.

21 *The Quest of the Historical Jesus* (Eng. tr. 1911) p. 387.

22 cf. Lundström, *Kingdom of God*, p. 76; O. Cullmann, *Christ and Time* (1951) p. 30.

23 E. N. Mozley, *The Theology of Albert Schweitzer for Christian Enquirers* (1950) p. 34.

24 Schweitzer, *The Mystery of the Kingdom* (Eng. tr. 1925) p. 97.

25 *The Kingdom of God and Primitive Christianity* (hereafter *KGPC*) (Eng. tr. 1968) p. 83.

26 *KGPC*, p. 81.

27 Ibid., p. 82.

28 cf. discussion in following chapters.

29 *The Mystery of the Kingdom*, p. 119–20.

30 *KGPC*, p. 85.

31 *Mysticism of St Paul* (Eng. tr. 1931) p. 294.

32 Ibid., p. 294.

33 Ibid., p. 296.

34 Ibid., p. 307.

35 Ibid., p. 309.

36 Ibid., p. 333.

37 cf. *My Life and Thought* (Eng. tr. 1933) pp. 156–7, and his article in *Christendom I* (Winter 1936) 2, pp. 225–39, reprinted as Appendix 1 in H. Clark, *The Ethical Mysticism of Albert Schweitzer*, (1962) pp. 180–94.

38 Ibid., pp. 182–3.

39 Ibid., p. 189.

40 A. N. Wilder, 'Albert Schweitzer and the N.T.', p. 76.

41 E. P. Sanders, *Jesus and Judaism* (1985), pp. 106–13.
42 A. N. Wilder, *Eschatology and Ethics*, p. 178; for other criticisms of Schweitzer, cf. pp. 39–41, 177–9.
43 cf. H. Windisch, *The Meaning of the Sermon on the Mount* (1951), pp. 39–40; more recently, H. Bald, 'Eschatological or Theological Ethics? Notes on the Relationship between Eschatology and Ethics in the Teaching of Jesus', in B. D. Chilton (ed.), *The Kingdom of God* (1984), pp. 133–53; A. P. Winton, *The Proverbs of Jesus* (1990), esp. pp. 161–7.
44 Bultmann, *Jesus and the World* (Eng. tr. 1958), pp. 44–7.
45 Wilder, 'Albert Schweitzer and the N.T.', p. 80.
46 cf. cognitive dissonance theories as in L. Festinger, *When Prophecy Fails* (1956), R. P. Carroll, *When Prophecy Failed* (1979); and 'reversal' theories as in A. Verhey, *The Great Reversal: Ethics and the New Testament* (1984).
47 *My Life and Thought*, p. 232.
48 Wilder, 'Albert Schweitzer and the New Testament', p. 78.
49 cf. L. Newbigin, *The Gospel in a Pluralist Society* (1989), *passim*.
50 Wilder, 'Albert Schweitzer and the N.T.', p. 73.
51 cf. *The Idea of the Holy* (Eng. tr. 1923), *passim*.
52 *The Kingdom of God and the Son of Man* (Eng. tr. 1938).
53 Otto, *Kingdom*, p. 62.
54 G. Lundström, *The Kingdom of God*, p. 191.
55 Criticism has extended from his Iranian hypothesis to his use of source criticism: cf. Lundström, pp. 178–81.

4 EXISTENTIAL ETHICS

1 *Jesus and the Word* (henceforth, *Jesus*) (Eng. tr. 1943, rev. 1958), p. 83. Rudolf Bultmann (1884–1976), form critic and principal proponent of existential interpretation, drew particularly on Heidegger and Collingwood. In his earlier work, *Jesus* (1926), he discounted several attempted solutions to the relation of ethics and the kingdom: the fulfilling of the will of God as the condition for entering; or entry to it as a reward for obedience; the kingdom as an inner spiritual possession (the dominant liberal view in the nineteenth century), and its identification with the actual fellowship of believers. Also rejected is the contention that the eschatological preaching does not come from Jesus, but from the church: form critical analysis tended to identify an older eschatological stratum to which later churchly sayings were added. In any case, the Passion story makes little sense unless Jesus spoke as a messianic prophet. If anything, tradition may have toned down this element.

2 cf. Barth, *The Epistle to the Romans* (1929), pp. 176–7, 502–3.
3 cf. *Romans*, on 13.1.
4 In exegesis, because Barth does not do a close contextual reading of the text; in ethics, because he simply appeals to freedom and the Spirit: his ethical position is, in fact, act deontology; and in theology, because he often seems to assert the negative rather than the positive: cf. H. Zahrnt, *The Question of God*, pp. 29–34.
5 *Jesus* 1926.
6 *Jesus and the Word* (Eng. tr. 1934), p. 96.
7 Ibid., p. 100.
8 Ibid., pp. 98–109.
9 Ibid., p. 110.
10 Ibid., p. 66.
11 Ibid., p. 53.
12 Ibid., p. 60. It might be credible to argue that a messianic prophet could be carried beyond the position he envisaged by the power of his rhetoric or the dynamic of his mission. But how does Bultmann know? Such an interpretation seems to presuppose the kind of psychological understanding which he expressly rejected.
13 His discussion of 'the Jewish conception of God' and 'God the Remote and Near', for example, is unmistakably a Christian theological reading of the data: *Jesus*, pp. 98–109.
14 On Dodd, see next chapter, and for Bultmann, cf. *Jesus* p. 87.
15 *Jesus*, pp. 87–8.
16 cf. D. O. Via, Jr., *Self-Deception and Wholeness in Paul and Matthew* (1990), esp. pp. 1–18. The chief limitation is that it requires that the ethical analysis be conducted at the level of philosophical generality in accordance with the Western academic tradition.
17 See above, pp. 56–7, 83–4..
18 Dibelius, *Jesus* (Eng. tr. 1963), p. 97.
19 Ibid., pp. 113–14.
20 Ibid., p. 165.
21 Bultmann's consideration of the Sermon and the question of justice is discussed below.
22 Modern sociological approaches to New Testament ethics, for example, emphasises the early Christian groups as 'moral communities'; and in Christian ethics, cf. similar emphases in writers such as Gustafson, Lehmann, and Hauerwas.
23 Bornkamm, *Jesus of Nazareth* (Eng. tr. 1960/73), p. 105.
24 Ibid., pp. 87–8, 106–8.
25 Barth, *The Epistle to the Romans*, especially on 12.21 and 13.1.
26 cf. E. Fuchs, *Studies of the Historical Jesus* (1964), pp. 213–28; G. Ebeling, 'Hermeneutic', *RGG* II (1959), cols. 242–62.

27 cf. J. L. Austin, 'Performative Utterances', in his *Philosophical Papers* (1961), pp. 220–39.
28 See above, p. 67.
29 A stalwart champion of the traditions of the fathers (Gal. 1.14), Paul was converted to the Christian faith through the preaching of the Hellenistic Church, surrendering what had hitherto been precious to him (Phil. 3.4–7). He became immersed in its missionary activity while keeping his distance from the churches of Judaea and even Jesus' disciples in Jerusalem (cf. Gal. 1–2). He professed not to base his message on mere human knowledge of Jesus nor on human tradition, and, while he occasionally cited or reflected a 'word of the Lord', he did not recapitulate Jesus' teaching.
30 *Theology of the New Testament (TNT)*, I, p. 335.
31 Paul can relate ethics directly to the coming divine judgement: cf. 1 Cor. 3.17; cf. Käsemann 'Sentences of Holy Law in the New Testament', *New Testament Questions of Today* (Eng. tr. 1969), pp. 66–81. Some critics have endorsed this proposal unequivocally as showing the pluralistic base of Paul's ethics: 'the imperative of the tenets of holy law is not *based upon, grounded in* the indicative of justification as is otherwise normally the case for the ethical imperatives Paul uses': J. T. Sanders, *Ethics in the New Testament* (1975), p. 49. Even if Käsemann has overstated the case for the 'sentences', the force of the observation remains.
32 But the coherence of this picture is open to challenge, as is the way in which Paul's ethics is informed by the *Torah*. In his struggle both to revalue the *Torah* in the light of Christ and to describe the basis of the Christian way, Paul did not evince a single invariable attitude: cf. his use of *Haustafeln*, even though their realm of discourse was inconsistent with the main thrust of his ethics. On the 'end' of the Law, cf. W. S. Campbell, 'Christ the End of the Law: Romans 10.4', *Paul's Gospel in an Intercultural Context* (1991), pp. 60–7.
33 cf. chapter five below, and cf. Sanders, *Paul, the Law and the Jewish People* (1983), p. 10.
34 The implications for ethics are discussed in chapter five below.
35 *TNT*, II, p. 82; *Gospel of John*, pp. 527–9; *The Johannine Epistles*, p. 28; cf. V. P. Furnish, *The Love Commandment* (1973), pp. 143–8, 152–4.
36 *TNT*, II, p. 82.
37 Käsemann, *Testament of Jesus*, p. 59.
38 J. T. Sanders, *Ethics in the N.T.*, p. 100.
39 Ibid.

40 Houlden, *Ethics and the New Testament*, p. 39. The reference here is to the community reflected in 1 John.

41 *TNT*, I, 270–87.

42 cf. Paul Tillich, *Love, Power and Justice*, 1954.

43 cf. P. Ricoeur, 'Preface to Bultmann', in L. S. Mudge (ed.), *Essays on Biblical Interpretation: Paul Ricoeur* (1980), pp. 49–72; J. P. Mackey, *Jesus: The Man and the Myth* (1979), pp. 30–4, 75–85, 173–204, 210–40.

44 cf. 'Is Exegesis without Presuppositions Possible?' in S. M. Ogden, *Existence and Faith* (1961), p. 292.

45 D. Sölle, *Political Theology*, p. 44.

5 THE ETHICS OF COVENANT AND COMMAND

1 A. N. Wilder, *Eschatology and Ethics* (rev. 1950), p. 160.

2 J. Muilenburg, *The Way of Israel* (1962), p. 15.

3 cf. W. Kaiser, *Towards Old Testament Ethics* (1983); C. J. H. Wright, *Living as the people of God*, 1983. B. C. Birch, *Let Justice Roll Down* (1991), 202.

4 E. P. Sanders, *PPJ*, p. 422; his definition of covenantal nomism is 'the view that one's place in God's plan is established on the basis of the covenant and that the covenant requires as the proper response of man his obedience to its commandments, while providing means of atonement for transgression': *PPJ*, p. 74, cf. p. 236.

5 T. W. Manson (1893–1958) was professor at Mansfield College, Oxford (1932–36) and subsequently Rylands Professor of Biblical Criticism at Manchester. His best-known works are probably *The Teaching of Jesus* (1931) and *The Sayings of Jesus*, first published as Part 2 of *The Mission and Message of Jesus* (ed., H. D. A. Major), in 1937.

6 *Teaching of Jesus* (henceforth, *TJ*), pp. 14–21.

7 *TJ*, p. 227.

8 Ibid., p. 166.

9 Ibid., pp. 63–4.

10 Ibid., p. 81.

11 Ibid., pp. 290–1.

12 Ibid., p. 295.

13 Ibid., p. 302.

14 *Ethics and the Gospel* (*EG*), p. 52.

15 *EG*, p. 59.

16 cf. *On Paul and John*, p. 57.

17 *EG*, p. 66.

18 Ibid., p. 63.

19 *TJ*, pp. 307–8.
20 *EG*, pp. 63–4.
21 *TJ*, p. 311; cf. *On Paul and John*, pp. 104–10.
22 Even in his later work he resists the full implications of form criticism: cf. *EG*, pp. 46–50.
23 cf. *The Sayings of Jesus*, pp. 9–38.
24 cf. 'The Old Testament in the Teaching of Jesus', *BJRL*, 34,2 (1952), pp. 312–32; cf. *EG*, p. 93.
25 Manson related the Great Commandment/Golden Rule traditions to two great principles of Kant's moral theory: the unique importance of good will and the supreme law of pure practical reason: 'Act so that the maxims of your will may be in perfect harmony with a universal system of laws': cf. *TJ*, pp. 302–8. It is noticeable that Manson did not explicitly differentiate Jesus' position from that of Kant in the way he differentiated it, for example, from Judaism or Calvinism. He was perhaps unaware of the extent to which he retained in himself the 'liberal, rational, evolutionary' presuppositions which he recognised as having a distorting effect on others' interpretations.
26 See below.
27 *EG*, p. 103.
28 C. H. Dodd (1884–1973), classicist and Congregational minister, held professorships at Mansfield College, Oxford, and the Universities of Manchester and Cambridge. His scholarly contribution ranged from discussion of the authority of the Bible (cf. *The Authority of the Bible*, 1928) to the importance of the parables for the understanding of the kingdom of God (*Parables of the Kingdom*, 1935) and the centrality of *kerygma* in the New Testament (*The Apostolic Preaching and its Development*, 1936). He later wrote important studies of the Fourth Gospel (1953 and 1963), as well as commentaries and popular theological studies. He also evinced a strong interest in ethics, of which *Gospel and Law* is evidence.
29 See chapter one.
30 *Parables of the Kingdom (PK)*, p. 45.
31 *PK*, p. 45.
32 *PK*, p. 49.
33 *PK*, p. 49.
34 *GL*, p. 27.
35 cf. *The Apostolic Preaching and its Development*.
36 cf. Jülicher, *Die Gleichnisse Jesu* (1899–1910), who emphasised the moralistic, and J. T. Sanders, *Ethics in the New Testament*, who reinforced 'interim ethics': see chapter one.
37 *GL*, p. 57.

38 Ibid., p. 59.
39 *PK*, p. 109.
40 *GL*, p. 31.
41 Ibid., p. 32.
42 *The Meaning of Paul for Today (MPT)*, p. 122.
43 *MPT*, p. 126.
44 cf. Ibid., p. 127.
45 cf. Ibid., p. 129–30.
46 *MPT*, p. 147.
47 *GL*, pp. 35–6.
48 Ibid., p. 39.
49 Ibid., p. 41.
50 Ibid., p. 42.
51 Ibid., p. 42.
52 Ibid., p. 44.
53 Ibid., p. 71.
54 Ibid., p. 81.
55 cf. J. I. H. McDonald, *Kerygma and Didache* (1980). The relation-ship he posits between *kerygma* and *didache* seems to assume that practice follows creed or at least sermon. But practice may itself serve as proclamation. *Kerygma* may be implicit in *didache*. The book called the 'Didache' seems to place moral education in the forefront. In any case, *kerygma* and *didache* are at once more complex, more integrated and more fluid than Dodd allows.
56 cf. *The Authority of the Bible*, pp. 26–31.
57 *PK*, p. 80.
58 Ibid., p. 197.
59 cf. J. Knox, *The Ethic of Jesus and the Teaching of the Church* (1962), p. 15.
60 cf. J. Knox, *Chapters in a Life of Paul*, p. 148; for a reply, cf. C. F. D. Moule, 'Obligation in the Ethic of Paul', in W. R. Farmer, C. F. D. Moule and R. R. Niebuhr (eds.), *Christian History and Interpretation* (1967).
61 W. D. Davies (1911–) combined expertise in ancient Judaism and contextual studies of Paul and Jesus (his *Setting of the Sermon on the Mount (SM)* is a classic in its field, as is *Paul and Rabbinic Judaism (PRJ)*) with a lively interest in the ethics of the New Testament and its relevance for today: cf. his article on 'Ethics in the New Testament' *(ENT)* in the *Interpreter's Dictionary of the Bible*, and his essay 'The Relevance of the Moral Teaching of the Early Church' *(RMT)* in Ellis and Wilcox (eds.), *Neotestamentica et Semitica* (1969), pp. 30–49.
62 *ENT*, p. 169.
63 Ibid., p. 168.

64 Ibid., p. 172.
65 *SM*, p. 90.
66 Ibid., p. 150.
67 Like Manson, Dodd, Wilder and others, Davies accepted the force of Jesus' call to repentance in view of the coming kingdom. E. P. Sanders questioned the place of repentance in the ministry of Jesus, apparently on the grounds that its true context was to be found in Judaism, with its clear penitential requirements, or even in the ministry of the Baptist, but that it was intrusive upon Jesus' simple call to people to accept him and his message of the kingdom. The approach of the kingdom is good news; eschatology has assumed a smiling face: *Jesus and Judaism* (*JJ*), pp. 203–11. But, much earlier, Wilder had shown that, in the Jewish context, repentance was thought of as hastening the kingdom, rather than as a qualification for entry. Repentance is part of the blessing the kingdom brings. Sanders may evince residual theological overtones here; a more cautious statement of the case would have been appropriate. For further important contributions from Sanders, cf. *Jewish Law from Jesus to the Mishnah*, London (1990) and *Judaism: Practice and Belief*, London (1992).
68 *JJ*, p. 252.
69 Ibid., pp. 252–5. Sanders comments that, in the new age, God would go beyond the law; he would admit even the wicked to his kingdom: *JJ*, p. 336.
70 *PRJ*, p. 16.
71 Ibid., p. 324.
72 Ibid., pp. 36–57; cf. pp. 31–5.
73 cf. *Paul and Palestinian Judaism* (*PPJ*), pp. 442–7.
74 cf. my discussion of this feature in *Resurrection: Narrative and Belief* (1989), pp. 25–48.
75 *PPJ*, p. 497.
76 Ibid., p. 513.
77 Ibid., p. 513.
78 Ibid., p. 517.
79 Collins Dictionary of the English Language. Sanders held that, for Paul, people who are 'in' keep the law, but they do not get 'in' by keeping the law.
80 cf. I. H. Marshall, 'Some observations on the covenant in the New Testament', in *Context. Essays in Honour of Peder Borgen* (1987), pp. 121–56.
81 Marshall, ibid., pp. 135–6.
82 *JJ*, pp. 333–4.
83 Ibid., p. 333.
84 *RMT*, p. 42.

6 THE PROBLEM OF CHRISTIAN SOCIAL ETHICS

1 R. Niebuhr, *An Interpretation of Christian Ethics* (1937), p. 41–2.
2 M. Keeling, *The Foundations of Christian Ethics* (1990), p. 1.
3 cf. W. Pannenberg, *Christian Spirituality and Sacramental Community* (Eng. tr. 1983); J. Moltmann, *The Trinity and the Kingdom of God* (Eng. tr. 1981).
4 cf. P. Tillich, *Love, Power and Justice* (1954), pp. 24–34.
5 'The Relevance of the Moral Teaching of the Early Church' (*RMT*), p. 36.
6 Ibid., p. 37–8, where Davies cites 1 Corinthians 11.13ff., Romans 1.28, Romans 2.14–15, and the Apostolic Decree in Acts 15 (with its dependence on the Noachian commandments).
7 *RMT*, p. 38.
8 Ibid., p. 40.
9 Ibid., p. 40–1.
10 *SM*, pp. 237ff.
11 *RMT*, p. 43.
12 Ibid., p. 45.
13 Ibid., pp. 45–6.
14 Ibid., p. 47.
15 Ibid., p. 47.
16 Ibid., pp. 47–8.
17 *JJ*, p. 129.
18 Paul Ramsey was much involved in the norm versus context debate: cf. J. M. Gustafson, 'Context Versus Principles: A Misplaced Debate in Christian Ethics', in Marty and Peerman, *The New Theology*, 3 (1966), pp. 69–102. On the notion of justice, cf. Tillich (n. 4 above) and Old Testament discussion as in B. C. Birch, *Let Justice Roll Down* (1991), pp. 153–7.
19 The 'later' Ramsey was much preoccupied with specific issues in ethics, from war and peace to medical ethics. The prophetic ardour of *Basic Christian Ethics* (1953 – henceforth *BCE*) yielded to a stance of rule-agapism which was intended to contain it, but at the cost of a degree of distortion. Yet when, in the course of his argument for the use of the 'just war' theory today, he writes that Christians should 'live together in covenant love no matter what the morrow brings, even if it brings nothing', we recognise a familiar theme, even if there is a retreat to community ethics; cf. *BCE*, p. 3.
20 Ibid., p. 10.
21 Ibid., p. 17. Ramsey dissented from Brunner's view of the world of systems, on the grounds that he neutralised not merely selfish

concern, but effective neighbourly concern, and left *agape* in some kind of transcendental isolation. With acknowledgements to Rousseau, Ramsey thought of justice as establishing order based on 'objective generality'. At this point Ramsey attempted to go beyond the 'community view' of Christian ethics and to engage with social ethics proper. Christian love has a critical role to play in reshaping the institutions of society through Christian involvement in them, and it has a similarly critical and modifying role in relation to other theories of social ethics with which it may be associated from time to time.

22 BCE, p. 41.
23 Ibid., p. 89.
24 Ibid., pp. 327–37.
25 Ibid., p. 340.
26 cf. Ramsey, *The Just War: Force and Political Responsibility* (1968); cf. M. Walzer, *Just and Unjust Wars* (1977), pp. 270–2, 278–83; D. S. Long, 'Ramseyian Just War and Yoderian Pacifism: Where is the Disagreement?' *Studies in Christian Ethics*, 4/1 (1991) p. 68.
27 E. Brunner, *The Divine Imperative* (Eng. tr. 1937), p. 434.
28 cf. Brunner, *Justice and the Social Order* (1945), p. 129; cf. chapter 15 *passim*.
29 *BCE*, p. 3.
30 cf. J. A. T. Robinson, *The Body* (1952).
31 *An Interpretation of Christian Ethics*, p. 47.
32 Ibid., p. 67. Schweitzer's influence is operative here: significantly, Niebuhr cites Matthew 10.23.
33 *An Interpretation of Christian Ethics*, pp. 113–45.
34 cf. P. Tillich, *Love, Power and Justice, passim*.
35 *An Interpretation of Christian Ethics*, p. 145.
36 Ibid., p. 208.
37 D. B. Forrester, *Beliefs, Values and Policies* (1989), p. 76.
38 J. L. Crenshaw, 'The influence of the Wise upon Amos', *ZAW* 79 (1967), pp. 42–52.
39 Totalitarian contexts raise special problems and demand special praxis: the Barmen Declaration is a good example.
40 *The Relevance of the Impossible: A Reply to Reinhold Niebuhr* (1941), p. 37 (cited below as *Relevance*). Macgregor's major exegetical study is *The New Testament Basis of Pacifism* (1936).
41 *Relevance*, p. 39.
42 Ibid., p. 41; cf. C. E. Raven, *The Gospel and the Church* (1939), pp. 40–2; *War and the Christian* (1938), pp. 123–59.
43 *Relevance*, p. 49.
44 See chapter seven.

45 *Relevance*, p. 52.
46 Ibid., p. 75.
47 Ibid., p. 77.
48 Ibid., p. 58.
49 It is noteworthy that Martin Luther King in his ethics and praxis combined scriptural understanding with spiritual discipline, a keen analysis of the socio-political structures, communication, negotiation, compromise, action and forgiveness. Contextually, it was important that he could make the Federal constitution work in his favour: cf. Fairweather and McDonald, *The Quest* (1984), pp. 201–7.
50 cf. Barth, *Church and State* (1939), p. 64.
51 cf. O. Cullmann, *The State in the New Testament* (1957).
52 cf. A. N. Wilder, *Eschatology and Ethics in the New Testament* (1950).
53 Particular mention might be made of G. H. C. Macgregor, 'Principalities and Powers: The Cosmic Background of St Paul's Thought', *New Testament Studies*, 1, 1954, pp. 17–28; G. B. Caird, *Principalities and Powers* (1956); C. D. Morrison, *The Powers That Be* (1960); and, much later, W. Carr, *Angels and Principalities*, Cambridge (1981).
54 *Theology of the New Testament*, 1 (Eng. tr. 1952, pp. 254–9).
55 *Kerygma and Myth I* (Eng. tr. 1953), p. 5.
56 'The Interpretation of Romans 13', in *New Testament Questions of Today* (Eng. tr. 1969), pp. 203–5.
57 cf. Part Three below.
58 W. Wink, *Naming the Powers: The Language of Power in the New Testament* (1984), p. 5; cf. also *Unmasking the Powers: The Invisible Forces that Determine Human Existence* (1986).
59 cf. W. Wink, *The Bible in Human Transformation* (1973), esp. pp. 19–80.
60 Wink, *Unmasking the Powers*, p. 25.
61 Ibid., p. 95.
62 Ibid., p. 96.
63 cf. D. B. Forrester, *Beliefs, Values and Policies*, pp. 65–77.

PART THREE   A DOUBLE ETHICAL RESPONSIBILITY

1 R. N. Bellah, *Beyond Belief* (1970), p. 257.
2 cf. J. Habermas, *Reason and the Rationalisation of Society* (Eng. tr. 1, 1981), p. 135; H. Gadamer, *Truth and Method* (Eng. tr. 1975); P. Ricoeur, 'Gadamer and Habermas in Dialogue', *Philosophy Today* 17.2/4 (1973), pp. 153–165.
3 cf. M. Pusey, *Jurgen Habermas* (1987), pp. 61–4, whose outline is broadly followed here.

4 cf. W. G. Jeanrond, 'Hermeneutics', in *DBI* (1990), p. 283. In his anxiety to avoid undue 'objectivism', Gadamer underestimated the importance of the methodological dimension of interpretation, which Habermas and Ricoeur supplied.

5 Pusey, *Jurgen Habermas* (1987), p. 63.

6 Communication is the catalyst that binds together language, interpretation and ethics. Habermas followed Austin, Searle and Strawson in understanding language as action or performance, and posited three basic orientations: the cognitive, which has to do with understanding the 'world out there'; the interactive, which has to do with regulating our social world (norms and rightness); and the expressive, which relates to self-expression: cf. Pusey, *Jurgen Habermas* (1987), pp. 78–85; see Habermas, *Communication and the Evolution of Society* (1979), chapter 1. The ethics of reading involves rational criticism of oneself and rational awareness of the critical process as enabling the most meaningful reading of the text. Reception involves an act of trust, a relationship with the text that involves openness: allowing scope for the imagination to bring to life the world presented in the text. It also involves the responsibility to discriminate between genres, to establish the ethos of the text and to take up an appropriate stance in relation to it. On the ethics of reading, cf. G. Steiner, *Real Presences* (1989), and Wayne Booth, *The Company We Keep* (1988). On reader response, cf. R. C. Holub, *Reception Theory: A Critical Introduction* (1984); J. P. Tomkins (ed.), *Reader-Response Criticism* (1980).

7 cf. Pusey, *Jurgen Habermas*, pp. 64–5.

8 Deconstruction (cf. Derrida), or 'the hermeneutics of suspicion' is of positive assistance in eliciting the hidden agenda of the text. It is destructive only when it seeks to dissolve the text in its own critical acids.

9 cf. Ch. Perelman and L. Olbrechts-Tyteca, *The New Rhetoric: a Treatise on Argumentation* (1969), pp. 59–62. On the rhetorical or persuasive aspect to the text, cf. G. Kennedy, *New Testament Criticism through Rhetorical Criticism* (1984); B. L. Mack, *Rhetoric in the New Testament* (1990); W. Wuellner, 'Where is Rhetorical Criticism Taking Us'?, *CBQ*, 49,3 (1987), pp. 448–63.

10 Peter Berger presupposed a procedural neutrality, as if 'social determinant' was the veritable Archimedean fulcrum – in spite of the fact that sociological analysis is itself interpretive and by no means value free. David Martin, John Milbank and Robin Gill have protested strongly against tendencies in sociological studies to reduce religion merely to its empirical aspects: cf. P. Berger, *The Social Reality of Religion* (1973), p. 7; D. Martin, *The Breaking of the Image: A Sociology of Christian Theory and Practice* (1980); J. Milbank,

Theology and Social Theory: Beyond Secular Reason (1990); R. Gill, *Christian Ethics in Secular Worlds* (1991), esp. pp. 38–41. Sociology is itself part of the circular movement in interpretation and is affected, no less than other disciplines, by that significant cultural sea change which is sweeping away the great subject/object divide, with its pretensions to neutrality and objectivity, and establishing a more intersubjective *modus operandi*. Gill speaks of 'a somewhat humbled sociology' today, and warns against imperialistic claims by any one discipline. R. Gill, *A Textbook of Christian Ethics* (1985), p. 25.

11 Parsons claimed to stand in the tradition of Durkh'eim, Pareto and Weber. He pointed to cultural institutions and activities (churches and schools among them) which serve as the *means* of maintaining stable patterns and defusing tensions in society, while elements within the social system (the legal, health and welfare services, for example) work towards securing the *goals* of integration and solidarity. External goals for attainment are set out by politics and religion in particular. People are also required to adapt to the conditions (for example, the economic situation) in which they find themselves and thus themselves become the means by which society advances; cf. B. J. Malina, 'The Social Sciences and Biblical Interpretation', in N. K. Gottwald (ed.), *The Bible and Liberation* (1983), pp. 16–17.

12 On cognitive dissonance, cf. R. P. Carroll, *when Prophecy Failed* (1979), and L. Festinger, '*A Theory of Cognitive Dissonance*' (1957); note also J. G. Gager, *Kingdom and Community* (1975). The widespread use of the concept of equilibrium in psychology, at least from P. Janet, *L'Evolution psychologique de la personalité*, Paris (1929), may also be noted. Piaget observed that models of equilibrium are to be found in mechanics, thermo-dynamics, physical chemistry and other fields, and that they evince considerable variety: cf. J. Piaget, 'The Role of the Concept of Equilibrium in Psychological Explanation', in D. Elkind (ed.), *Jean Piaget: Six Psychological Studies* (1980), pp. 100–15, esp. pp. 107–8.

13 Following Merton in particular, Ashley, Cohen and Slatter, *An Introduction to the Sociology of Education* (1969), p. 38, conclude: 'both consensus and conflict are admitted as fundamental processes in a social system'; cf. Malina, 'The Social Sciences and Biblical Interpretation', p. 17.

14 cf. Malina, 'The Social Sciences and Biblical Interpretation', p. 18; see also 'Social-Scientific Criticism of the New Testament: More on Methods and Models' (*Semeia*, 35 (1986), pp. 11, 18–22). In relation to religious groups, Weber's distinction between the ideal types of 'church' and 'sect', the one associational and the

other sectarian, may also contribute towards this kind of analysis, although its limitations must be recognised; cf. R. Gill, *Prophecy and Praxis* (1981), pp. 21–30.

15 It is certainly possible to argue for the absorption of moral values from religious tradition, as Habgood and Gill do: J. Habgood, *Church and Nation in a Secular Age* (1983); R. Gill, *Christian Ethics in Secular Worlds* (1991), pp. 97–113. But, as Alasdair MacIntyre has indicated, there is great difficulty in maintaining the notion of a moral consensus in a complex, secularised society. A. MacIntyre, *Whose Justice? Which Rationality?* (1988), pp. 1–11; *After Virtue* (1981), p. 245; cf. D. B. Forrester, *Beliefs, Values and Policies* (1989), esp. pp. 3–49. Rationality itself is an insufficient guarantor of it, for it can fuel conflict and contradiction as well as counter them. Dialogue is a more real possibility. MacIntyre finds the hub of the issue in the reluctance or inability of many societies to recognise and appraise the 'fiduciary foundations' on which their value systems are in fact built. A systemic model of society would entail recognising such inherent tensions and estimating their significance.

16 E.-Schüssler Fiorenza, 'The Ethics of Biblical Interpretation; Decentering Biblical Scholarship', *JBL*, 107/1 (1988), pp. 14–15.

7 THE ETHICS OF HISTORICAL INTERPRETATION

1 E. Schüssler Fiorenza, 'The Ethics of Biblical Interpretation: Decentering Biblical Scholarship', *JBL*, 107/1 (1988), p. 14.

2 J. E. Bernhart, 'The Relativity of Biblical Ethics', in R. J. Hoffmann and G. A. Larue, *Biblical and Secular Ethics. The Conflict* (1988), p. 114.

3 E. Schüssler Fiorenza, as in note 1.

4 W. Meeks, *The Moral World of the First Christians* (1986).

5 J. Bright, *A History of Israel*, 1960.

6 G. E. Mendenhall, *The Tenth Generation: The Origin of the Biblical Tradition*, 1973; 'The Hebrew Conquest of Palestine', *BAR* 3 (1970), pp. 100–20 = *BA* 25 (1962), pp. 66–87; cf. N. K. Gottwald, *The Tribes of Yahweh* (1979), pp. 599–602.

7 Ibid., p. 600.

8 Ibid., p. 601.

9 Ibid., p. 611.

10 Ibid., pp. 618–21.

11 On economics, cf. B. C. Birch, *Let Justice Roll Down* (1991), pp. 178–82.

12 The use of terms such as 'totalitarian', 'omni-competent' and the like may well be anachronistic.

13 B. Childs described the consequences of Gottwald's work as 'a massive theological reductionism': *Old Testament Theology in a Canonical Context* (1985), p. 25. But to take Gottwald's position as simply identifying theology and social reality fails to do justice to the sophistication of his argument, however carelessly stated it may be at times.

14 cf. Birch, *Let Justice Roll Down*, pp. 145–84.

15 F. Belo, *A Materialist Reading of the Gospel of Mark* (Eng. tr., 1981).

16 cf. the incorporation of the originally independent wisdom tradition.

17 L. Schottroff, 'Experience of Liberation', *Concilium* 172/2, 1984, p. 68.

18 cf. 1 Sam. 9–20; 4.1–7.2; 2 Sam. 6; J. Bright, *A History of Israel*, pp. 163–248.

19 In 1 Kings 21 interest centres on the clash of quite different symbolic systems. Jezebel's system reflects the absolute power of Tyrian kings; Naboth reflects the independent rights of the covenantal landholder in Israel; Ahab is caught between the two; and Elijah represents the moral power of Yahwism.

20 cf. J. Lindblom, *Prophecy in Ancient Israel* (Eng. tr., 1962), esp. pp. 210–19.

21 cf. Isa. 42.1–4; 49.1–6; 50.4–9; 52.13–53.12. The traditional position is set out in C. R. North, *The Suffering Servant in Deutero-Isaiah* (1948); more recent scholarship emphasises the context of the passages: cf. T. N. D. Mettinger, *A Farewell to the Servant Songs* (1983); Birch, *Let Justice Roll Down*, pp. 297–300. The figure is taken as a collective characterisation of a significant section of the community in exile.

22 J. G. Gager, *Kingdom and Community: The Social World of Early Christianity* (1975); L. Festinger, *A Theory of Cognitive Dissonance* (1957).

23 G. Theissen, *The First Followers of Jesus* (Eng. tr. 1978).

24 W. Meeks, *The Moral World of the First Christians*, pp. 97–160.

25 J. H. Elliott suggests a 'multivariate matrix model' which allows comparison of interest groups in terms of, for example, socio-economic factors, political–legal factors, culture or belief systems, and strategy and ideology.

26 H. C. Kee, *Christian Origins in Sociological Perspective* (1980), p. 101.

27 M. Machovec, *A Marxist Looks at Jesus* (Eng. tr. 1976); G. V. Pixley, *God's Kingdom* (1981); F. Belo, *A Materialist Reading of the Gospel of Mark* (1981); W. Stegemann, *God of the Lowly* (1984); M. Clévenot, *Materialist Approaches to the Bible* (1985).

28 cf. D. E. Oakman, *Jesus and the Economic Questions of his Day* (1986).

29 Stegemann, *God of the Lowly*, p. 19.
30 cf. W. Horbury, 'The Temple Tax', in Bammel and Moule (eds.), *Jesus and Politics* (1984), pp. 277f.
31 Clévenot (1985), p 44.
32 cf. M. Hengel, *The Zealots* (Eng. tr. 1989), p. 323; R. Horsley and J. S. Harrison, *Bandits, Prophets and Messiah* (1985), p. 31; R. Horsley, 'The Zealots', Nov.T. 28 2 1986, pp. 159–92; W. R. Farmer, *Maccabees, Zealots and Josephus* (1956).
33 John's preaching attracted crowds of ordinary people, and he appears to have counselled people deeply affected by the situation in the land: tax-collectors who came to be baptised (Luke 3.12) and who were accounted impure or polluted by reason of their calling; and serving soldiers (the reference is unlikely to be to freedom fighters!) who asked about the implications of his message for them. (Luk. 3.14)
34 On rhetorical criticism, see p. 271, n. 9.
35 Belo, *A Materialist Reading*, pp. 187–8.
36 Ibid., p. 187.
37 Ibid., p. 193.
38 cf. E. P. Sanders, *JJ*, pp. 294–318.
39 Belo, *A Materialist Reading*, p. 180.
40 D. E. Nineham, *The Gospel of Mark* (1963), p. 301.
41 cf. Chilton and McDonald, *Jesus and the Ethics of the Kingdom*, pp. 16–20, 29–31 etc.
42 L. Schottroff, *Concilium*, 172/2, pp. 69, 71.
43 cf. K. Füssel, 'The Materialist Reading of the Bible', in Gottwald (ed.), *The Bible and Liberation* (1983) pp. 134–46.
44 cf. R. Horsley, *Jesus and the Spiral of Violence* (1987).
45 An obvious *crux interpretum* is Luke 19.12–27.
46 cf. Belo, *A Materialist Reading*, p. 113, where the heart is 'the place where decisions are made': the hardened heart cannot read Jesus' praxis, that is, his narrative.
47 cf. ibid., p. 109.
48 L. Schottroff, *Concilium*, 172/2, p. 70.
49 cf. T. H. Groome, *Christian Religious Education* (1980) and A. Verhey, *The Great Reversal: Ethics and the New Testament*, Grand Rapids (1984).
50 cf. W. Schrage, *The Ethics of the N.T.*, pp. 291–3.
51 cf. ibid., pp. 297, 308–14.
52 cf. Schrage, pp. 341–2.
53 cf. G. Theissen, *The Social Setting of Pauline Christianity* (Eng. tr. 1982), pp. 28–35.
54 cf. 2 Cor. 11.7–10; 12.13–18; cf. Phil. 4.10–18.

55 cf. Theissen, pp. 35–46.
56 1 Cor. 7.21 is ambiguous: it may refer to the opportunity of gaining freedom or the opportunity to use one's slave status to the glory of God (cf. 1 Cor. 7.17).
57 cf. Meeks, *Moral World*, pp. 32–8.
58 J. C. O'Neill, *Paul's Letter to the Romans* (1975) recognised the Stoic connection, but argued for an interpolation: pp. 208–9.
59 cf. J. I. H. McDonald, 'Romans 13.1–7: A Test Case for New Testament Interpretation', *NTS*, 35/4, 1989, pp. 546–7.
60 cf. Polycarp, *Martyrdom*, 17.
61 cf. Ibid., 10.
62 cf. Meeks, *Moral World*, pp. 45–61.
63 H. C. Kee, *Christian Origins*, pp. 75.
64 Dominant ancient cultures tended to have a mythology of race. The superiority of the Greek was a general Greek assumption which Plato at one point attempted to explain in environmental terms. He indicated, however, that its correlative, 'barbarian', was problematic and insupportable as a division of humankind. It remained a cultural factor in Hellenistic imperialism, although it stood in tension with the cosmopolitanism that was also a feature of the period. Once again it is to the more popular philosophies that we look for the best expression of this cosmopolitanism.
65 Athens in its heyday was relatively conservative, at least as regards the role of wives. Plato, in the *Laws*, suggested that the state could not afford to neglect to employ the talents of half its citizens, but this is part of a rather ideal scenario: Pamela Huby, *Plato and Modern Morality* (1972), pp. 32–8; Aristotle was more negative: cf. A. W. Gomme, *Essays in History and Literature* (1937). In the dramatists women emerged as fitting agents for expressing alternative values. In time, the Epicureans were able to express a quite different status for women in their communities.
66 See above, n. 56.
67 cf. J. M. G. Barclay, 'Paul, Philemon and the Dilemma of Christian Slave-Ownership', *NTS*, 37/2 1991, pp. 161–86. In relation to Hellenic culture, Luise Schottroff pointed to the social ambivalence in the use of the term 'freedom'. Freemen, she observes, 'were the people with full civic rights who let others work for them as bondsmen or slaves', *Concilium* 172/2 (1984), pp. 67–73. Slaves – even educated slaves – were animated possessions or tools, as far as status went. Thus, liberty in classical writings tends to be an internalised liberty which is adopted in spite of external conditions and leaves the latter largely undisturbed. The dominant order could be questioned and alternatives could be set forth on an

individual or community basis, but there is little evidence of real subversion – although the Roman imperial defensiveness in relation to secret societies indicates that the possibility was not ruled out. The most feared counter-force was outright rebellion.

8 ETHICS AND CONTEMPORARY READING

1 W. Wink, *The Bible in Human Transformation* (1973), p. 74.
2 E. Schüssler Fiorenza, 'The Ethics of Biblical Interpretation', *JBL* 107/1 (1988), p. 15.
3 This does not mean that one cannot read the Bible in private! When we do so, however, we presuppose the community which shaped and sustains us.
4 D. Tracy, *Blessed Rage for Order*, 1978.
5 cf. 'New Testament and Mythology', in Bartsch (ed.), *Kerygma and Myth I*.
6 E. Fuchs and G. Ebeling take the language aspect much more seriously and make their mark in literary discussions: cf. R. Detweiler and V. K. Robbins, 'From New Criticism to Poststructuralism: Twentieth-Century Hermeneutics', in S. Prickett (ed.), *Reading the Text*, pp. 241–3.
7 cf. W. Wink on human transformation (n. 1 above) and P. Ricoeur's discussion of Bultmann in 'Preface to Bultmann', in L. S. Mudge, *Paul Ricoeur, Essays on Biblical Interpretation*, (Eng. tr.) 1981.
8 cf. Ricoeur, 'Preface to Bultmann', p. 56.
9 D. Sölle, *Thinking About God* (1990), p. 38.
10 T. H. Groome, *Christian Religious Education* (1980), pp. 207–14.
11 cf. L. M. Russell (ed.), *Feminist Interpretation of the Bible* (1985), pp. 21–51; cf. A. Loades (ed.), *A Feminist Reader* (1990); and *Searching for Lost Coins: Explorations in Christianity and Feminism* (1987).
12 cf. D. Sölle, *Thinking About God* (1990), p. 70.
13 cf. J. P. Mackey, 'The Use and Abuse of Mary in Roman Catholicism', in R. Holloway (ed.), *Who Needs Feminism?* (1991).
14 cf. Ruether, R. R. *Mary – The Feminine Face of the Church*, London (1979); *Sexism and God-Talk*, London (1983).
15 C. Mesters, 'The Use of the Bible in Christian Communities of the Common People', in N. K. Gottwald (ed.), *The Bible and Liberation* (1983), p. 122.
16 E. Cardinale, *The Gospel in Solentiname* (1977–80); cf. J. L. Segundo, *The Community Called Church* (1980), *passim*.
17 Mesters, pp. 119–33.
18 Ibid., p. 126.

19 Ibid., p. 123.
20 Ibid., p. 122.
21 J. L. Segundo, *The Liberation of Theology*, Dublin (1977), pp. 13–25.
22 cf. Ricoeur, 'The Hermeneutics of Testimony', in Mudge (ed.), *Essays on Biblical Interpretation* (1981), pp. 18–21.
23 Mudge, *Essays*, p. 23.
24 Ibid., pp. 21–7.
25 Ibid., p. 27.
26 cf. 'Freedom in the Light of Hope', in ibid., pp. 155–80.
27 Wink, *Bible in Human Transformation*, p. 22.
28 Ibid., pp. 27–8.
29 Ibid., p. 29.
30 Ibid., p. 65, cf. p. 31.
31 Ibid., p. 29, cf. p. 31.
32 Ibid., p. 39.
33 On psychoanalysis, cf. ibid., pp. 46–65.
34 Ibid., p. 66.
35 cf. W. Wink, *Transforming Bible Study* (2nd edn. 1990), pp. 17–151; and the 'shared praxis' approach of T. H. Groome below.
36 Wink, *Bible in Human Transformation*, pp. 62–3; cf. p. 75.
37 Wink, *Naming the Powers* (1984).
38 Groome, *Christian Religious Education* (1980), p. 217.
39 E. Schüssler Fiorenza, *In Memory of Her* (1983), on Mark 14.3–9.
40 The Hebrew scriptures present a challenge to the feminist interpreter, who may well go in search of 'texts of terror' involving women, as Phyllis Trible did (cf. *Texts of Terror* (1984)). More positive is the rereading of the story of Adam and Eve which properly emphasises the interdependence of the sexes, and can even claim the support of etymology. The word *adam* is properly 'earth creature' (*adamah* is 'earth'), rather than 'man'; and the *adam* Yahweh created was both male and female (Gen. 1.27). Not until Genesis 2.22–3 were they differentiated as *ish* and *isha*.
41 D. Sölle, *Thinking about God*, pp. 74–5.
42 Guttiérez, *Theology of Liberation* (1974), p. 3.
43 cf. Wink, *Bible in Human Transformation*, p. 15.
44 cf. Paulo Freire, *Pedagogy of the Oppressed* (1972).
45 Guttiérez, *Theology of Liberation*, p. 60.
46 L. and C. Boff, *Introducing Liberation Theology* (1987) *passim*.
47 C. Boff, *Theology and Praxis* (1987), pp. 147–9.
48 cf. J. S. Croatto, *Exodus. A Hermeneutics of Freedom* (Eng. tr. 1981); also, 'Socio-historical and Hermeneutical Relevance of the Exodus', *Concilium*, 189 (1987), pp. 125–33. Croatto writes with an awareness of Ricoeur and the Western hermeneutical debate.

49 J. L. Segundo, *The Community Called Church* (1980).

50 cf. A. MacIntyre, *After Virtue* (1981), p. 263.

51 Story is one of the most characteristic literary forms in the Bible: cf. H. Frei, *The Eclipse of Biblical Narrative* (1974); *Identity* (1975); G. W. Stroup, *The Promise of Narrative Theology* (1981); G. Genette, *Narrative Discourse. An Essay in Method* (1980); R. W. Funk, *The Poetics of Biblical Narrative* (1988). Stories have to do with identity: whether of God's people Israel, or Jesus as messenger of the kingdom, of Paul the apostle, or of the hearer; and with relationships, whether to God, neighbour, alien or enemy, the powerful or the dependent. They are a public declaration of internalised experience, an invitation to see new perspectives, to discover how *this* story intersects *my* story or *our* story, and to identify with it and be transformed. On the tension between 'story' and 'concept', cf. J. L. Houlden, *History, Story and Belief*, King's College, University of London (1988). It may be that the approach of *Heilsgeschichte* – cf. G. E. Wright, *The God Who Acts* (1952), O. Cullmann, *Salvation in History* (Eng. tr., 1967), G. von Rad, *Old Testament Theology* (Eng. tr. 1962–5); criticised by J. Goldingay, 'Salvation History', in *DBI* (1990), pp. 606–7 – could have a future if recast as narrative theology.

52 cf. Habgood, Gill and others.

53 M. Vidal, 'Is Morality based on Autonomy compatible with the ethics of Liberation?' *Concilium*, 172/2 (1984), pp. 80–6.

54 F. M. Réjon, 'Seeking the Kingdom and its Justice', pp. 38–9, in *Concilium*, 172/2 (1984), pp. 38–9.

55 cf. Fairweather and McDonald, *The Quest* (1984), pp. 219–57; one might properly emphasise 'respect for persons' as the essential condition for creative, critical dialogue: cf. W. W. Bartley III, *The Retreat to Commitment* (1984), p. 165.

56 E. Dussel, *Ethics and Community* (Eng. tr., 1988), p. 28.

57 Ibid., pp. 27–36.

58 Ibid., pp. 47–57.

59 cf. chapter seven, above.

60 J. C. O'Neill, *Paul's Letter to the Romans* (1975), p. 209.

61 cf. E. Käsemann, 'Principles of the Interpretation of Romans 13', *New Testament Questions of Today*', p. 198; cf. pp. 196–216. There is room, he argued, neither for dogmatic theology nor for ethics in the sense of a 'logically articulated system designed to be normative for Christian behaviour.' Moral guidance in an eschatological ethos takes the form of paraenesis: single injunctions like the love command and exhortations to obedience, operating almost in casuistical fashion. Although he is essentially post-Bultmannian,

280 *Notes for pages 224–231*

Käsemann presents remarkable similarities with Otto in his emphasis on charismatic power and joy. The basic question is how dependent this standpoint is on Paul, and how far it represents Käsemann's own *Sitz im Leben*.

62 'Principles', p. 199.
63 Käsemann probably overstates a valid case. The Nazi debacle illustrates the danger of investing the human ruler with divine prerogatives; and demonisation may well have corresponding dangers. However, Paul's imagery or *theologumenon*, carefully interpreted, may be serviceable for social ethics: cf. A. N. Wilder, *The Bible and the Literary Critic*, 1991, p. 69; D. B. Forrester, *Beliefs, Values and Policies*, 1989, 65–77: cf. chapter six above.
64 'Principles', p. 207. The statement at least requires further discussion: see on Macgregor, in chapter six.
65 'Principles', p. 215.
66 cf. J. I. H. McDonald, 'Romans 13.1–7: a Test Case for New Testament Interpretation', *NTS*, 35/4, 1989, pp. 540–9.
67 cf. C. S. Cooley, *Social Organization* (1909), p. 23; W. J. H. Sprott, *Human Groups* (1958), p. 57.
68 E. Fuchs, *Sexual Desire and Love* (1983), pp. 41–5.
69 Ibid., pp. 172–91.
70 Erasmus made three criticisms: the 'sacramental' view was not patristic; it raised controversy about the nature of a sacrament; and 'mysterion' should be translated as 'mystery', not 'sacrament'. The basic *mysterion* is the union of Christ and his church (not marriage in itself).
71 *Casti Connubi* (Pius IX, 1930).
72 Apart from feminism, socialist perspectives have shown ambivalence towards the family. The radical socialist regarded the family as part of the capitalist system, to be swept away as the new order dawned. Nevertheless, since the family located value in human relationships rather than the market as such (however much it was, and is, affected by the market), the Fabian wing (and others) affirmed the family and concentrated on eliminating the poverty which so brutalised it. Capitalism, however, has shown remarkable resilience, whatever moral problems it raises, and has obstinately refused to fade away like an old soldier. Hence, socialist perspectives on the family now tend to see a positive aspect to the family as signalling a new social order based not on market values and competition, but on co-operation and love of others; and emphasis is put on allocating resources to release families from worry, anger, distrust and insecurity.
73 D. J. West, *Homosexuality Reexamined* (1977), p. 1; cf. J. Boswell,

Christianity, Social Tolerance, and Homosexuality, 1980. Earlier works of note are D. S. Bailey, *Homosexuality and the Western Christian Tradition* (1955); and *The Man–Woman Relation in Christian Thought* (1959).

74 L. Virgo, 'Homosexuality', in *A Dictionary of Pastoral Care*' (ed. Campbell, 1987), p. 113.
75 R. Scroggs, *The New Testament and Homosexuality*, (1983), p. 127.
76 cf. Pseudo-Phocylides 3.190–2, Philo, *Special Laws*, 3.39–40, *The Contemplative Life* 59–62, and *Abraham* 133–41 (cf. *Sibylline Oracles*).
77 L. W. Countryman, *Dirt, Greed and Sex* (1988), p. 62.
78 For a balanced review, cf. M. Banner, 'Directions and Misdirections in Christian Sexual Ethics', *ER* 19/3 (1992), pp. 95–107.
79 Countryman, *Dirt* (1988), p. 118.
80 cf. Virgo's article, n. 74 above.
81 cf. Ogletree, *The Use of the Bible in Christian Ethics* (1983).
82 cf. chapter seven above.
83 There is some evidence that Christian attitudes varied according to socio-political context. The Pauline churches, with their close ties to commercial life, were less detached from material things, and made their wealth work on behalf of the church, but were constantly warned against wrong values. The letter of James is outspoken in its condemnation of tendencies within Christian communities to place value on wealth and worldly status.
84 On the 'jubilee year', cf. R. de Vaux, *Ancient Israel* (1961), pp. 175–7.
85 R. M. Grant, 'Early Christianity and the Creation of Capital', in P. Berger (ed.), *The Spirit of Capitalism*, 1990.
86 After the death of Herod the Great, Archelaus went off to Rome to ask Augustus to nominate him as his father's successor: Josephus, *Antiquities* 17.9.1. His petition was countered by an embassy of fifty Jews: *Antiquities* 17.11.1–2.
87 Professor of economics in the Free University, Amsterdam.
88 'Freedom and Justice', *ER*, 19/3 (1992), p. 29.
89 CFCs = chlorofluorohydrocarbons.
90 L. White, 'The Historical Roots of our Ecologic Crisis', in W. Granberg-Michaelson, *Ecology and Life: Accepting our Environmental Responsibility* (1988), p. 134. The article originally appeared in *Science*, 155, pp. 1203–7.
91 White, 'Historical Roots', p. 135; cf. also J. Black, *The Dominion of Man*, Edinburgh (1970), pp. 19–42; E. Breuilly and M. Palmer (eds.), *Christianity and Ecology* (1992).
92 J. C. L. Gibson, *Genesis*, Daily Study Bible. On population, cf. P. and A. Ehrlich, *The Population Explosion* (1990).

93 cf. De Vaux, *Ancient Israel* (1961), pp. 480–2.

94 White, 'Historical Roots', p. 137.

95 C. Gunton, *Enlightenment and Alienation* (1985), p. 25. The tendency to pillory Christianity or selected targets within it – Calvinism is a favourite whipping boy, at least in popular writing – requires to be offset by reference to wider context. Against Gunton, it should be noted that the physical and the moral were divided long before the Enlightenment, as in the scholastic view that, since animals had no souls, humans had no obligation to them.

96 Cited in the bibliographical introduction by C. H. Bishop to Jules Isaac, *The Teaching of Contempt* (1964), p. 5.

97 cf. E. L. Abel, *The Roots of Anti-Semitism* (1975).

98 Isaac, *The Teaching of Contempt*, pp. 39–149.

99 Ibid., pp. 69–71.

100 Ibid., pp. 79–107.

101 Ibid., p. 117.

102 cf. P. Richardson (ed.), *Anti-Judaism in Early Christianity*, I (1986); J. G. Gager, *The Origins of Anti-Semitism* (1983).

103 cf. J. C. Hurd, 'Paul Ahead of His Time: 1 Thess, 2.13–16', in P. Richardson (ed.), *Anti-Judaism*, pp. 21–36.

104 R. R. Ruether, 'The *Faith and Fratricide* Discussion: Old Problems and New Dimensions', in A. T. Davies, *Anti-Semitism and the Foundations of Christianity* (1979), p. 234; cf. L. Newbigin, *The Gospel in a Pluralist Society*, 1989.

105 H. J. Schoeps, *The Jewish Christian Argument: A History of Theologies in Conflict* (1963), p. 8; cited in P. Richardson (ed.), *Anti-Judaism*, p. 19.

Select bibliography

Abel, E. L., *The Roots of Anti-Semitism*, London 1975.
Alexander, A. B. D., *The Ethics of St Paul*, Glasgow 1910.
   Christianity and Ethics, London (1914) 1931.
   The Shaping Forces of Religious Thought, Glasgow 1920.
   The Thinkers of the Church, London 1924.
   'The Kingdom of God and the Ethics of Jesus', *Expository Times*,
      1928–9.
Althaus, P., *The so-called Kerygma and the Historical Jesus* (Eng. tr.)
      Edinburgh 1959.
Ashley, B., Cohen, H. S., and Slatter, R. G., *An Introduction to the
      Sociology of Education*, Edinburgh 1969.
Austin, J. L., 'Performative Utterances', in his *Philosophical Papers*
      (eds. J. O. Urmson, G. J. Warnock), Oxford 1961.
Bailey, D. S., *Homosexuality and the Western Christian Tradition*, London
      1955.
   The Man–Woman Relation in Christian Thought, London 1959.
Bald, H. 'Eschatological or Theological Ethics? Notes on the
      Relationship between Eschatology and Ethics in the Teaching of
      Jesus', in Chilton (ed.), *The Kingdom of God in the Teaching of Jesus*,
      London 1984.
Bammel, E. and C. F. D. Moule (eds.), *Jesus and the Politics of his Day*,
      Cambridge 1984.
Banner, M., 'Directions and Misdirections on Christian Sexual
      Ethics', *Epworth Review*, 19.3, 1992.
Barclay, J. M. G., 'Paul, Philemon and the Dilemma of Christian
      Slave-Ownership', *New Testament Studies* 37/2 1991.
Barrett, C. K., *Westcott as Commentator*, Cambridge 1959.
Barth, K., *Der Römerbrief* (5th edn. München 1929).
   The Epistle to the Romans Eng. tr.) London 1933.
   Church and State (Eng. tr.) London 1939.
   Ethics (ed. D. Braun), (Eng. tr.) Edinburgh 1981.
Bartley, W. W., III, *The Retreat to Commitment*, La Salle 1984.

Bartsch, H. W. (ed.), *Kerygma and Myth I* (Eng. tr.) London 1954.
Bellah, R. N., *Beyond Belief*, London 1970.
Belo, F., *A Materialist Reading of the Gospel of Mark* (Eng. tr.) Maryknoll, New York 1981.
Bennett, J., *Christian Ethics and Social Policy*, New York 1946.
Bentley, J., *Between Marx and Christ*, London 1982.
Berger, P., *The Social Reality of Religion*, Harmondsworth 1973.
Berger, P. (ed.), *The Spirit of Capitalism*, San Francisco 1990.
Bernhart, J. E., 'The Relativity of Biblical Ethics', in R. J. Hoffmann and G. A. Larue, *Biblical and Secular Ethics* (q.v.).
Best, G. F. A., *Bishop Westcott and the Miners*, Cambridge 1967.
Birch, B. C., *Let Justice Roll Down: The Old Testament Ethics and Christian Life*, Louisville, Kentucky 1991.
Blumhardt, C., *Ihr Menschen seid Gottes*, Erlenbach-Zurich and Leipzig 1936.
Boff, C., *Theology and Praxis: Epistemological Foundations*, Maryknoll, New York 1987.
Boff, L. and Boff, C., *Introducing Liberation Theology*, New York 1987.
Booth, W., *The Company We Keep: An Ethics of Fiction*, Berkeley 1988.
Bornkamm, G., *Jesus of Nazareth* (Eng. tr.), London 1960.
Boswell, J., *Christianity, Social Tolerance and Homosexuality*, Chicago 1980.
Bowden, J., *Karl Barth*, London 1971.
Breuilly, E. and M. Palmer (eds.), *Christianity and Ecology*, London 1992.
Bright, J., *A History of Israel*, London 1960.
Brown, S., *Secular Alternatives to Religion* ('Man's Religious Quest', Unit 22), Milton Keynes 1978.
Brunner, E., *The Divine Imperative* (Eng. tr.) London 1937.
 Justice and the Social Order, London 1945.
Bultmann, R., *Jesus*, Berlin 1926.
 Theology of the New Testament I (Eng. tr.) London 1952.
 'New Testament and Mythology', in *Kerygma and Myth I*, (ed. Bartsch) London 1954.
 Jesus and the Word (Eng. tr.) London (1943) rev. 1958.
Cadbury, H. J., *The Peril of Modernising Jesus*, New York 1937.
Caird, G. B., *Principalities and Powers*, Oxford 1956.
Campbell, A. V. (ed.), *A Dictionary of Pastoral Care*, London 1987.
Campbell, W. S., *Paul's Gospel in an Intercultural Context*, Frankfurt-on-Main, 1991.
 'Christ the end of the Law: Romans 10.4', in *Paul's Gospel in an Intercultural Context*.
Cardinale, E., *The Gospel in Solentiname*, London 1977–1980.

Carr, W., *Angels and Principalities*, Cambridge, 1981,
Carroll, R. P., *When Prophecy Failed*, London 1979.
Childs, B., *Old Testament Theology in a Canonical Context*, London 1985.
Chilton, B., and McDonald, J. I. H., *Jesus and the Ethics of the Kingdom*, London 1987.
Clark, H., *The Ethical Mysticism of Albert Schweitzer*, Beacon, Boston 1962.
Clévenot, M., *Materialist Approaches to the Bible*, Maryknoll, New York 1985.
Collingwood, R. G., *The Idea of History*, London 1946.
Cooley, C. S., *Social Organization*, New York 1909.
Corner, M., see Rowland, C.
Countryman, L. W., *Dirt, Greed and Sex*, London 1988.
Crenshaw, J. L., 'The influence of the Wise upon Amos' *ZAW*, 79, 1962.
Croatto, J. S., *Exodus. A Hermeneutics of Freedom* (Eng. tr.) New York, 1981.
Cullmann, O., *Christ and Time* (Eng. tr.) London 1967 (1951).
  The State in the New Testament (Eng. tr.) London 1957.
  Salvation in History (Eng. tr.) London 1967.
Curran, T. H., 'Schleiermacher: True Interpreter' in D. Jasper (ed.) *The Interpretation of Belief* (q.v.).
Davie, G., *The Scottish Enlightenment and Other Essays*, Edinburgh 1991.
Davies, A. T. (ed.), *Anti-Semitism and the Foundations of Christianity*, New York 1979.
Davies, W. D., *Paul and Rabbinic Judaism*, London 1948.
  'Ethics in the New Testament', in *Interpreter's Dictionary of the Bible*, New York 1962.
  The Setting of the Sermon on the Mount, Cambridge 1964.
  'The Relevance of the Moral Teaching of the Early Church', in E. E. Ellis and M. Wilcox (eds.), *Neotestamentica et Semitica* (q.v.).
Detweiler, R., and Robbins, V. K., 'From New Criticism to Post-structuralism: Twentieth-Century Hermeneutics' in S. Prickett, (ed.), *Reading the Text* (q.v.).
Dibelius, M., *Jesus* (Eng. tr.) London 1963.
Dilthey, W., *Leben Schleiermachers*, Berlin 1922.
Dodd, *The Meaning of Paul for Today*, London 1920.
  The Authority of the Bible, London 1928.
  Parables of the Kingdom, London 1935.
  The Apostolic Preaching and its Development, London 1936.
  Gospel and Law, Cambridge 1952.
Dunn, J. D. G., *Unity and Diversity of the New Testament*, London 1977.
Dussel, E., *Ethics and the Theology of Liberation*, Maryknoll, N.Y. 1978.

Ethics and Community (Eng. tr.) Maryknoll, N.Y. 1986.
Ebeling, G., 'Hermeneutic', *RGG*, II, 1959.
Ehrhardt, E., *Der Grundcharakter der Ethik Jesu*, Freiburg 1895.
Ehrlich, P. and A., *The Population Explosion*, London 1990.
Ellis, E. E., and Wilcox, M., *Neotestamentica et Semitica*, Edinburgh 1969.
Fairweather, I. C. M., and McDonald, J. I. H., *The Quest for Christian Ethics*, Edinburgh 1984.
Farmer, W. R., *Maccabees, Zealots and Josephus*, New York 1956.
Ferguson, R., *George Macleod*, London 1990.
Festinger, L. (with H. W. Riecken and S. Schechter), *When Prophecy Fails*, New York (1956) 1964.
  '*A Theory of Cognitive Dissonance*', Evanston, Ill., 1957.
Fiorenza, E. S., 'The Ethics of Biblical Interpretation: Decentering Biblical Scholarship', *JBL*, 107/1, 1988.
  Bread not Stone: The Challenge of Feminist Biblical Interpretation, Edinburgh, 1984.
  In Memory of Her, London 1983.
  (with D. Tracy), 'The Holocaust as Interruption', *Concilium* 175, Edinburgh 1984.
Fierro, A., *The Militant Gospel*, London 1977.
Fletcher, J., *Situation Ethics*, London 1966;
  Moral Responsibility, London 1967.
Forrester, D. B., *Christianity and the Future of Welfare*, London 1985.
  Beliefs, Values and Policies, London 1989.
Frei, H., *The Eclipse of Biblical Narrative*, New Haven 1974.
  Identity, Philadelphia 1975.
Freire, P., *Pedagogy of the Oppressed*, Harmondsworth 1972.
Fuchs, E., *Studies of the Historical Jesus* (Eng. tr.) London 1964.
  Sexual Desire and Love (Eng. tr.) Clarke, Cambridge, 1983.
Funk, R., *The Poetics of Biblical Narrative*, Sonoma 1988.
Furnish, V. P., 'The Jesus–Paul Debate: From Baur to Bultmann', *BJRL*, 47, 1964–5.
  The Love Commandment in the New Testament, London 1973.
Füssel, K., 'The Materialist Reading of the Bible', in Gottwald (ed.), *The Bible and Liberation* (q.v.).
Gadamer, H.G., *Truth and Method* (Eng. tr.) London (1975) 1981.
Gager, J. G., *Kingdom and Community: The Social World of Early Christianity*, Englewood Cliffs N.J., 1975.
  The Origins of Anti-Semitism, New York 1983.
Genette, G., *Narrative Discourse. An Essay in Method* (Eng. tr.) Cornell 1980.
Gill, R., *The Social Context of Theology*, London 1975.

Theology and Social Structure, London 1977.
Prophecy and Praxis, London 1981.
A Textbook of Christian Ethics, Edinburgh 1985.
Christian Ethics in Secular Worlds, Edinburgh 1991.
Gladstone, W. E., *On Ecce Homo*, 1868 originally published as a series of articles in the monthly *Good Words*.
Goldingay, J., 'Salvation History', in *DBI*, 1990.
Gomme, A. W., *Essays in Greek History and Literature*, Oxford 1937.
Gooch, G. P., *The Cambridge Modern History XII*, Cambridge 1910.
Gottwald, N. K., (ed.) *The Bible and Liberation*, Maryknoll, N.Y. 1983.
The Tribes of Yahweh, London 1979.
Granberg-Michaelson, W., *Ecology and Life: Accepting our Environmental Responsibility*, Waco Texas 1987.
Grant, R. M., 'Early Christianity and the Creation of Capital', in P. Berger (ed.), *The Spirit of Capitalism* (q.v.).
Groome, T. H., *Christian Religious Education*, San Francisco 1980.
Gunton, C., *Enlightenment and Alienation*, London 1985.
Gustafson, J. M., 'Context Versus Principles: A Misplaced Debate in Christian Ethics', in Marty and Peerman *The New Theology* (q.v.).
Gutiérrez, G., *Theology of Liberation*, London (1974) 1975.
Habermas, J., *Communication and the Evolution of Society* (Eng. tr.) London 1979.
The Theory of Communicative Action: Reason and the Rationalisation of Society, 1 (Eng. tr.) London 1984.
Habgood, J., *Church and Nation in a Secular Age*, London 1983.
Harnack, A., *Das Wesen des Christentums*, Leipzig 1900.
What is Christianity? (Eng. tr.) London 1901.
History of Dogma (Eng. tr.) London 1897–9 (r.p. 1957).
(with W. Herrmann), *Essays on the Social Gospel* (Eng. tr.) London 1907.
Harrison, J. S., see Horsley, R.
Hauerwas, S., *A Community of Character*, Notre Dame 1981.
Hefner, P. *Faith in the Vitalities of History*, New York 1966.
Heitmüller, W., *Im Namen Jesu*, Gottingen 1903.
Hengel, M., *The Zealots* (Eng. tr.) Edinburgh 1989.
Herrmann, W., and Harnack, A. (eds.) 'The Social Mission of the Church', in *Essays on the Social Gospel*: see Harnack.
Hiers, H. H., and Holland, D. L. (eds.), *Johannes Weiss: Jesus' Proclamation of the Kingdom of God* (Eng. tr.) London 1975.
Hoffman, R. J., and Larue, G. A., *Biblical and Secular Ethics. The Conflict*, Buffalo, N.Y. 1988.
Holland, D. L., see Hiers, H. H.

Holloway, R., (ed.), *Who Needs Feminism?* London 1991.
Holub, R. C., *Reception Theory: A Critical Introduction*, London 1984.
Horbury, W., 'The Temple Tax', in Bammel and Moule, *Jesus and Politics* (q.v.).
Horsley, R., and Harrison, J. S., *Jesus and the Spiral of Violence*, San Francisco 1987.
Bandits, Prophets and Messiah, San Francisco, 1988.
Houlden, J. L., *Ethics and the New Testament*, London 1973.
Huby, P., *Plato and Modern Morality*, London 1972.
Hurd, J. C., 'Paul Ahead of His Time: 1 Thess. 2.13–16' in P. Richardson *Anti-Judaism*, Waterloo, Ontario 1986.
Isaac, J., *The Teaching of Contempt: Christian Roots of Anti-Semitism* (Eng. tr.) New York 1964.
Jasper, D., (ed.), *The Interpretation of Belief: Coleridge, Schleiermacher and Romanticism*, London 1986.
Jeanrond, W. G., 'The Impact of Schleiermacher's Hermeneutics on Contemporary Interpretation Theory' in D. Jasper (ed.) *The Interpretation of Belief* (q.v.).
'Hermeneutics', in *DBI*, 1990.
Jülicher, A., *Die Gleichnisreden Jesu II*, 1910.
Kähler, M., *Historische Jesus*, Leipzig 1892.
Kaiser, W. C., Jr., *Toward Old Testament Ethics*, Grand Rapids (1983) 1991.
Kant, I., *Der Kritik der reinen Vernunft*, 1781/87; *The Critique of Pure Reason* (Eng. tr.) London 1933.
The Moral Law: Kant's Groundwork of the Metaphysics of Morals (Eng. tr.) London 1948.
Käsemann E., *New Testament Questions of Today* (Eng. tr.) London 1969.
Testament of Jesus (Eng. tr.) London.
Kee, H. C., *Christian Origins in Sociological Perspective*, London 1980.
Keeling, M., *The Foundations of Christian Ethics*, Edinburgh 1990.
Kennedy, G., *New Testament Criticism Through Rhetorical Criticism*, Chapel Hill 1984.
Knox, J., *The Ethic of Jesus and the Teaching of the Church*, London 1962.
Chapters in a Life of Paul, New York 1950.
Kümmel, W. G., *The New Testament: The History of the Investigation of its Problems* (Eng. tr.) London 1973.
Larue, G. A.: see Hoffmann, R. J.
Lindblom, J., *Prophecy in Ancient Israel* (Eng. tr.) Oxford 1962.
Loades, A., *Searching for Lost Coins*, London 1987.
(ed.) *A Feminist Reader*, Louisville, 1990.
(ed.,) *Hermeneutics, The Bible and Literary Criticism*, Basingstoke 1992.

Lodge, O., Preface to the Everyman edition of *Ecce Homo* (see Seeley).
Long, D. S., 'Ramseyian Just War and Yoderian Pacifism: Where is the Disagreement?', *Studies in Christian Ethics*, 4.1, 1991.
Lundström, *The Kingdom of God in the Teaching of Jesus* (Eng. tr.) Edinburgh 1963.
Luthardt, C. E., *History of Christian Ethics* (Eng. tr.) Edinburgh 1889.
McDonald, J. I. H., *Kerygma and Didache*, Cambridge 1980.
  Resurrection: Narrative and Belief, London 1989.
  Jesus and the Ethics of the Kingdom (with Chilton, B. q.v.).
  The Quest for Christian Ethics (with Fairweather I. C. M. q.v.).
  'Romans 13.1–7: A Test Case for New Testament Interpretation', *New Testament Studies*, 35.4 1989.
  'The Bible and Christian Practice', in D. B. Forrester (ed.), *Theology and Practice*, London 1990.
Macgregor, G. H. C., *The Relevance of the Impossible: A Reply to Reinhold Niebuhr*, London 1941.
  'Principalities and Powers: The Cosmic Background of St Paul's Thought', *New Testament Studies*, 1, 1954.
  The New Testament Basis of Pacifism (1936), London 1958.
MacIntyre, A., *After Virtue*, London 1981.
  Whose Justice? Which Rationality?, London 1988.
Machovec, M., *A Marxist Looks at Jesus* (Eng. tr.) London 1976.
Mack, B. L., *Rhetoric in the New Testament*, Fortress 1990.
Mackey, J. P., *Jesus: The Man and the Myth*, London 1979.
  'The Use and Abuse of Mary in Roman Catholicism,' in R. Holloway (ed.), *Who Needs Feminism?* (q.v.).
Mackintosh, H. R., *Types of Modern Theology*, London 1937.
Macquarrie, J., *An Existentialist Theology*, London 1955.
  The Scope of Demythologizing, London 1960.
Major, H. D. A., (ed.) *The Mission and Message of Jesus*, London 1937.
Malina, B. J., 'The Social Sciences and Biblical Interpretation', in N. K. Gottwald (ed.), *The Bible and Liberation* (q.v.).
Manson, T. W., *The Teaching of Jesus*, Cambridge 1931.
  The Sayings of Jesus, first published as Part II of *The Mission and Message of Jesus*, (ed.), H. D. A. Major (q.v.).
  Ethics and the Gospel, London 1960.
  On Paul and John, London 1963.
  'The Old Testament in the Teaching of Jesus', *BJRL*, 34.2, 1952.
Marshall, I. H., 'Some observations on the Covenant in the New Testament', in P. W. Bockman and R. E. Kristiansen (eds.), *Context. Essays in Honour of Peder Borgen*, Tapir 1987.
Martin, D., *The Breaking of the Image: A Sociology of Christian Theory and Practice*, Oxford 1980.

Marty, M. E., and Peerman, D. G. (eds.), *The New Theology 3*, New York 1966.

Mathews, S., *The Social Teaching of Jesus: An Essay in Christian Sociology*, 1910.

Meeks, W., *The Moral World of the First Christians*, London 1986.

Mendenhall, G., *The Tenth Generation: The Origin of the Biblical Tration*, 1973.

'The Hebrew Conquest of Palestine', *BAR*, 3 1970 = *BA*, 25, 1962.

Mettinger, T. N. D., *A Farewell to the Servant Songs*, Lund 1983.

Milbank, J., *Theology and Social Theory: Beyond Secular Reason*, Oxford 1990.

Moltmann, J., *The Trinity and the Kingdom of God* (Eng. tr.) London 1981.

Morrison, C. D., *The Powers That Be*, London 1960.

Moule, C. F. D., *The Birth of the New Testament*, London (1962) 1981.

'Obligation in the Ethic of Paul', in W. R. Farmer, C. F. D. Moule and R. R. Niebuhr (eds.), *Christian History and Interpretation*, Cambridge 1967.

See Bammel.

Mozley, E. N., *The Theology of Albert Schweitzer for Christian Enquirers*, London 1950.

Mudge, L. S. (ed.), *Paul Ricoeur, Essays on Biblical Interpretation*, London 1981.

Muilenburg, J., *The Way of Israel*, London 1962.

Murdoch, I., *The Sovereignty of the Good*, London 1970.

Newbigin, L., *The Gospel in a Pluralist Society*, London 1989.

Nicholls, D., *Deity and Domination*, London 1989.

Niebuhr, R., *An Interpretation of Christian Ethics*, London 1937.

Nineham, D. E., *The Gospel of Mark*, Harmondsworth 1963.

North, C. R., *The Suffering Servant in Deutero-Isaiah*, London (1948) 1950.

Oakman, D. E., *Jesus and the Economic Questions of his Day*, Lewiston, New York 1986.

Ogden, S. M. (ed.), *Existence and Faith*, London 1961.

Ogletree, T. W., *The Use of the Bible in Christian Ethics*, Fortress 1983.

Olbrechts-Tyteca, L., see Perelman, C.

Oldham, J. H., see Visser't Hooft, W. A.

O'Neill, J. C., *Paul's Letter to the Romans*, Harmondsworth 1975.

Otto, R., *The Idea of the Holy* (Eng. tr.) Oxford 1923.

The Kingdom of God and the Son of Man (Eng. tr.) London 1938.

Page, R., 'The Bible and the Natural World' and 'The Influence of the Bible on Christian Belief about the Natural World', in Breuilly and Palmer (q.v.).

Palmer, M., see Breuilly, E.

Pannenberg, W., *Christian Spirituality and Sacramental Community* (Eng. tr.) London 1983.

Pauck, W., *Harnack and Troeltsch*, New York 1968.

Peerman, see Marty.

Perelman, C., and Olbrechts-Tyteca, L., *The New Rhetoric: A Treatise on Argumentation*, Notre Dame, Ind., 1969.

Piaget, J., 'The Role of the Concept of Equilibrium in Psychological Explanation', in D. Elkind (ed.) *Jean Piaget: Six Psychological Studies*, Brighton 1980.

Pixley, G. V., *God's Kingdom*, London 1981.

Polanyi, M., *Personal Knowledge: Towards A Post-Critical Philosophy*, London 1962.

Preston, R. H., *Church and Society in the Late Twentieth Century: The Economic and Political Task*, London 1983.

Prickett, S. (ed.), *Reading The Text: Biblical Criticism and Literary Theory*, Oxford 1991.

'Romantics and Victorians', in *Reading The Text*, 1991.

Pusey, M., *Jurgen Habermas*, Chichester 1987.

Rad, G. von, *Old Testament Theology* (Eng. tr.) Edinburgh 1962–5.

Ramsey, P., *Basic Christian Ethics*, London 1953.

The Just War: Force and Political Responsibility, New York 1968.

Rauschenbusch, W., *Christianity and the Social Crisis*, New York 1907.

Christianizing the Social Order, New York 1916.

A Theology for the Social Gospel, New York 1918.

Raven, C. E., *War and the Christian*, London 1938.

The Gospel and the Church, London 1939.

Reardon, B. M. G., *Liberal Protestantism*, London 1968.

Roman Catholic Modernism, London 1970.

Réjon, F. M., 'Seeking the Kingdom and its Justice', in *Concilium* 172.2, 1984.

Reumann, J., *Variety and Unity in New Testament Thought*, Oxford 1991.

Reuther, R., 'The Faith and Fratricide Discussion: Old Problems and New Dimensions', in A. T. Davies, *Anti-Semitism and the Foundations of Christianity* (q.v.).

Richardson, P., (ed.) *Anti-Judaism in Early Christianity vol. I*, Wilfred Laurier, 1986.

Ricoeur, P., 'Gadamer and Habermas in Dialogue', *Philosophy Today*, 17.2/4, 1973.

'Preface to Bultmann' and 'Freedom in the Light of Hope', in *Essays on Biblical Interpretation*, see Mudge L. S.

Riecken, H. W., see Festinger, L.

Ritschl, A., *Die Christliche Lehre von der Rechtfertigung und Versöhnung*,

292   *Select bibliography*

Bonn 1870–4. *The Christian Doctrine of Justification and Reconciliation* (Eng. tr.) Edinburgh 1922.
Robbins, V. K., see Detweiler, R.
Robinson, J. A. T., *The Body*, London 1952.
Rowland, C., and Corner, M., *Liberating Exegesis*, London 1990.
Rumscheidt, M., (ed.), *Adolf von Harnack: Liberal Theology at its Height*, London 1989.
Russell, L. M., (ed.) *Feminist Interpretation of the Bible*, Oxford 1985.
Sanders, E. P., *Paul and Palestinian Judaism*, Philadelphia 1977.
Jesus and Judaism, Philadelphia 1985.
Sanders, J. T., *Ethics in the New Testament*, Philadelphia 1975.
Schachter, S., see Festinger, L.
Schleiermacher, F. D. E., *On Religion: Speeches to its Cultured Despisers*, Berlin 1899.
Christian Faith in Outline (Eng. tr.) Edinburgh 1922.
Schnackenburg, R., *The Moral Teaching of Jesus* (Eng. tr.) Freiburg 1965.
Schoeps, H. J., *The Jewish Christian Argument: A History of Theologies in Conflict*, New York 1963.
Schottroff, L., 'Experiences of Liberation', *Concilium*, 172, 2. 1984.
Schrage, W., *The Ethics of the New Testament* (Eng. tr.) London 1988.
Schweitzer, A., *Von Reimarus zu Wrede. Eine Geschichte der Leben-Jesu-Forschung*, Tubingen 1906; (Eng. tr.) *The Quest of the Historical Jesus*, London (1911) 1948.
Paul and His Interpreters (Eng. tr.) London 1912.
The Mystery of the Kingdom of God (Eng. tr.) London 1925.
Mysticism of St Paul (Eng. tr.) London 1931.
My Life and Thought (Eng. tr.) London 1933.
The Kingdom of God and Primitive Christianity (Eng. tr.) London 1968.
Scott, E. F., *Man and Society in the New Testament*, 1947.
Scroggs, R., *The New Testament and Homosexuality*, Fortress 1983.
Seeley, J. R., *Ecce Homo* London 1865.
Natural Religion, London 1882.
Segundo, J. L., *The Community Called Church*, Dublin 1980.
Sölle, D., *Thinking about God*, London 1990.
Political Theology (Eng. tr.) Philadelphia 1974.
Spencer, S., 'History and Society in William Temple's Thought', in *Studies in Christian Ethics* 5.2. 1992.
Sprott, W. J. H., *Human Groups*, Harmondsworth 1958.
Stack, G. J., *Kierkegaard's Existential Ethics*, Alabama 1977.
Stegemann, W., *God of the Lowly: Socio-Historical Interpretation of the Bible*, Maryknoll, N.Y., 1984.
Steiner, G., *Real Presences: is there anything in what we say?*, London 1989.
Stroup, G. W., *The Promise of Narrative Theology*, London 1984.

Suggate, A., *William Temple and Christian Social Ethics Today*, Edinburgh 1987.
Temple, W., *Mens Creatrix*, London 1917.
Christus Veritas, London 1924.
Nature, Man and God, London 1934.
Christianity and the Social Order, Harmondsworth 1942.
Theissen, G., *The First Followers of Jesus* (Eng. tr.) London 1978.
The Social Setting of Pauline Christianity (Eng. tr.) Edinburgh 1982.
Psychologische Aspecte Paulinischer Theologie, Göttingen 1983.
Biblical Faith: An Evolutionary Approach (Eng. tr.) London 1984.
Tillich, P., *The Protestant Era* (Eng. tr.) Chicago 1948.
Love, Power and Justice, London 1954.
Tomkins, J. P., (ed.), *Reader-Response Criticism*, Baltimore 1980.
Tracy, D., *Blessed Rage for Order*, New York 1978.
Trible, P., *Texts of Terror*, Philadelphia 1984.
Troeltsch, E., *The Social Teaching of the Christian Churches* (Eng. tr.) London 1931.
Religion and History (Eng. tr.) Edinburgh 1991.
'Stoic-Christian Natural Law and Modern Secular Natural Law' in *Religion and History* (q.v.).
Vaux, R. de, *Ancient Israel*, London 1961.
Via, D. O., *Self-Deception and Wholeness in Paul and Matthew*, Fortress 1990.
Vidal, M., 'Is Morality based on Autonomy compatible with the Ethics of Liberation? *Concilium*, 172.2, 1984.
Villa-Vicencio, C., *A Theology of Reconstruction*, Cambridge 1992.
Virgo, L., 'Homosexuality', in A. V. Campbell (ed.), *A Dictionary of Pastoral Care* (q.v.).
Visser't Hooft, W. A., and Oldham, J. H., *The Church and its Function in Society*, London 1937.
The Background of the Social Gospel in America, St Louis, Mo. (1928) 1963.
Walzer, M., *Just and Unjust Wars*, Harmondsworth 1977.
Weber, M., *The Protestant Ethic and the 'Spirit' of Capitalism*, New York 1958.
The Sociology of Religion, London 1965.
Weiss, J., *Die Predigt Jesu vom Reiche Gottes*, Göttingen 1892;
Paul and Jesus (Eng. tr.) London 1909.
(Eng. tr.) *Jesus' Proclamation of the Kingdom of God*, London 1971.
West, D. J., *Homosexuality reexamined*, London (1955) 1977.
Westcott, B. F., *Social Aspects of Christianity*, London (1888) 1900.
White, L., 'The Historical Roots of our Ecologic Crisis', in W. Granberg-Michaelson, *Ecology and Life* (q.v.).
Wilcox, M., see Ellis, E. E.

Wilder, A. N., *Eschatology and Ethics in the New Testament*, New York 1950.
'Albert Schweitzer and the N.T.', in *The Bible and the Literary Critic* (q.v.).
The Bible and the Literary Critic, Minneapolis 1991.
Windisch, H., *The Meaning of the Sermon on the Mount* (Eng. tr.) Philadelphia 1951.
Wink, W., *The Bible in Human Transformation*, Philadelphia 1973.
Naming the Powers: The Language of Power in the New Testament, Philadelphia 1984.
Unmasking the Powers: The Invisible Forces that Determine Human Existence, Philadelphia 1986.
Transforming Bible Study, London 1990.
Winter, G., *Social Ethics*, London 1968.
Winton, A. P., *The Proverbs of Jesus*, Sheffield 1990.
Wrede, W., *Das Messiasgeheimnis in den Evangelion*, Göttingen 1901.
Wright, C. J. H., *Living as the People of God*, London 1983.
Wright, G. E., *The God Who Acts*, London 1952.
Wuellner, W., 'Where is Rhetorical Criticism Taking Us?', *CBQ*, 49.3, 1987.
Zahrnt, H., *The Question of God* (Eng. tr.) London 1969.

Index

NAMES

Abel, E. L. 282
Acton, Lord 16
Alexander, A. B. D. 36–44, 46, 251–3, 255, 260
Alison, A. 16
Allport, G. W. 253
Althaus, P. 259
Archelaus 236
Aristotle 148, 276
Ashley, B. 272
Augustine, St. 42
Austin, J. L. 106, 263, 271

Baab, O. J. 147
Bailey, D. S. 281
Bald, H. 261
Bammel, E. 275
Banner, M. 281
Barclay, J. M. G. 276
Barrett, C. K. 254
Barth, K. 6, 34, 55, 68, 74, 96–7, 106, 155, 158, 200, 221, 256, 262, 270
Bartley (III), W. W. 279
Bartsch, H. W. 257, 277
Baur, F. C. 252
Bellah, R. N. 163, 270
Belo, F. 176, 180–1, 274–5
Bennett, J. 147, 255
Bentham, J. 12
Bentley, J. 256
Berger, P. 271, 281
Bernhart, J. E. 273
Best, G. F. A. 255
Birch, B. C. 4, 247, 264, 268, 273–4
Bishop, C. H. 282
Black, J. 281
Bloch, E. 55

Blumhardt, C. 53–5, 57, 95, 256, 259
Blumhardt, J. 53–5, 57, 95, 259
Boff, C. 216–17, 278
Boff, L. 216, 278
Bonhoeffer, D. 114, 230
Booth, W. 271
Bornkamm, G. 104–5, 107, 262
Bosanquet, B. 256
Boswell, J. 232, 280
Bousset, W. 106
Bowden, J. 256
Bradley, F. H. 256
Breuilly, E. 281
Bright, J. 170, 273–4
Brown, S. 249
Brunner, E. 150–1, 268–9
Buber, M. 161
Bultmann, R. 6, 36, 66–8, 71, 73–4, 90, 96–102, 104, 106–16, 150, 159, 163, 200, 202–3, 250, 261–2
Burrows, M. 147

Cadbury, H. J. 60, 257
Caird, G. B. 270
Calvin, J. 42, 48, 226, 254
Campbell, A. V. 281
Campbell, W. S. 263
Cardinale, E. 205, 277
Carlyle, T. 16
Carr, C. D. 270
Carroll, R. P. 261, 272
Childs, B. S. 274
Chilton, B. 260–1, 275
Clark, H. 257, 260
Clévenot, M. 176, 178, 274, 275
Cohen, H. 272
Coleridge, S. T. 13

295

Index

299

Strawson, P. F. 271
Stroup, G. W. 279
Suetonius 194
Suggate, A. 52, 255–6

Tacitus 194
Temple, W. 51–3, 255–6
Theissen, G. 175, 189–90, 253, 274–6
Tillich, P. 64, 115, 144, 264, 268–9
Tolstoy, Count Leo 31, 56–7
Tomkins, J. P. 271
Tracy, D. 202, 277
Trible, P. 278
Troeltsch, E. 48, 61, 63–4, 257
Tyler, E. B. 12

Vaux, R. de 281–2
Verhey, A. 261, 275
Via, D. O. 254, 262
Vidal, M. 220–1, 279
Villa-Vicencio, C. 53, 256
Virgo, L. 281
Voltaire, F. M. A. de 10

Walzer, M. 269
Weber, M. 12, 48, 53, 61, 64, 254, 257, 272

Weiss, J. 66, 75–81, 84, 89, 125, 253, 257, 259, 260
West, D. J. 280
Westcott, B. F. 49–53, 254–5
White, L. 238, 240, 281–2
Wilcox, M. 266
Wilder, A. N. 89–90, 93, 117, 158, 257, 260–1, 264, 267, 270, 280
Windisch, H. 57, 90, 256, 261
Wink, W. 161–2, 200, 209–11, 270, 277–8
Winter, G. 47, 254
Winton, A. P. 261
Wogaman, J. P. 247
Wolff, H. W. 10
Wordsworth, W. 10, 248
Wrede, W. 37, 66, 82–3, 257
Wright, C. J. H. 247, 264
Wright, G. E. 279
Wuellner, W. 271
Wuttke, A. 250

Zahn, T. 252
Zahrnt, H. 65, 257, 259, 262
Ziegler, T. 25, 251

SUBJECTS

accessibility 2
accountability 168, 201
agape (love) passim, esp. 129–32, 146–56
antinomianism 26, 66, 111, 133–4
anti-Semitism 240–3
apocalyptic, apocalypticism 65–6, 69, 89, 103, 111, 119, 148, 153, 175, 182
application 6
Aufklärung: see Enlightenment
authenticity, authentic 71, 107–11, 144, 165
autonomy (of ethics), autonomous ethics 6, 94–5, 98, 110, 151, 220

biblical ethics 169, 199
biblical interpretation 1, 5, 7, 8, 13, 17, 18, 21, 41, 44–5, 52, 60, 64, 124, 142, 147, 150, 157–60, 162–3, 168, 185, 199, 201, 223, 231, 234, 244–5

Body of Christ 111, 123, 128–9, 151–2

capitalism 230
character 40, 42, 46
Christian ethics passim, esp. 78–81, 243–6
Christian principle 63
church, church type 48, 55, 61, 63
civilisation 32–3, 37, 44, 78, 97, 148
command, command theory 43, 103–5, 112, 114, 117–42, 144–7, 155, 157–8
communion (of horizons) 210–12
community: see also moral community passim, esp. 218–19
conflict model 166, 175
conscience 34, 42, 56, 122, 130, 226–9
context, contextuality, contextual (see also non-contextual use) passim, esp. 169–99, 215–17
correlation 205–6, 208, 233–5, 240–1

BIBLICAL QUOTATIONS

Printed in the United States
37415LVS00002B/565-567

9 780521 020282